Praise for *American Taliban*

"*American Taliban* makes it clear that in a blind taste test the only way you'd be able to tell the difference between the GOP and Taliban philosophies would be beard hair."
—**Sam Seder**, *F.U.B.A.R: America's Right Wing Nightmare*

"Markos Moulitsas vividly exposes how the radical right and many leaders in the Republican Party, contrary to their incessant claims, actually hate the cherished American values of freedom, justice, tolerance, and diversity of thought and expression. With sparkling clarity, *American Taliban* sounds the alarm on the well-funded, highly placed authoritarians in this country who work daily to strip away civil liberties and viciously malign gays, women, and other groups—and he shows why they are treacherous to American democracy. We better listen."
—**Michelangelo Signorile**, *The Michelangelo Signorile Show*

"While not afraid to laugh at the American Taliban, Markos Moulitsas sees the culture warriors for the insidious, dangerous force they present to a free and democratic society."
—**Amanda Marcotte**, executive editor, Pandagon.net

"Markos Moulitsas exposes Limbaugh, Palin, Beck, O'Reilly, Boehner, Gingrich, the Teabaggers, and the Birthers as mullahs of a modern American Taliban hell-bent on imposing their narrow-minded political jihad on us all."
—**John Aravosis**, editor, AMERICAblog.com

"*American Taliban* shines a blinding light on the conservative right's dark agenda. Anyone who genuinely cares about America should read this book."
—**David Coverdale**, Whitesnake

D0027921

AMERICAN TALIBAN

AMERICAN TALIBAN

How War, Sex, Sin, and Power Bind Jihadists and the Radical Right

MARKOS MOULITSAS

PoliPointPress

American Taliban: How War, Sex, Sin, and Power
Bind Jihadists and the Radical Right

Copyright © 2010 by Markos Moulitsas

14 13 12 11 10   2 3 4 5

Production management: BookMatters
Book design: BookMatters
Cover design: Debra Naylor Design
Editor: Safir Ahmed
Consulting Editor: Susan Gardner
Researcher: Barb Morrill

Library of Congress Cataloging-in-Publication Data

Moulitsas Zúñiga, Markos, 1971–
    American Taliban : how war, sex, sin, and power bind
Jihadists and the radical right / Markos Moulitsas.
        p. cm.
    Includes bibliographical references and index.
    ISBN 978-1-936227-02-0 (alk. paper).
    1. Conservatism — United States — History — 21st century.
2. Right and left (Political science) — History — 21st century.
3. United States — Politics and government — 2009–   I. Title.
    JA83.M68 2010
    320.520973 — dc22   2010021216

Published by:
PoliPointPress, LLC
80 Liberty Ship Way, Suite 22
Sausalito, CA 94965
(415) 339-4100
www.p3books.com

Distributed by Ingram Publisher Services
Printed in the USA

For the *Daily Kos* community

Contents

Introduction

The truth tends to slip out of politicians at unguarded moments, when they're not spewing a scripted speech.

Pete Sessions, a top House Republican and head of the GOP's election committee, was telling *Hotline* editors in February 2009 about the Republican strategy for dealing with the new Democratic president and congressional majority. "Insurgency, we understand perhaps a little bit more because of the Taliban," Sessions said. "And that is that they went about systematically understanding how to disrupt and change a person's entire processes. And these Taliban—I'm not trying to say the Republican Party is the Taliban . . . "

Too late, Pete. Cat's out of the bag. May you have more unguarded moments so you speak the truth more often. Yes, the Republican Party, and the entire modern conservative movement is, in fact, very much like the Taliban.

In their tactics and on the issues, our homegrown American Taliban are almost indistinguishable from the Afghan Taliban. The American Taliban—whether in their militaristic zeal, their brute faith in masculinity, their disdain for women's rights, their outright hatred of gays, their aversion to science and modernity, or their staunch anti-intellectualism—share a litany of mores, values, and tactics with Islamic extremists.

Hence the irony watching conservatives, ever since 9/11, charging that liberals "want the terrorists to win." Former Republican House Majority Leader Tom DeLay never missed an opportunity to accuse his political foes of treason. "These are people that don't want to protect the American people," he said of Democrats. "They will do anything, spend all the time and resources they can, to avoid confronting evil." Ohio Republican Representative John Boehner, now the Republican leader in the House, said, "I listen to my Democrat friends, and I wonder if they are more interested in protecting the terrorists than protecting the American people." These are ludicrous charges and would be amusing were they not spoken from such high places.

Fact is, progressives hate the Taliban and other Islamic fundamentalists precisely for the same reason we hate rabid conservatives at home: their fear of change, their contempt for nontraditional lifestyles, their mania for militaristic solutions, and their fascistic efforts to impose their narrow worldview on the rest of society. Conservatives may hate to admit the obvious, but we liberals see both these enemies for what they are—dangerous threats to the ability of free people to live their lives in accordance with their own principles and conscience. Their militant nature and their "our-way-or-the-highway-to-hell" approach to everything they deem sacrilegious is absolutely anti-democratic—and therefore *anti-American*.

As we've seen from the day that Barack Obama was elected president, our American Taliban go beyond a rejection of science, progress, tolerance, and multiculturalism, to an utter disregard for the United States Constitution and our democratic traditions. When you have the Grand Mullah of the American Taliban, Rush Limbaugh, chortling on the air that "we all agree with the Taliban and Iran" about hating Obama and boldly saying he hopes the president of his own country "fails," and when you have governors of states like Texas seriously entertaining secession from the United States because of the Obama presidency, well then, the reality is quite clear—these aren't people who love America and what she stands for; these are people who only love America when they have control and can impose their authoritarian ideology.

Nine days after the devastating 9/11 terrorist attacks on the United States, President George W. Bush stood before a joint session of Congress and announced America's resolve to strike back at this new enemy. "These terrorists . . . we have seen their kind before," he said. "They're the heirs of all the murderous ideologies of the 20th century. By sacrificing human life to serve their radical visions, by abandoning every value except the will to power, they follow in the path of fascism, Nazism, and totalitarianism. And they will follow that path all the way to where it ends in history's unmarked grave of discarded lies."

Setting aside the eloquence, the product of a trained speechwriter, Bush was right about the perpetrators of the 9/11 attacks. They *were* murderous ideologues, and they *did* attack us, in large part, because they hate our freedoms. But let's be honest, the freedoms the jihadists hate are the very same freedoms that our own homegrown regressive ideologues hate: freedom of thought, of inquiry, of lifestyle. If America shared the values of the modern conservative movement, there would've been little reason for Al Qaeda to attack us. Heck, we would be cultural allies!

Everything Bush said about those radical jihadists could be said about our very own American Taliban—that they have "sacrificed human life to serve their radical visions" (Iraq, for starters), and that "by abandoning every value except the will to power, they follow in the path of fascism, Nazism, and totalitarianism."

Our homegrown cabals may masquerade as cultured and respectful leaders, but behind that façade lies a fanaticism that presents a clear and present danger to our nation.

1

POWER

Christian evangelism always surges during troubled times. The 1930s was the time of the Great Depression, a time when communism was alive and well in the international arena, and when trade unions packed far more clout in America than they do today. It was in this context that Abraham Vereide, a Methodist evangelist, began to sponsor prayer breakfast meetings with business and civic leaders in several cities, including Seattle and San Francisco. On a fateful night in 1935, Vereide had a vision.

"God came to him one night in April 1935 and said Christianity has been focusing on the wrong people, the poor, the suffering, the down and out," said Jeff Sharlet, author of *The Family*, on NPR's Fresh Air. "'I want you to be a missionary to and for the powerful,' those whom he calls the 'up and out.' They can dispense blessings to everybody else through a sort of kind of trickle-down religion."

Vereide and his fellow evangelists were intensely concerned about the chaos of democracy, about uppity trade unionists on the rise, and about communist ideas seeping into America. Convinced that democracy was part of the problem, they looked to fascism for solutions. "They come up with this idea of a third way, that they later start calling 'totalitarianism for Christ,'" explained Sharlet. "And they predict that the United States will pretty quickly embrace this and will get rid of political parties because democracy doesn't work. People arguing and debating doesn't work. They don't want a Republican Party, a Democratic Party. They want one big party—theirs."

This brand of evangelism had little to do with charity or nourishing the soul, connecting with God or becoming a better human being. That was for chumps. Rather, their Jesus was all about union busting and an aggressive, expansionist foreign policy. They began to organize prayer breakfast groups around the country, and over the next decade they succeeded in setting up groups in major cities and in the nation's seat of power on Capitol Hill. These evangelists operated under various monikers—the National Committee for Christian Leadership, the Fellowship House, and the International Foundation, among others—but were mostly identified as "The Family." The other benign-sounding, bureaucratic names helped mask The Family's secretive work: the cultivation as allies of the most influential and wealthy members of society, those in control of the levers of power. The Family has been one of the radical Right's most successful efforts, always working quietly, in the shadows. To this day, the organization boasts some of the top members of Congress and has sponsored the National Prayer Breakfast, which every president since 1953 has attended.

At its heart, The Family is an elitist, anti-democratic effort, driven by its authoritarian and theocratic mission, but it isn't the only outpost of such thought in conservative circles. In fact, our nation's political Right has been taken over by what can not-so-affectionately be called the American Taliban, a cabal of ideologues who are fundamentalist in their beliefs, intolerant of dissent, and xenophobic in matters of foreign policy.

"Our culture is superior. Our culture is superior because our religion is Christianity and that is the truth that makes men free," declared Pat Buchanan, former Republican presidential candidate, prominent media personality, and a leading light for followers of the movement.

Leaders of the American Taliban currently rule in corporate boardrooms, in state capitols, on Capitol Hill, and even in the White House when Republicans are elected to the highest office. President George W. Bush's first attorney general, John Ashcroft, was one such stealth jihadist, ignoring his own promises during Senate confirmation hearings to put the national agenda ahead of his own religious convictions. Ashcroft saw no distinction between the public good and his private aims, and he immediately set out to use the nation's premier law enforcement machine to support his theocratic agenda. He instituted daily prayer meetings at the Justice Department and tried to overrule local laws he believed violated biblical principles, such as Oregon's euthanasia law and Puerto Rico's death penalty ban. And he ignored critical pre-9/11 anti-terror efforts so agents could focus on issues that piqued his moral policing sensibility, like shutting down prostitution rings—normally the job of local authorities.

Such missionary zeal is dangerous and indicative of a totalitarianism of mind, of thought, of deed. It is indeed, as Sharlet points out, "totalitarianism for Christ," and its genesis is a corrupted and twisted theology, a distortion of the religious book to serve the crass ideological aims of the political fundamentalists. Which, of course, is no different than the totalitarianism of those Islamic extremists half a world away that American conservatives claim to loathe.

Sounding little different from Pat Buchanan when he spouts gibberish about the superiority of Christianity, Osama bin Laden has essentially distorted *his* holy book, the Quran, to serve his own militant message and extremist ideology. "Allah, the Most High, sent down His orders in His Sacred Books like the Torah and Evangel and sent with them the Messengers (Allah's prayers and peace be upon them) as bearers of good news to the people," bin Laden sermonized in a 2007 propaganda video on the sixth anniversary of 9/11.

> And everyone who believes in them and complies with them is a believer from the people of the Garden. Then when the men of knowledge altered the words of Allah, the Most High, and sold them for a paltry price, as the rabbis did with the Torah and the monks with the Evangel, Allah sent down His final Book, the magnificent Quran, and safeguarded it from being added to or subtracted from by the hands of men, and in it is a complete methodology for the lives of all people.

Having lost the intellectual arguments, having seen their worldview assailed by modernity, change, science, and more tolerant cultures, these religious extremists—whether Al Qaeda or the Afghan Taliban or the American Taliban—set out to re-create a holier-than-thou version of their religion-based ideologies, which command subservience from their flocks and allow no room for debate or open discussion. "Freedom," in the upside-down world of these self-righteous extremists, means acquiescence.

Sermonizing at a church in his Texas district, then House Majority Whip (and soon to be Majority Leader) Tom DeLay said,

> Ladies and gentlemen, Christianity offers the only viable, reasonable, definitive answer to the questions of "Where did I come from?" "Why am I here?" "Where am I going?" "Does life have

any meaningful purpose?" Only Christianity offers a way to understand that physical and moral border. Only Christianity offers a comprehensive worldview that covers all areas of life and thought, every aspect of creation. Only Christianity offers a way to live in response to the realities that we find in this world—only *Christianity*.

For DeLay, only Christianity offers a methodology for daily life, whereas for Osama bin Laden, only Islam does. And although Christians and Muslims have had numerous conflicts over the centuries that have cost countless lives, the similarities between their two doctrines when carried to extremes are downright eerie. Try to guess whether an Islamic or a Christian radical said the following:

> [Our religion's] message is in contradiction to the message spread by the devils of the world. Well, the devils find it hard to put up with this message. There are Satans in today's world too. They find it hard and, therefore, confront and challenge [our message]. There is no other alternative to victory in this challenge and confrontation except by standing firm with faith. There is no alternative but to believe in ourselves and our chosen path. This is the only alternative. We must believe in our path. All the believers of this path must join hands and stand firm. We must demonstrate steadfastness. This is the path to progress and victory. If all the believers do so, their victory will be certain.

That was the Iranian Grand Ayatollah Ali Khamenei, but the message is interchangeable with that of the American Taliban. Heck, half of President George W. Bush's speeches borrowed from these themes—glorifying belief over behavior, blind faith over scientific inquiry, and conformity over dissent. This "freedom" they all claim to seek is, to put it mildly, a limited one: freedom to worship *their* god and subscribe to *their* ideology, not freedom to live one's life as one sees fit. At its core is the idea that all laws of the land must flow from *their* holy book, and that all else is deviation that must be banned.

Holding such beliefs is fine, but foisting them on the rest of us is not. Filled with a moral certitude born of religious conviction, these fundamentalists want a society in which "freedom" means being free to submit to their god. "When the Christian majority takes over this country, there will be no satanic churches, no more free distribution of pornography, no more talk of rights for homosexuals," thundered Gary Potter, president of Catholics for Christian Political Action. "After the Christian majority takes control, pluralism will be seen as immoral and evil and the state will not permit anybody the right to practice evil."

Never mind that the "right to practice evil" is at the heart of most religions' understanding of the personal quest for faith— that believers wrestle with doubt and temptation, and sometimes fail. This insistence on state control of all "evil" behavior ultimately short-circuits the redemptive process recognized by theologians as the basis for true, growing faith. No, there will be no "right to practice evil" here! The ideal theocratic state will outlaw it! "Totalitarianism for Christ," indeed.

This level of intolerance is not the domain of loons and fringe characters but rather the very lifeblood coursing through the entire body of the modern conservative movement. People like the late Jerry Falwell, the key architect of the mainstreaming of the Christian evangelical movement, facilitated the entry of these totalitarian ideas into the political realm. He was the founder of the Christian Liberty University and, more significantly, the Moral Majority—the first major lobby promoting a Christian-Right agenda in government. Falwell pined for a theocratic regime that would do away with dissent and diversity. "If we are going to save America and evangelize the world, we cannot accommodate secular philosophies that are diametrically opposed to Christian truth." Gary North, of the now defunct Institute for Christian Economics, was equally blunt. "The long-term goal of Christians in politics should be to gain exclusive control over the franchise. Those who refuse to submit publicly to the eternal sanctions of God by submitting to His Church's public marks of the covenant—baptism and holy communion—must be denied citizenship." According to North, "This is God's world, not Satan's. Christians are the lawful heirs, not non-Christians."

Statements like North's sound extremist and fascistic; the more mainstream faces of the American Taliban are savvy enough to couch their rhetoric in softer language. "Civilized people—Muslims, Christians, and Jews—all understand that the source of freedom and human dignity is the Creator," preached John Ashcroft at a convention of Christian Broadcasters in 2002. "Civilized people of all religious faiths are called to the defense of His creation. We are a nation called to defend freedom—a freedom that is not the grant of any government or document, but is our endowment from God." The implications are crystal clear: only true believers in the Judeo-Christian-Islamic deity are "civilized people," and no "government or document" will stand in the way of such believers in their crusade to "defend freedom." No wonder Ashcroft, Bush, Cheney, and their missionary neocon warriors—civilized people all—didn't let any "government or document" (read: U.S. Constitution) stand in their way as they launched the bloodbath in Iraq the year after Ashcroft spoke to the Christian group.

Such certitude manifests itself in particularly virulent religious intolerance. The Buddhas of Bamyan were two glorious statues, roughly 180 feet tall, carved into the side of a cliff in the Bamyan Valley of Afghanistan in AD 507. Under Taliban rule, they were at first protected, primarily because they brought in tourist money. "The government considers the Bamyan statues as an example of a potential major source of income for Afghanistan from international visitors. The Taliban states that Bamyan shall not be destroyed but protected," said Mullah Mohammed Omar in 1999. But less than two years later, in March 2001, Mullah Omar changed his mind, declared them "idols" forbidden by Shariah (Islamic law), and had them dynamited. "Muslims should be proud of smashing idols. It has given praise to God that we have destroyed them," he declared. Such actions, aside from their sheer horror, betray a sense of deep insecurity, a fear of those who believe otherwise. Along with the Taliban's ideological and theological zeal and passion, along with their distortion and perversion of religious law, comes deep hatred for those who believe in other gods, or in no gods at all.

And of course, Muslim and Christian fundamentalists save some of the strongest vitriol for use against each other. Ironic, because both worship the same god.

Charles Gibson: Do we all worship the same God, Christian and Muslim?

George W. Bush: I think we do. We have different routes of getting to the Almighty.

Seems pretty obvious, but extremists have twisted the original holy texts to justify turning their weapons against each other. Some of the most vicious disagreements, after all, can be internecine, and when the American Taliban take on their Muslim cousins, they are enraged because they see so much of themselves in their supposed enemies.

"The Christian God encourages freedom, love, forgiveness, prosperity and health," said the Reverend Ted Haggard, former president of the National Association of Evangelicals. "The Muslim god appears to value the opposite. The personalities of each god are evident in the cultures, civilizations, and dispositions of the peoples that serve them. Muhammad's central message was submission; Jesus' central message was love. They seem to be very different personalities." Haggard, forced to resign his leadership role after admitting to buying meth and hiring a homosexual prostitute, apparently hadn't read the Old Testament. Not a lot of love or forgiveness happening in that tome. More like carnage and curses. Regardless, Islamic fundamentalists see things the same way as Christian fundamentalists. Haggard sees his god as "encouraging freedom, love, forgiveness, prosperity, and health"; the Iranian Grand Ayatollah Safi-Golpaygani says the Prophet Muhammad expects Muslims ". . . to advocate and spread fraternity, generosity, compassion, and fairness in the society." Brothers under the skin, clearly.

Paradoxical as it seems to those standing outside the fundamentalist struggle, the vitriol flows freely. "They would have us believe that Islam is just as good as Christianity," sermonized Rev. Jerry Vines, a former president of the Southern Baptist Convention, the world's largest Baptist denomination. "Christianity was founded by the virgin-born son of God, Jesus Christ. Islam was founded by Muhammad, a demon-possessed pedophile who had 12 wives, the last one of which was a nine-year-old girl." Former Alabama Chief Justice Roy Moore, on trial after installing a monument to the Ten Commandments in front of his courthouse, was asked whether non-Christian faiths were protected under the First Amendment. "I don't think so, sir, that Buddhists and other faiths—and I won't speak to all faiths because I'm not a theologian—recognize the Creator, God," Moore answered. "Some might, but if they do, it's not the God of the Holy Scriptures. And that's why the Bible is used for the very foundation upon which we take our oaths."

The American Taliban couldn't even stomach the rote proclamations Bush used for public consumption to temper the crazy talk, like when he said that America wasn't at war with the *religion* of Islam. Joe Glover, of the virulently anti-gay Family Policy Network, led the charge.

> Lots of people I've spoken to—not just the grassroots but also leaders of other pro-family organizations—are bewildered at why George Bush is doing so much to pay homage to Islam. Conservative evangelicals love Muslims. They care for them. They want to provide religious freedom for them. However, they are diametrically opposed to Islam. It's the same difference we have with the homosexual community. We care about homosexuals, yet we're opposed to their agenda because we know it destroys their lives. Likewise, we care about Muslims, but we're opposed to even any tacit endorsement of Islam because it's against the will of God.

Get it? Saying that we're not at war with a religion is endorsing it. Whether it's Islamic extremism in Afghanistan or Pakistan or Sudan, or Christian fanaticism in Alabama or Texas or Florida, the *political fundamentalism* driving them is the same: power must be wielded in the name of god, and everyone else must submit. The Bible or the Quran are to be the source of law, and there's zero tolerance for dissent or deviation from the norm.

This is at the heart of theocratic ideology: It is fascism with a religious face.

When voters in Minnesota's Fifth Congressional District (in the Minneapolis area) elected Keith Ellison to the U.S. Congress in 2006, Ellison became not only his state's first African-American representative but the nation's first Muslim representative in Congress. The response from the American Taliban was predictably vicious.

Dennis Prager, a columnist at conservative website Townhall .com, was outraged that Ellison chose a Quran (once owned by Thomas Jefferson, no less) for the photo-op reenactment of his swearing-in ceremony. In a piece with a long, strange title— "America, Not Keith Ellison, decides what book a congressman takes his oath on"—Prager raged: "He should not be allowed to do so—not because of any American hostility to [the Quran], but because the act undermines American civilization." How so? "First, it is an act of hubris that perfectly exemplifies multiculturalist activism—my culture trumps America's culture," wrote Prager, self-styled arbiter of American culture. "What Ellison and his Muslim and leftist supporters are saying is that it is of no consequence what America holds as its holiest book; all that matters is what any individual holds to be his holiest book." It did not matter to Prager (if he even knew at the time) that members of Congress get sworn in as a group and no religious books are used, or that the U.S. Constitution specifically prohibits religious tests for holding office. Given our nation's founding as a haven from religious persecution, this kind of sentiment from self-proclaimed "patriots" is breathtakingly un-American. Yet such sentiments are widespread among the American Taliban.

Jay Sekulow of the American Center for Law and Justice (ACLJ), where he describes himself as a "nationally respected defender of religious freedom," whined on Fox News in January 2007 that Ellison should have "abstained" from using the Quran, as it represented a "danger" to the nation's "Judeo-Christian tradition"—an odd way to defend religious freedom, indeed. Perhaps one should expect such doublespeak from the chief counsel of the ACLJ, which was founded in 1990 by none other than Pat Robertson, who holds a special place in the sanctum of the American Taliban as one of their institutional architects and most public faces. Robertson is the founder and driving force behind the Christian Broadcasting Network and the Christian Coalition, an organization several million strong dedicated to promoting the religious-Right agenda in government. His Bible-centered Regent University serves as a feeder system that injects fundamentalists into the political mainstream as conservative politicians hire its graduates.

Robertson would be the first to sound the alarm when someone of a different faith gets involved in government. Based on his own understanding of the purpose of government—to serve *someone's* religious agenda—he went nuts when Ellison took office. On his *700 Club* show in March 2007, he warned godly Americans that Muslims like Ellison wanted to "take over" our country and "institute Shariah." "You're going to lose your country if Christians don't mobilize and vote," he said, as if Christians were becoming an endangered species in Congress—where more than 90 percent are self-defined Christians. But the important implication of Robertson's statement is that this country *belongs* to Christians, and electing people of other faiths meant they were in mortal danger of losing it.

After Ellison's swearing-in, then U.S. Rep. Virgil Goode, an arch-conservative from Virginia, mailed a screed to his constituents that warned, "If American citizens don't wake up and adopt the Virgil Goode position on immigration there will likely be many more Muslims elected to office and demanding the use of the [Quran]." All you had to do was send good ol' Goode some money, and he'd fight to stem the flow of Muslim congressmen flooding across the border.

Caught up in the hysteria over Ellison's election was Fox News personality Glenn Beck, then at *CNN Headline News*. Weirdly enough, Beck admitted feeling threatened by Ellison's election—literally scared about interviewing him on CNN. "I have been nervous about this interview with you, because what I feel like saying is, 'Sir, prove to me that you are not working with our enemies.' And I know you're not. I'm not accusing you of being an enemy, but that's the way I feel, and I think a lot of Americans will feel that way." Even knowing his fears were irrational, Beck couldn't stop trembling at the thought of an American Muslim serving our great nation. As in most cases when the American Taliban quiver, shake, and shout, that interview revealed far more about Beck's cowardice and paranoia than it did about Ellison's qualifications for office.

These prejudices have created a bizarre victim complex among the American Taliban—bullying and confident in their dominant numbers, yet incessantly whining about being oppressed. "Just like what Nazi Germany did to the Jews, so liberal America is now doing to the evangelical Christians. It's no different," claimed Robertson in 1993. "More terrible than anything suffered by any minority in history." Perhaps the liberal media covered up the murder of *seven million* evangelicals. And maybe having a single Muslim and a single atheist in the U.S. House of Representatives (along with 29 Jewish members) is a disaster on a par with the plight of the Sudanese in Darfur. But I doubt it.

What's bizarre is that Robertson *really* believes this craziness. The American Taliban believe *all* their craziness. This phenomenon isn't just theological—it's dangerous.

The American Taliban's ideology—with its rigid conformity and lack of tolerance for dissent—extends far beyond biblical matters and spills over into areas of domestic and foreign policy. Take, for instance, Ronald Reagan, the patron saint of the modern conservative movement and a deity so revered that Republican politicians must swear undying loyalty to his legacy. After Reagan's death in 2004, California Governor Arnold Schwarzenegger, no doctrinaire Republican, wrote an op-ed in *USA Today* hilariously titled, "Ronald Reagan: My hero, and eternal light for the world." The 2008 presidential Republican primary was a contest over who could best claim Reagan's mantle. In a 90-minute debate at the Ronald Reagan Presidential Library, the candidates and moderators cited Nancy and Ronald Reagan's names 54 times. John McCain claimed three times that he was a "foot soldier" in the Reagan revolution. Mitt Romney *channeled* the former president.

> Ronald Reagan would look at the issues that are being debated right here and say, one, "We're going to win in Iraq, and I'm not going to walk out of Iraq until we win in Iraq." Ronald Reagan would say, "Lower taxes." Ronald Reagan would say, "Lower spending." Ronald Reagan would—is pro-life. He would also say, "I want to have an amendment to protect marriage."

Really? The only divorced U.S. president ever would say that, Mitt? Asked to comment on Supreme Court Justice Sandra Day O'Connor, a Reagan appointee and frequent target of GOP critics, Mike Huckabee weaseled out of it. "I'm not going to come to the Reagan Library and say anything about Ronald Reagan's decisions. I'm not that stupid. If I was, I'd have no business being president." Even criticizing Reagan's *mistakes* was off limits and would disqualify a Republican from holding office.

The funny thing is, Reagan was a flaming liberal compared with today's American Taliban. In the conservative canon, Reagan was a heroic tax cutter and fiscal hawk, who brought the Soviet

Union down with his steely resolve and soaring rhetoric ("Mr. Gorbachev, tear down this wall!") and who made America proud of itself again. Reagan's record, though, was a bit different. He certainly passed massive tax cuts his first year in office, but he reversed many of them when he signed into law the Tax Equity and Fiscal Responsibility Act of 1982 (TEFRA). Former Reagan advisor Bruce Bartlett wrote in 2003 that "according to a recent Treasury Department study, TEFRA alone raised taxes by almost 1 percent of the gross domestic product, making it the largest peacetime tax increase in American history." Moreover, Reagan also backed a $3.3 billion gasoline tax and increased the Social Security tax rate. Sure, the Soviet Union fell soon after his presidency ended, but Reagan met and *negotiated* with Gorbachev—the head of the "evil empire," as Reagan himself labeled the Soviet Union. As for his reputation as a fiscal hawk, it would be laughable were it not for the fact that Reagan initiated the steep slide into deficit spending that inflicted long-term damage. And for a party that has worked tirelessly to destroy the civil rights of homosexuals, Reagan was a maverick in his strident opposition to the Briggs Initiative in California, which would have banned gays and lesbians from teaching in the public schools, and his opposition helped defeat the measure. Last, let's not forget that Reagan granted amnesty to millions of illegal aliens in 1986, a position antithetical to current American Taliban ideology.

Today, any Republican talking or governing like Ronald Reagan would be labeled a tax-raising, terrorist-negotiating, gay-loving, amnesty-granting, big spender. Nonetheless, the American Taliban has elevated Reagan to sainthood, airbrushing out his more nuanced beliefs and actions, while throwing far less nuanced Republicans to the curb for far lesser offenses.

Take Anthony Adams, a California state assemblyman from

San Bernardino. In 2009, the state of California was in dire financial straits, and the legislature and Governor Schwarzenegger were desperately seeking to plug a projected budget deficit of $42 billion. Schwarzenegger's budget included $12.5 billion in tax increases, which made the budget toxic for the Taliban faction of his party. Although Republicans held only 29 seats in the 80-seat state assembly, they could still block passage of any budget because a two-thirds vote is required. The state GOP was willing to tank its state rather than vote for any budget that included tax increases—no matter how many spending cuts it had (and the budget *was* draconian in its spending cuts). Adams was a doctrinaire Republican: anti-gay, anti-choice, anti-government spending, and he had signed an anti-tax increase pledge. But he also knew that in the budget vote the stakes were high and human lives would be drastically affected. "State people were not getting paychecks," Adams told the *Washington Post* in December 2009. "We faced the possibility of paying those people off in IOUs for quite some time . . . I thought it was unconscionable not to pay people we owe." Those people included police, firefighters, nurses, and other essential personnel.

The budget impasse was broken at the eleventh hour, when Schwarzenegger got Adams to join a handful of Republicans in supporting his budget. The backlash against Adams was swift. Death threats prompted state Highway Patrol protection for Adams and his wife, and his own mother-in-law turned against him. "It hurts, but there is a new push by the purists out there," he lamented. "*This Taliban mentality*: it's trying to get rid of people in our party." His words, my emphasis.

In the world of the radical Right, logic and rationality have no place. Things are definitely not what they seem. Their world is full of doublespeak and deception: tax cuts are the answer to

every problem, *even* budget deficits; homosexuals destroy hetero-
sexuals' marriages; and the more bombs we drop on other lands,
the more the world will love and respect us. In the American Taliban's worldview, Christians are an oppressed minority, even when
they are the majority, and Christmas is under siege from secularist
forces (and Kwanzaa!). In their world, the mythical "heartland"
is the only real America, even if their leaders and heroes live in
coastal cities like New York and Palm Beach, Florida (and in the
case of Rush Limbaugh and Ann Coulter, both those places). They
wouldn't be caught dead living in the heartland. What's more,
government invading our privacy—tapping our phones without
judicial approval—is fine, but government guaranteeing adequate
health care for all is taboo.

In their world, everything is nuance-free, all black or white,
good or evil, us versus them. Like their Islamic extremist counterparts, the American Taliban are motivated not by love, compassion, forgiveness, or freedom, but rather by fear and hatred. Both
sides *need* to feed off the hatred of the other. "The curse of God
is to bring in people who don't share your point of view and then
ultimately destroy your civilization," said Pat Robertson. Indeed,
their worldview is one of Old Testament fire and brimstone, their
way or eternal damnation. Their approach to life is angry and
vengeful, and they cling desperately to scriptural certainty in a
tumultuous world. Too bad that the tolerant and the rational elements of each society get caught in the crossfire of dueling extremist insanity.

Such certainty, manifested merely as intolerance, would be
problematic but not dangerous. However, the American Taliban,
like their Islamic extremist brethren across the globe, seek to force
their rigid views on the rest of society. Such totalitarianism is
incompatible with freedom and democracy. If a democratic elec-

tion does not go the way they want, their response is not to accept the results and try harder the next time, but to resort to militancy.

In 1996, the prospect of Bill Clinton getting re-elected president was getting some of our own Taliban virtually apoplectic. Here's nationally syndicated columnist Cal Thomas fulminating:

> Conservative religious believers are now faced with a clear choice. They can abandon their political interests and claim resident alien status in a land that has forgotten their God . . . Or they can remember what the Founders said: When, in the course of human events, it becomes necessary for one people to dissolve the political bands which have connected them with another, and to assume, among the powers of the earth, the separate and equal station to which the laws of nature and of nature's God entitle *them*."

That quote from the Declaration of Independence, as every American school child can tell you, refers to revolution.

Yet such seditious thoughts, whether justifiable or not, only seem to arise when a Democratic president is in office, betraying a fundamental truism about the American Taliban: no matter how much they quote the Founding Fathers or our foundational documents, they are only paying lip service to those principles. In reality, they have no loyalty to the country or its Constitution or its laws, and they only invoke them when it suits their purpose.

Such attitudes are little different than those of the Afghan Taliban, who justify their mad power grab in theological terms. "I want to tell you clearly when we rose up in Afghanistan in 1994 we did not rise up to be the government," claimed Zabiullah Mujahid, one of Mullah Omar's two spokesmen, in a May 2009 interview with CNN. "[W]e rose up not for power and government, we rose up just to force Islamic law and to help our widows in Afghanistan." Although it's ludicrous to argue that "to force Islamic law"

is not the same as rising up for "power and government," the sentiment is clearly shared by the American Taliban. In essence, god's
law supersedes man's law, and any institution designed to provide
for secular governance is by nature illegitimate.

"The Constitution of the United States, for instance, is a mar-
velous document for self-government by the Christian people," Pat
Robertson said on his *700 Club* show in 1981. "But the minute
you turn the document into the hands of non-Christian people
and atheistic people they can use it to destroy the very foundation
of our society." The American Constitution as a deadly weapon.
Nice. And the American Taliban haven't mellowed in the three
decades since Robertson's paranoid statement.

"I want you to just let a wave of intolerance wash over you,"
said Randall Terry, founder of the militant anti-abortion protest
group Operation Rescue, in 1993. "I want you to let a wave of
hatred wash over you. Yes, hate is good. . . . Our goal is a Christian
nation. We have a biblical duty, we are called by God, to conquer
this country. We don't want equal time. We don't want pluralism." Indeed, the very concept of *democracy* is infuriating to this
crowd, as Robert Simonds of the National Association of Christian Educators attests: "As the church watches from the sidelines,
the ungodly elect atheists and homosexuals to school boards and
legislatures to enact policies and laws that destroy our Christian
children and discriminate against Christian families." His solution? "Atheistic secular humanists should be removed from office
and Christians should be elected." Clearly, he forgot to add "by
any means necessary."

Lest you dismiss this crowd as fringe, ponder the case of John
Hagee. This pastor has built a media empire from the altar of his
19,000-member megachurch in San Antonio, Texas. John Hagee
Ministries broadcasts his work to 160 television and 50 radio sta-

tions in the United States, and he has several best-selling books
to his name. After Hurricane Katrina hit New Orleans in 2005,
Hagee blamed the natural disaster on residents. "New Orleans
had a level of sin that was offensive to God." He has called the
Catholic Church "the great whore" and a "false cult." In his 1987
book, *Should Christians Support Israel*, which Hagee said was a
"declaration of war" against anti-Semitism, he blamed the Holocaust on the Catholic Church.

> *Where are the Jews of Spain?*
> They were murdered in cold blood by the Roman Church!

> *Where are the Jews of Portugal?*
> They were murdered in cold blood by the Roman Church!

> *Where are the Jews of Italy and France?*
> They were murdered in cold blood by the Roman Church!

> *Where are the Jews of Austria and Hungary?*
> A Godless theology of hate that no one dared try to stop for a
> thousand years, produced a harvest of horror. When the Pale
> Rider of Death thrust in the sickle, the rivers of Europe turned
> red with the blood of the Jews.

In 2008, John McCain, desperate to shore up his bona fides
with the evangelicals that make up such a key segment of the GOP
base, ardently wooed Hagee for his endorsement. At a speech
for a Hagee event, McCain looked at Hagee and said, "I thank
you for your spiritual guidance to politicians like me who need
it fairly often." After working him for over a year and traveling
together several times, the Arizona senator finally won the Hagee
sweepstakes.

What kind of worldview was McCain's spiritual guide promoting? "As soon as Jesus sits on his throne he's gonna rule the world

with a rod of iron. That means he's gonna make the ACLU do what he wants them to. That means you're not gonna have to ask if you can pray in public school. We will live by the law of God and no other law." So much for allegiance to the U.S. Constitution. Or for the compassionate Jesus. Or for the notion that these Taliban nuts have no say in our contemporary political process. Fact is, they are very relevant, very engaged, and very dangerous.

Bob Jones, president of the fundamentalist Bob Jones University in South Carolina, was so elated about Bush being re-elected president in 2004, that he wrote him a letter.

> In your re-election, God has graciously granted America— though she doesn't deserve it—a reprieve from the agenda of paganism. Put your agenda on the front burner and let it boil. You owe liberals nothing. They despise you because they despise your Christ.

Next in line was Fox News personality Bill O'Reilly, who, unhappy that alleged terrorists were being tried in New York as required by the Sixth Amendment, thundered at a guest on his show on November 16, 2009, "I don't care about the Constitution!" Obviously. Nice to have him state it out in the open. Yes, the Constitution is, well, an inconvenience that often gets in the way of these radicals. But that is a feature, not a bug. It is a document specifically designed to thwart those seeking absolute power, so it should be no surprise that O'Reilly finds it a nuisance. There is no shortage of conservative disdain for the rights and protections afforded to us by our nation's supreme laws.

Take Article III, for example, which establishes the judicial branch of the government, including the U.S. Supreme Court. Enshrined in the Constitution are the ideas of "separation of powers" between the executive, legislative, and judicial branches, and a system of "checks and balances" that prevents the usurpation of powers by any one of the three branches. But these Civics 101 lessons are completely lost on members of the American Taliban, like Pat Robertson, who misinformed *700 Club* viewers, when he said, "A Supreme Court ruling is not the Law of the United States. The law of the United States is the Constitution, treaties made in accordance with the Constitution, and laws duly enacted by the Congress and signed by the president . . . I don't think the Congress of the United States is subservient to the courts . . . They can ignore a Supreme Court ruling if they so choose." Poor Pat. One can only be thankful that his quixotic attempt to become president in 1988 was unsuccessful.

It's no wonder that the Supreme Court, despite its strongly conservative bent, remains a favorite target of the American Taliban. "Who are the beneficiaries of the Court's protection?" asked Pat Buchanan, another unsuccessful presidential contender. "Members of various minorities, including criminals, atheists, homosexuals, flag burners, illegal immigrants (including terrorists), convicts, and pornographers." In his rant, Buchanan blasted the desegregation of whites-only schools as an example of the Supreme Court's "judicial dictatorship in America." For a movement that is built on subjugating and eliminating its enemies, any institution that works to protect besieged minority rights from the tyranny of demagogues will drive those thwarted demagogues to distraction. Just listen to Michael Schwartz, no less than a chief of staff to a U.S. Senator, Tom Coburn of Oklahoma: "I'm a radical! I'm a real extremist. I don't want to impeach judges. I want to impale them!"

Nothing like a little medievalism to brighten up an otherwise boring disagreement about separation of powers.

The American Taliban seek a tyranny of the believers in which the popular will, the laws of the land, and all of secular society

are surrendered to their clerics and ideologues. But, alas, we are a
nation of laws and democratic traditions, which, after eight years
of the Cheney-Bush death-and-destruction machine, enabled
Barack Obama's ascension to the presidency in January 2009.

And that is when the American Taliban went completely
bananas.

Orly Taitz is a Southern California real estate agent, dentist, and
lawyer, originally from the Soviet Union, who immigrated to the
United States in the early 1990s by way of Israel. You could be
diplomatic and refer to her as "colorful," though "batshit insane"
would be more accurate.

Unhappy with Obama's election as the nation's 44th president,
she led a crusade to delegitimize his administration. She described
Obama as a "usurper" and an "arrogant jerk from Africa and Indo-
nesia," and called for "Nurenberg [sic] style trials" for "crimes perpetrated upon American citizens," and has used her (questionable)
legal skills to seek a temporary restraining order to stop Obama
from deploying troops abroad because, well, he is not really the
president. She believes Obama has murdered his gay lovers, that
he "represents radical Communism and radical Islam," that he has
killed a "goon" who tampered with his passport, and that he's tried
to have her killed several times. She thinks Venezuelan President
Hugo Chavez has been stealing U.S. elections, that the flu vaccine
is contaminated, and that Google and the entire internet is in on a
conspiracy to protect Obama from all this seedy business. There's
more, but you get the idea.

But what *really* sets Taitz off is her unshakable conviction that
Obama is not an American citizen because he was born in Kenya, a
fact that would render him constitutionally unqualified to serve as
president. In a series of lawsuits, including one on behalf of former

Republican presidential candidate Alan Keyes (a fellow marcher in the parade of lunacy), Taitz claimed that Obama falsified his U.S. birth certificate in an elaborate conspiracy in which his parents placed two birth announcements in Hawaii newspapers after Barack was born in Kenya. Sad to say, Taitz didn't invent this conspiracy theory; she only borrowed it and took it for a long, long walk. It emerged in mid-2008 from the turgid swamps of the conservative internet during the presidential campaign, where rumors abounded that the birth certificate would show that "Muhammad" was his middle name or that "Barry" was his first name, which would be proof that . . . who knows. It's not as if "Barry Muhammad Obama" would make him *far* less electable than "Barack Hussein Obama." When the Obama campaign released a duplicate "Certificate of Live Birth" from Hawaii—after the director of the Hawaii Department of Health said she had seen the original certificate and because state law bars release of the original to anyone who does not have "tangible interest"—that did not satiate the American Taliban. In fact, it emboldened these "birthers."

Taitz rose to prominence in this environment, with her blizzard of lawsuits and aggressive media hustling. Reporters were fed increasingly grandiose claims about her escapades, like bragging that she had to hire *five* people to accept all the friend requests she was receiving on her Facebook page. (A quick check revealed she had an unremarkable 3,000 friends. Being Taitz's "Facebook friend responder" was obviously easy work, if you could get it.)

Her difficulties with the truth quickly became legendary—and entertaining. For instance, she gleefully filed what she believed was a Kenyan birth certificate for Obama in the various courts where her lawsuits were pending, trumpeting her "proof" to everyone. Yet it didn't take long for the online birther debunking movement (yes, there *is* such a thing) to tear the forgery apart: it had Obama's age off by a year, was marked as an official February 1964 document from the "Coast Province" of the "Republic of Kenya"—although no such province existed, nor did the "Republic of Kenya" exist until December of that year. It was "entered at the District Registry Office" on August 5, 1961, but that was a Saturday when government offices would be closed. Finally, the source of the forgery was discovered—a crudely photoshopped Australian birth certificate. A woman and a movement that had spent months "debunking" Obama's certificate of live birth, had been easily punk'd by a forgery so poor, it appeared to be a trick to make them look bad. One liberal blogger even claimed responsibility for the forgery. Yet this episode is emblematic of the typical American Taliban approach to reality: eager to embrace information that validates their worldview, yet refusing to accept reality.

Her legal efforts in shambles, facing court sanctions for her antics, her reputation in tatters, Taitz resorted to that final trope for dejected and demoralized members of the American Taliban, and no, it was not organizing for the 2012 elections. "The simple fact is that we are long overdue for another rebellion in this nation, and I heartily endorse the idea of having one again very soon, preferably starting *this* year!"

One might be tempted to dismiss Taitz and her merry band of birthers as fringe wingnuts, but the sad reality is that Taitz and her lunatic ranting actually fall well within the Republican mainstream. A January 2010 poll of self-identified Republicans by independent pollster Research 2000 asked, "Do you believe Barack Obama was born in the United States, or not?" A full 36 percent said he was not born in the United States; 22 percent were unsure. A Public Policy Polling poll from September 2009 showed that 39 percent of self-identified Republican respondents were birthers and that another 22 percent were flirting with the idea. About a third of Republican respondents to a *Washington Post/ABC News* poll in May 2010 couldn't accept the fact that Obama was born in Hawaii.

Heck, even Sarah Palin, fast becoming the queen bee of the American Taliban hive, went birther, saying, "I think [Obama's birth certificate] is a fair question just like I think past associations and past voting records. All of that is fair game." Other Republicans like Reps. Roy Blunt of Missouri and Jean Schmidt of Ohio, and Senator Richard Shelby of Alabama, have expressed their sympathies for the birther cause, feeding a ludicrous conspiracy theory that shows no sign of abating.

What originally came together as a lonely band of kooks in early 2009 grew rapidly, and the birthers were no longer lone warriors in their crusade against Obama. They were joined—perhaps the better word is "co-opted"—by a "Tea Party" movement seeking the destruction of the Obama/Democratic agenda. And they're not doing a bad job of it, either.

The "teabaggers" are rabid conservative activists who have taken to the streets to protest the Obama administration and its allies in Congress. They compare themselves to participants in the historic Boston Tea Party, in which angry colonists dumped British East India Company tea into Boston Harbor to protest the violation of their right to be taxed by their own elected representatives. The battle cry was "no taxation without representation," which is *exactly* like the teabaggers in the Obama era, who apparently are only "represented" when their chosen candidate wins an election. Otherwise, it's like living in a monarchy or a dictatorship. Or something like that.

A typical teabagger rally is like a dozen ditzy Orly Taitzes in one place, at one time, on steroids. Sure, there's the birther stuff, but there's a lot more demented crap, too: pictures from the Holocaust of dead Jewish children, Obama pics with Hitler mustaches, anti-immigrant bigotry, signs proclaiming "Obama Bin-Lyin, Free our Markets, Not the Terrorists," "Obama's Plan, White Slavery," and so on. What's more, they've been fueled by the GOP's leadership. The conservative movement's chief propaganda arm, Fox News, relentlessly promoted the teabagger protests. In fact, the network was even caught moving protesters around to get better camera shots, essentially directing the protests, rather than merely reporting on them like a legitimate news organization. At a teabagger protest in Washington DC called by Rep. Michelle Bachmann of Minnesota (also "batshit insane"), the entire House Republican leadership, including Minority Leader John Boehner of Ohio, spoke to the crowd. "I do think there is a rebellion going on in this country," Boehner told the protesters. "How else could you get 10,000 people to show up with only a few days notice?" If the mathematically challenged Boehner thought 10,000 people showing up constituted a "rebellion" in a nation of 300 million, I wonder what he made of the real millions who marched in 2003 in opposition to the Iraq War; 10,000 people would have been a rounding error at the mostly ignored anti-war rallies.

But it's hard to doubt the teabaggers' effectiveness, at least at commanding media attention. They exploded onto the national political scene in August 2009, disrupting the town halls of elected officials. Indeed, their goal wasn't to engage in rational debate or a civil exchange of ideas. A widely circulated memo among teabagging circles provided a peek into their strategy of orchestrated disruption.

- Artificially inflate the size of the protesters: "Spread out in the hall and try to be in the front half. The objective is to put the Rep on the defensive with your questions and follow-up. The Rep should be made to feel that a majority, and if not, a significant portion of at least the audience, opposes the socialist agenda of Washington."

- Disrupt. "You need to rock-the-boat early in the Rep's presentation. Watch for an opportunity to yell out and challenge the Rep's statements early."

- Seek to unnerve the elected official. "The goal is to rattle him, get him off his prepared script and agenda. If he says something outrageous, stand up and shout out and sit right back down. Look for these opportunities before he even takes questions." Also, "The balance of the group should applaud when [teabagger] question is asked, further putting the Rep on the defensive. If the Rep tries a particularly odious diversion, someone from group should yell out to answer the question. These tactics will clearly rattle the Rep and illustrate some degree of his ineptness to the balance of the audience."

This blueprint for mob-style harassment got ugly when put into action. At a town hall meeting for Senator Arlen Specter in mid-August 2009, police and security guards had to fan out across the aisles to physically restrain the crowd. Long Island Democratic Representative Tim Bishop cancelled his town halls after an acrimonious one where police had to escort him safely to his car—the first time he'd had any such problem in over 100 town halls he'd held since being elected in 2002. "There is no point in meeting with my constituents [to] listen to them and have them listen to you if what is basically an unruly mob prevents you from having an intelligent conversation."

It wasn't just Democrats facing these hostile tactics. The teabaggers also targeted Republicans not sufficiently aligned with their radical agenda. South Carolina Senator Lindsey Graham came under assault at a mid-October 2009 event in Greenville for voting to confirm Supreme Court Justice Sonia Sotomayor and signaling his willingness to deal with the Obama administration on clean energy legislation. Graham is no liberal; his voting record garnered him a *National Journal* ranking as the 15th most conservative senator, and one from Progressive Punch as the 27th most conservative (more so than conservative stalwarts Tom Coburn, Chuck Grassley, John Thune, and Richard Shelby). But rationality and logic are not the strong points of the American Taliban, which would prefer 30 ideologically pure senators than a bigger tent with a 51-seat majority. One rabble-rouser elicited wild applause when he yelled, "When are you going to announce that you are switching parties?" Graham responded, "I'm going to grow this party, I'm not going to let it get [inaudible], I'm not going to let it be hijacked by Ron Paul. . . . I'm going to find people in Maine, Delaware, Illinois, other places . . ." The audience response? "Move there!"

The teabaggers weren't any more tolerant of others in the crowd who disagreed with them. At a November 14, 2009, Oak Lawn (in the Chicago area) town hall held by Democratic Representative Dan Lipinski, Dan and Midge Hough told the tragic story of their daughter-in-law Jenny, who was pregnant and unable to afford regular prenatal care, ending up in the emergency room with double pneumonia that turned into septic shock. The baby died in the womb, and Jenny died several weeks later. She left behind her husband and a two-year-old daughter.

As Midge Hough told the story, the teabaggers in the audience began to heckle her, and many laughed openly. After the event, Catherina Wajtowicz of the Chicago Tea Party Patriots claimed the story was fabricated and that the Houghs were Obama operatives who "go from event to event and (cry) the same story." The Houghs' story wasn't fabricated, and they didn't make a habit of attending events outside their district, but for the teabaggers, such details were irrelevant. Whether it was waving a sign that said, "Bury Obamacare With Kennedy" days after Senator Ted Kennedy's death, or proudly using the Twitter tag "#iamthemob" to describe themselves, subtlety and class are not the hallmarks of this gang.

Yet by early 2010, their successes were impossible to overlook. They were even willing to lose a reliably Republican seat in a special House election in northern New York, just to send a message to their party that any candidates less than ideologically pure would be sabotaged. Indeed, any elected official caught working with Democrats on *anything* was a candidate for a good teabagging. In Florida, popular Governor Charlie Crist, once seen as a sure shot for the state's open senate seat in November 2010, came under siege for backing Obama's legislation that provided states with billions in economic stimulus funds to protect jobs during a deep recession. The teabagger candidate—Marco Rubio—flipped nearly overnight from underdog to the favorite in the race, fueled by the outrage of the purity faction.

But their ability to influence public opinion paled in comparison to the way they raised money and promoted the candidacy of Scott Brown in Massachusetts, a long shot in the special election to fill the late Ted Kennedy's seat. Losing Teddy's seat to the first teabagger senator was a gut-punch to liberals, and evidence to teabaggers that their brand of populism, in a brutal anti-incumbent political environment, was a force to be reckoned with. Although the teabagger agenda, out of step with mainstream America, would prove problematic long-term for the GOP, its early successes bolstered its ability to impose ideological rigidity inside an already uncompromising political party.

In the teabaggers, the American Taliban found their enforcers.

Once "that Black Man" moved into the White House, the American Taliban lost whatever few marbles they had left. It's as if the

South had risen again, and it was time for an uncivil war. Alongside the birthers and the teabaggers, we saw the resurgence of, believe it or not, *secessionists*.

˙ Responding to a North Korean missile test on April 6, 2009, Sarah Palin declared, "I am deeply concerned with North Korea's development and testing program, which has clear potential of impacting Alaska, a sovereign state of the United States, with a potentially nuclear armed warhead." A *sovereign state* of the United States? The word "sovereignty" means supreme, independent authority over a territory, something clearly residing with the federal government. Maybe it was a typical Palin slip of the tongue, overburdened by the stress of her brief tenure as governor (something she quit soon thereafter)? Nope. Palin's not alone. A Texas House resolution declared, "Whereas, The Tenth Amendment assures that we, the people of the United States of America and each *sovereign state* in the Union of States, now have, and have always had, rights the federal government may not usurp . . ." At an April 9, 2009, press conference explaining his support, Texas Governor Rick Perry said,

> We think it's time to draw the line in the sand and tell Washington that no longer are we going to accept their oppressive hand in the state of Texas. That's what this press conference, that's what these Texans are standing up for. There is a point in time where you stand up and say enough is enough, and I think Americans, and Texans especially have reached that point.

Obama had been president for less than three months, and that's all it took to break Texas. Fox News personality Glenn Beck, a chief coach of the teabagger movement, couldn't contain his excitement. "I have to tell you, you know, I've been a little iffy on Governor Perry because of the way he's handled the border in the past. I didn't think he was real tough on the border, but holy cow. What a statement coming from him on state sovereignty." Sovereignty resolutions have been introduced in 37 state legislatures, and have passed in seven—Alaska, Idaho, North Dakota, South Dakota, Oklahoma, Louisiana, and Tennessee. Ironically, those are some of the largest recipients, per capita, of federal dollars. Alaska ranks 2nd, Louisiana 3rd, and North Dakota ranks 8th. Tennessee ranks lowest at 21st, meaning all are in the top half. Yet none of these "sovereign" states would dream of rejecting those federal dollars. And none of them cared about "sovereignty" when one of their own American Taliban members, George W. Bush, was in charge.

Governor Perry, locked in a tough Republican primary against popular Senator Kay Bailey Hutchison, worked to get the teabaggers on his side, positioning himself as quite the revolutionary and frequenting rallies and events full of sound, fury, and irrational "patriots." On April 15, 2009, addressing a rally in Austin, Perry embraced the teabaggers as his own. "I'm just not real sure you're a bunch of right-wing extremists. But if you are, we're with you!" He then launched into a tirade against the federal government amid chants of "Secede!" Speaking to reporters after his speech, he said people had a right to demand secession, "There's absolutely no reason to dissolve it. But if Washington continues to thumb their nose at the American people, you know, who knows what might come out of that." The leader of the Texas National Movement, a pro-secession outfit, was overcome with appreciation for Perry. "When [Perry] was giving a speech and the crowd began to shout what?—Secede! Secede! Secede!—That's what they chanted. So they asked him afterward, 'What do you think?' He said, 'Well, we reserve that right; if things get so bad we reserve the right to leave,'" said Daniel Miller. "And I gotta tell you it's the first solid thing he's done in his administration that I can agree with in many, many years."

Reserving the right to leave, eh? Guess that means the "America, love it or leave it" crowd doesn't love their country anymore.

Texas Representative Ron Paul, a two-time presidential contender (once as a Libertarian, once as a Republican), couldn't agree more.

> [Perry] really stirred some of the liberal media, where they started screaming about: "What is going on here, this is un-American." I heard one individual say, "This is treasonous to even talk about it." Well, they don't know their history very well, because if they think about it ... it is very American to talk about secession. That's how we came into being. Thirteen colonies seceded from the British and established a new country. So secession is a very much American principle.

Seceding from Britain? That *was* very American. Seceding from America? Not so much. Seems we fought a little war over this, in fact.

It sure ain't patriotism. Such talk is cowardly and treasonous. For a group of people obsessed with flag lapel pins and obnoxious jingoism, it was suddenly clear that their allegiance to their nation was a mile wide and an inch deep, and only operative as long as members of their own American Taliban controlled the levers of power in DC. Rather than respect the Constitution and our nation's democratic principles, they were quick to chant "Secede!" at the first sign of adversity. They are fair-weather patriots, loving America only when it carries out their agenda. They pledge allegiance to the flag of the United States of America, and to the *Republican* for which it stands, one nation, under god, indivisible, with justice and liberty for all—but *only* if the majority elected a president they supported. Otherwise, scratch that part about "one nation," and delete that part about "indivisible," and forget that part about "pledge allegiance," and certainly ignore that part about "for all." But don't mess with "under god," because that's the *one* phrase of the pledge that is sacrosanct to the American Taliban.

Crazy as it seems, Governor Perry and friends are speaking to a significant portion of the American Taliban when talking secession. In April 2009, the polling firm Research 2000 asked, "Do you think Texas would be better off as an independent nation or as part of the United States of America?" Forty-eight percent of Republican respondents in Texas said "an independent nation," whereas an equal percentage wanted Texas to remain part of America. Asked whether they approved of Perry's secession remarks, 51 percent of Republican respondents said "yes." That's a majority.

In another survey soon thereafter, Republican pollster Scott Rasmussen asked, "If you could vote on the issue, would you vote for Texas to remain in the United States, or for Texas to secede from the United States?" Over a quarter of self-identified conservative respondents—26 percent—said they'd vote for secession; another 12 percent were undecided about their patriotism. The ultimate poll, of course, was election day. Perry won the Republican nomination with 51.1 percent of the vote—21 percent more than the runner-up challenger.

All of this points up a major difference between liberals and the American Taliban. When George W. Bush was installed as president in 2000, California Governor Gray Davis didn't call for secession to the cheers of his constituents. Rather, out of respect for the democratic institutions of our country, liberals worked to persuade the American people to vote differently in the next election. Yet the American Taliban, like their ideological twins in the Islamic world, have nothing but disdain for democracy and the machinery that keeps it going.

After President Mahmoud Ahmadinejad stole the 2009 Iranian elections, Iran's Supreme Leader Ali Khamenei gave due credit to his god. "In the Islamic Republic, aside from the 1979 referendum, there has been no election like the one held last Friday with a turnout of almost 85 percent. This means almost 40 million voters. You can see the presence of the 12 and last Shia Imam behind this. This is a sign of God's blessing to us." American conservatives were beside themselves in anger at this usurpation of democracy, yet it wasn't so very long ago that their very own god supposedly handed one of their own, George W. Bush, the White House despite the wishes of the American electorate. "Why is this man in the White House?" asked Lt. Gen. William G. Boykin, a top-ranking Pentagon officer and a member of the American Taliban, who has stirred international anger and unnecessarily riled up the Muslim world by casting the "War on Terror" in biblical terms. "The majority of Americans did not vote for him. I tell you this morning that he's in the White House because God put him there for a time such as this." So Khameini says it's "God's blessing" to have an unelected leader in Iran and Boykin says "God put" the unelected leader in office in America. They're birds of a feather, even if they don't flock together.

But what happened in 2008? Why had their god, who so thoughtfully stole the 2000 election for them, failed to prevent Obama from becoming president? Ah, well. Funny story: turns out their god was no match for the all-powerful, all-knowing ACORN—the Association of Community Organizations for Reform Now, the most omnipotent group Americans had never heard of until it became the latest straw bogeyman.

In our January 2010 poll of Republicans, 21 percent of respondents believed that ACORN stole the election for Obama, whereas 55 percent were undecided on the matter. Just 24 percent rejected this absurd premise outright. So who or what is ACORN and why does the American Taliban believe it "stole" the election for Obama? ACORN is an activist organization focused on advocacy for low-income Americans with regards to affordable housing, the minimum wage, health care, and other social issues. Although ACORN is a nonpartisan organization, it has a legally separate, political-action component, which endorsed Obama in 2008. In addition, it conducted voter registration drives using signature gatherers who were paid based on the signatures they gathered. A small handful of them "registered" fake names, including the ubiquitous "Mickey Mouse." And thus another conservative conspiracy theory was born.

There was never any danger of Mickey Mouse or any other fictional registrant actually turning out to vote. Despite repeated GOP assertions, this was not *voter* fraud, it was *registration* fraud. And the fraud was perpetrated against ACORN, which was paying for valid and legitimate registrations, not against Republican candidates, who never had to *genuinely* worry about losing the cartoon mice demographic.

"By all indications, ACORN operates within the American political mainstream, though clearly it favors the left side of the ideological spectrum," wrote PolitiFact—a Pulitzer Prize–winning fact-checking operation of the *St. Petersburg Times*. "Its voter registration efforts tend to focus on the low-income, minorities and youth, all traditional Democratic constituencies. Obama received an endorsement from the group's political action committee in February 2008 when the Democratic primary was in full swing. But that's not to say Republicans never support ACORN's efforts: McCain himself appeared at a 2006 rally in favor of immigration reform, sponsored in part by ACORN."

That didn't stop Republicans from trying to make hay about ACORN's "voter fraud" on behalf of Obama and the Democratic Party. John McCain himself, in the final presidential debate, was nearly hysterical. "We need to know the full extent of Senator Obama's relationship with ACORN, who is now on the verge of maybe perpetrating one of the greatest frauds in voter history in this country, maybe destroying the fabric of democracy."

Conservative media took their cues from candidate McCain and amped up the ACORN hysteria. In the four-day period before the 2008 election, ACORN was mentioned 67 times on MSBNC, 112 times on CNN, and 706 times on Fox News. Obama's victory merely cemented the fiction that those low-income housing advocates had fraudulently generated Obama's nine-million-vote margin. And the anti-ACORN hysteria proved a strong GOP boogeyman through 2009. "A portion of ACORN's People's Platform manifesto drafted in 1970 reads, and I quote, 'We come before our nation not to petition with hat in hand, but to rise as one people and demand. We will no longer wait for the crumbs at America's door. We will continue our fight until the American way is just one way, until we have shared the wealth,'" reported Glenn Beck on his show, shaking in anger at the thought of low-income Americans demanding a piece of the American dream. "The question tonight is: How much has the radical Left influenced President Barack Obama and our government? Barack Obama has spent a large portion of his career working for ACORN and its subsidiaries. And now, in his first term, he begins to share the wealth."

Low-income housing advocates of the world, unite!

Beck isn't alone. From Rep. Michelle Bachmann, to Rush Limbaugh, to virtually the entire conservative online world, ACORN is an all-powerful organization pretty much *run* by Obama (even though his entire involvement with the organization was a court case and a training session with them early in his career), able to crush the will of American voters at the ballot box.

So the American Taliban think Obama is an illegitimate president because he was born in Kenya and had ACORN steal the election for him. Don't be surprised that they believe these crazy conspiracy theories. We saw the same phenomenon at work during the Iraq War, with large numbers of these same people believing that Saddam Hussein and Iraq perpetrated the 9/11 terrorist attacks and other similar nonsense. These beliefs persist because their ringleaders, with a heavy assist from their cheerleaders in the media (Fox News, Rush Limbaugh, etc.) keep repeating the lies until they are firmly embedded as "truth" in the collective American Taliban mind.

But the truth is, the American Taliban are prime fodder for duping, in thrall to conspiracy theorists and demagogues who see plots and plotters behind every door. Light a match, throw in craziness about Obama being a socialist (79 percent in our January 2010 poll believe it or aren't sure) who wants the terrorists to win (57 percent believe it or aren't sure), and it's no surprise that this crowd fantasizes about evicting him from the White House. In a December 2009 poll by Public Policy Polling (PPP), 35 percent of Republicans were demanding Obama's *impeachment*. In January, our poll found the number to be 39 percent, with another 29 percent mulling the idea. Just 32 percent of self-identified Republicans seemed sane enough to realize that absent any scandal suggesting high crimes or misdemeanors, there are no real grounds to impeach the president.

Of course, these were the people who lusted for pre-emptive war. What's a little pre-emptive impeachment after *that*?

In any case, from the American Taliban point of view, this "democracy" thing is messy and can churn out unsatisfactory results from time to time. A good ol' dictatorship would be easier and more efficient, as George W. Bush said after meeting with the top four congressional leaders in December 2000, before he took office the next month. "I told all four that there were going to be some times where we don't agree with each other. But that's OK. If this were a dictatorship, it'd be a heck of a lot easier, just so long as I'm the dictator."

So here we are a decade later, in the Obama era, and the American Taliban are now front-and-center in the Republican Party. They have little love for America, disrespecting its democratic traditions, its diversity of opinion, its pluralism. They rail irrationally against a president they deem illegitimate and pine for secession from a country they pretend to defend. They whine about the tyranny of secularism, yet openly dream of their own regressive brand of religious dictatorship.

Theirs isn't a movement built on the values that made America great but rather one dedicated, devoutly, to the unbridled pursuit of power at all costs. Their ideological certainty leaves them with little tolerance for the trappings of democracy. When challenged, they are all too quick to resort to violence.

2

WAR

On Interstate 70 in Lafayette County in northwestern Missouri, the local Republican Party celebrated the appearance of a new billboard in late 2009, proudly displaying an image of it on its website. The old billboard had featured a communist hammer and sickle and read, HOW DO YOU LIKE YOUR CHANGE NOW? OBAMA-NATION. THEY ARE COMING FOR YOU! THE TAX-PAYER. 1ST & 2ND AMENDMENTS ARE IN JEOPARDY. LIVE FREE OR DIE. Apparently, red-baiting wasn't doing the trick, so the sponsors replaced it with a somewhat harsher message. The new billboard:

A Citizens Guide to REVOLUTION of a corrupt government.

1. Starve the Beast.
2. Vote out incumbents.
3. If steps 1 & 2 fail?

PREPARE FOR WAR—LIVE FREE OR DIE!

The message was not, "Register to Vote—Take Back Your Country!" or "Send a Message to Obama—Vote Republican!" As we've seen, the American Taliban have a deep-seated disrespect for democracy, only embracing it when their own are elected. So what happens if step #2 in this "Citizens Guide" fails? They certainly have no interest in accepting the will of the voters. For them, it's either a ballot-box victory, or it's war.

This, of course, is emblematic of the American Taliban, just as it is for their anti-democratic brethren in the world of Islamic extremism. Democracy requires tolerating diversity and dissent and accepting the popular will, even if offensive to one's personal beliefs or religion. Both Talibans, however, see diplomacy and democratic process as an avenue for the weak or, to use the term popularized by Governor Arnold Schwarzenegger, "girlie men." This disregard for the give-and-take of democracy, for the legitimate use of persuasion and reason, would be troubling on its own. But coupled with the American Taliban's glorification of guns (a trait also shared with their Islamic counterparts), the testosterone-driven talk of violence underscores their latent militancy, their eagerness for war. It is what fueled the 9/11 attacks, and it is what fueled the Iraq war.

A rural Missouri billboard blaring "Prepare for War" expresses the same militant mindset as graffiti scrawled on a wall in Kabul saying "Death to America."

Much of the American Taliban's talk is directed at their favorite foe—the Islamic extremists so like themselves. "You've got to kill the terrorists before the killing stops and I am for the President— chase them all over the world, if it takes 10 years, blow them all away in the name of the Lord," said prominent American Taliban member, the late Jerry Falwell, speaking on national television in 2004. There's no qualitative difference between that and Osama bin Laden saying, "We are on the course of opening more fronts, with God's permission, so what would be better, my dear nation, than putting your hand in the hands of your sons the Mujahideen so we can continue Jihad against the enemies of the faith, so we can continue bleeding them out in these two wars, these two open fronts in front of you against the crusader Zionist alliance and their agents in the region in Palestine, Iraq, Afghanistan, and Waziristan and Islamic North Africa and in Somalia."

It's one thing for bin Laden to engage in his fiery rhetoric aimed at mobilizing uneducated Muslims to kill in the name of god. But it is quite another for Americans to sink to the same level, as Falwell does, expressing his bloodlust "in the name of the Lord." Once you do that, as soon as you respond to the 9/11 attacks—as horrific and tragic and unjustified as they were—with the same apocalyptic language and the same methods of motivation, you have effectively erased the difference between them and us, and lost the higher ground that a modern civilized democracy has over terrorism.

Our struggle against Al Qaeda is not a theological one, but you'd be hard pressed to know that from the rhetoric of the American Taliban. Listen to Lt. Gen. William G. Boykin sermonizing at an Oklahoma church in June 2002. "We in the army of God, in the house of God, kingdom of God, have been raised for such a time as this." At a speech in Daytona, Florida, he told the following story about a man in Mogadishu named Osman Atto, whom Boykin identified as a top lieutenant to Somali warlord Mohammed Farah Aidid. During an operation, Boykin's unit came within seconds of capturing him.

> He went on CNN and he laughed at us, and he said, "They'll never get me because Allah will protect me. Allah will protect me." Well, you know what? I knew that my God was bigger than his. I knew that my God was a real God and his was an idol.

When Atto was captured three days later, Boykin confronted Atto in his cell: "You underestimated our God."

Sounds like a bunch of 12-year-old boys bragging about the fighting prowess of their daddies, only it's grown-ups with guns, bombs, and fatal consequences.

Keep in mind that Boykin was not just some grunt shooting his mouth off; then Secretary of Defense Donald Rumsfeld had appointed him deputy undersecretary of defense for intelligence, in charge of tracking down bin Laden, Mullah Omar, Saddam Hussein, and others. As such, his public statements of a jihad-in-return—such as "our spiritual enemy will only be defeated if we come against them in the name of Jesus"—rise to the level of official policy, especially to people in the Muslim world hearing such messianic messages emanating from top American military leaders.

Nor does it help to have prominent members of the American Taliban egging Boykin on with their own jingoistic crap. Pat Buchanan was quick to defend Boykin, saying, "To a devout Christian, there is not only nothing wrong with the general's beliefs, everything is right about them. For just as Muslims do not accept Jesus as God, Christians do not accept Muhammad. Martyrs, whether to Christianity or Islam, do not die to testify that all faiths are equal."

William Arkin, a former U.S. Army intelligence officer, was a welcome voice of moderation, writing in 2003 in the *Los Angeles Times* why this kind of claptrap was dangerous.

> In describing the war against terrorism, President Bush frequently says it "is not a war against Islam." In his National Security Strategy, Bush declared that "the war on terrorism is not a clash of civilizations." Yet many in the Islamic world see the U.S. as waging a cultural and religious war against them.

Arkin quoted a report by a White House advisory group on public diplomacy for the Arab and Muslim world. "Arabs and Muslims respond in anger to what they perceive as U.S. denigration of their societies and cultures . . . The task for the U.S. is to wage a major struggle to expand the zone of tolerance and marginalize extremists."

The right tone was set by President Barack Obama in May 2009, when he delivered a speech at the National Archives, and said,

> From Europe to the Pacific we've been the nation that has shut down torture chambers and replaced tyranny with the rule of law. That is who we are. And where terrorists offer only the injustice of disorder and destruction, America must demonstrate that our values and institutions are more resilient than a hateful ideology.

Yet the American Taliban refuse to heed such calls to order and reason, embracing instead their very own bloodthirsty hateful ideology. "We know who the homicidal maniacs are," Ann Coulter famously snarled after the 9/11 attacks. "They are the ones cheering and dancing right now. We should invade their countries, kill their leaders, and convert them to Christianity."

Rather than marginalize and isolate the Islamic extremists, the American Taliban actively *seek* out that clash of civilizations. It's no different than Osama bin Laden and his ideological ilk. For the Saudi terrorist, his religion is no more a "religion of peace" than Christianity is for the American Taliban; both sides dehumanize the other to better rally the troops to their bloodthirsty cause. "Islam is a religion in which God requires you to send your son to die for him," U.S. Attorney General John Ashcroft said in November 2001. "Christianity is a faith in which God sends his son to die for you." God, maybe, but George W. Bush and the rest of the American Taliban have been all too eager to send the sons and daughters of other Americans to die for their misguided causes.

And heavens knows, there never is a shortage of war lust with that crowd, which presents a dilemma for them, given the general public's distaste for needless death and destruction, not to mention the budget-busting cost of warfare in a time of economic distress. The attacks on 9/11 were manna from heaven—as clear-cut a case for war as any. So clear-cut, in fact, that the administration quickly pivoted from the real enemy—Al Qaeda in Afghanistan and Pakistan—to an unnecessary and costly war in Iraq. Without 9/11, the trumped-up rationales for the Iraq invasion would never have existed.

Yet the American public has soured on our wars, even the justified one in Afghanistan, and clamors to bring our troops home, safe and sound, to their families. How can the American Taliban satiate their war lust, when the American people refuse to play ball, and a Democrat occupies the Oval Office? Simple. They inflate the influence of their enemies. In these exaggerated scenarios, Iran is *this* close to getting nuclear weapons, and Al Qaeda is the most nefarious and powerful force in the universe.

When the "crotch bomber" failed spectacularly to take down Northwest Airlines Flight 253 in December 2009, the only thing more pathetic than Al Qaeda taking "credit" for the buffoonish attack, was conservatives rushing to give the terrorists the very victory they had been denied. Bill Kristol, founder and editor of the conservative *Weekly Standard* and chief architect of the neo-conservative strategy that led us into the Iraq quagmire, was disappointed in the failed attempt. On *Fox News Sunday*, he declared, "This last week has been a victory for Al Qaeda." Fox anchor Brit Hume readily agreed, "If I were the Al Qaeda people, I think Bill's right. They could look at this as a success. This was an attack that didn't succeed on the scale it was expected to but did succeed." Lurita Doan, a Bush administration bureaucrat, wrote at the conservative Big Government website, "Everyone keeps saying how lucky we are that the 'crotch' bomber on Flight 253 was unable to ignite the explosives hidden in his underwear, but I am sorry to report that the attack was actually a huge success."

First, it was not an "attack," it was an *attempted* attack. Second, it was not a "success," it *failed*. Yet the nonsensical assertion went unchallenged. The Arab media ignored the incident, uninterested in sensationalizing a failure. Yet the American Taliban propaganda arm was gleeful, giving the story front-page treatment and using it as an opportunity to relive the glory post-9/11 days, when they scared the public into surrendering civil liberties and sending our men and women in uniform to die over there, so the terrorists didn't kill us over here. And if Al Qaeda actually proves to be a paper tiger, unable to follow up on its one spectacular attack? Doesn't matter. The mission has been accomplished—terror is in the news again! Thus you have the bizarre situation, where Al Qaeda's biggest champion and cheerleader building them up to be the biggest, baddest, scariest group on the planet, is the American Taliban. Just consider how often the Bush administration blamed "Al Qaeda" for every military attack in Iraq, despite the fact that most insurgent attacks were carried out by nationalist groups.

Ultimately, American conservatives are willing to hand Al Qaeda a huge propaganda victory as long as their own strategic goals of furthering war are advanced. Unfortunately for our country, the conservative fluffing of Al Qaeda's power has real-world repercussions.

In July 2007, Marc Lynch, a political scientist at George Washington University, author of *Voices of the New Arab Public*, and an expert in Arab media, wrote,

> The real harm comes in the wider Arab and Muslim world, where the exaggeration of al-Qaeda's role works directly and devastatingly against American goals. It magnifies al-Qaeda's perceived power, strengthening its own media campaign and feeding its most powerful propaganda instrument . . .
>
> The [Bush] administration in effect claims more power and military success for al-Qaeda in Iraq than al-Qaeda claims for itself—for which the al-Qaeda leadership can only be bemusedly grateful. If you're looking for a real public diplomacy fiasco, you'll be hard pressed to do worse than the US acting as al-Qaeda's agent in promoting its Iraqi success.

As John Brennan, a senior counterterrorism advisor to Obama, noted in a *USA Today* opinion piece in February 2010, "Terrorists are not 100-feet tall. Nor do they deserve the abject fear they seek to instill." They don't deserve it, but the American Taliban will do everything they can to give our enemies that power anyway. Without that enemy, without instilling fear, the American Taliban's hold on the public is tenuous at best.

Once they have identified their enemy, these fundamentalists (from both sides of the world) delight in their own versions of shock and awe. Asked to respond to the assertion that Islam was spread by the sword, radical Sheikh Muhammed Salih Al-Munajjid of Saudi Arabia wrote on his website, Islam-QA.com, "Islam was spread by proof and evidence, in the case of those who listened to the message and responded to it. And it was spread by strength and the sword in the case of those who stubbornly resisted, until they had no choice and had to submit to the new reality." A sermon recorded by Australian Sheik Feiz Mohammad gave a new reason for having children. "We want to have children and offer them as soldiers defending Islam," said the crazy cleric, who was also head of the Global Islamic Youth Center in western Sydney. "Teach them this: there is nothing more beloved to me than wanting to die as a *mujahid*. Put in their soft, tender hearts the zeal of jihad and a love of martyrdom." Over in England, the imam of Finsbury Park Mosque, Abu Hamza al-Masri, was no less incendiary. "The real weapons of mass destruction are the desire for martyrdom. Millions of you are ready to be *shaheed*. Half a million martyrdom *shaheed* is enough for Muslims to control the whole of earth forever. In the end of the day, Islam must control earth, whether we like it or not." He was convicted by a British court on 11 counts of encouraging the murder of non-Muslims and inciting racial hatred.

And let's not forget the "Blind Sheikh" of Brooklyn, Omar Abdel-Rahman. After his 1995 conviction on sedition charges for his involvement in the first World Trade Center bombing and later schemes to hit targets like the United Nations, the George Washington Bridge, the Lincoln and Holland Tunnels, and the FBI's New York City headquarters, a defiant Abdel-Rahman called on Muslims to "dismember their nation, tear them apart, ruin their economy, provoke their corporations, destroy their embassies, attack their interests, sink their ships, shoot down their planes, kill them on land, at sea, and in the air. Kill them wherever you find them."

That hateful war lust is easily matched by the American Taliban. Jerry Falwell, on Phil Donahue's television show, couldn't contain his glee at the coming religious war.

> *Caller:* Hi, Phil. I would like to say that what kind of a normal person creates thousands and thousands of gallons of chemical and biological agents? Then you have President Bush, who's a noble man, saying, look, this is a threat. We have—I have to

protect my people. I am the leader. He's a noble man, and he's getting beat up for trying to fight and protect us!

Falwell: Amen!

Caller: And let me tell you another thing. We're going to have to face this threat one time or another. And we'd better get it now, before this guy gets stronger . . .

Falwell: Amen!

Funny what a potent mix religion and war make. The covers of the daily intelligence briefings that Secretary of Defense Donald Rumsfeld hand-delivered to President Bush were typically adorned with gung-ho images of American soldiers alongside biblical quotes. One cover featured a picture of an F/A-18 Hornet fighter jet on the deck of an aircraft carrier, with Psalm 139:9–10: "If I rise on the wings of the dawn, if I settle on the far side of the sea, even there your hand will guide me, your right hand will hold me fast, O Lord." Another featured a photograph of Saddam Hussein with a passage from 1 Peter 2:15: "It is God's will that by doing good you should silence the ignorant talk of foolish men." Rumsfeld and Bush were so satisfied with their holy war that they didn't even need to be subtle about it. When Pentagon officials argued against the covers, fearful that any leaks would further inflame Arab passions and prove costly to troops on the ground, the official behind the covers, Major General Glen Shaffer, brushed off the criticism, noting that his work was "appreciated by my seniors"—Bush and Rumsfeld.

Yet as disastrously wrong as the American Taliban's neocons were about their pet war in Iraq, their appetites remain unsated. They want more. More conflict, more drama, more blood. In the 2008 presidential campaign, John McCain thought it hilarious to sing, to the tune of the Beach Boys' "Barbara Ann," "Bomb,

bomb, bomb, bomb bomb Iran . . ." And the American Taliban's latest enemy de jour, Iran, remains an obsessive target for those who don't believe America has suffered enough war in the past decade. Sarah Palin, for example, thought it would be fantastic as a way for Obama to cynically secure his re-election campaign. "Say [Obama] played the war card. Say he decided to declare war on Iran or decided really [to] come out and do whatever he could to support Israel, *which I would like him to do*, but—that changes the dynamics in what we can assume is going to happen between now and three years."

These political fundamentalists, whether Islamic or American, have zero problem playing the war card for domestic gain, sending our bravest to die in distant wars as thoughtlessly as they would move pieces around a game of Risk. Such reckless warmongering behavior results in death and destruction, all in service to their god or their political ambitions.

Yet, as bad as it is when the American Taliban direct such violent sentiment at our external enemies, it is a direct threat to our democracy when aimed at domestic targets.

Certain segments of the American Taliban have always been particularly prone to violent action, such as the anti-abortion movement. "We proclaim that whatever force is legitimate to defend the life of a born child is legitimate to defend the life of an unborn child," claims the Army of God, an extremist organization that supports the assassination of abortion doctors, on its website. It grants its followers permission to take "all Godly action necessary, including the use of force, to defend innocent human life (born and unborn)."

Among the nine people murdered by these extremists was Dr. George Tiller, a physician in Wichita, Kansas, and a long-time target of anti-abortion violence. In 1986, his clinic was firebombed and in 1993, an anti-abortion activist shot Tiller in both arms. Among the doctor's critics was Bill O'Reilly, who used his widely watched program on Fox News to attack Tiller. Starting in 2005, O'Reilly discussed Tiller at least 28 times, repeatedly referring to him as "Tiller the baby killer." O'Reilly's hard work demonizing Tiller finally paid off when, on May 31, 2009, Tiller was assassinated at his Wichita church. He was serving as an usher and handing out church bulletins when Scott Roeder walked up to him and shot him through his eye at point-blank range. Roeder had a checkered past as a long-time anti-government and anti-abortion crusader, having done jail time in the late 1990s on an explosives charge.

The ascendancy of Barack Obama that began in 2008 radicalized ever-growing numbers of fearful, hard-right conservatives. Vice-presidential candidate Sarah Palin's claims that Obama was "palling around with terrorists" would provoke near-riots at Republican rallies, with supporters screaming "Terrorist!" and "Kill him!" Responding to negative news reports, John McCain's campaign was forced to order Palin to tone down her rhetoric. At the same time, the Secret Service warned the Obama family of an unprecedented surge of threats against them, even as Palin was lobbing her verbal attacks. At least two assassination plots against Obama were busted during the campaign season.

The post-election season hasn't been much easier. On August 28, 2009, CNN's Rick Sanchez reported, "A CNN source with very close ties to the U.S. Secret Service confirmed to me today that threats on the life of the president of the United States have now risen by as much as 400 percent since his inauguration, 400 percent death threats against Barack Obama—quote—'in this environment' go far beyond anything the Secret Service has seen with any other president." The Secret Service told *Newsweek* in November 2009 that while the number of threats was high after the election and around the inauguration, they decreased throughout 2009 to normal levels.

Yet that return to normalcy does not erase the initial, violent reaction to Obama's inauguration. His historic election as the nation's first African American president was bound to stir up the racist fringe. Add to that the hysterical reaction to Democratic efforts to reform energy, health care, and immigration policy, and you had a volatile mix. The Southern Poverty Law Center, in an August 2009 report titled "Return of the Militias," examined this disturbing trend.

> The 1990s saw the rise and fall of the virulently anti-government "Patriot" movement, made up of paramilitary militias, tax defiers and so-called "sovereign citizens." Sparked by a combination of anger at the federal government and the deaths of political dissenters at Ruby Ridge, Idaho, and Waco, Texas, the movement took off in the middle of the decade and continued to grow even after 168 people were left dead by the 1995 bombing of Oklahoma City's federal building—an attack, the deadliest ever by domestic U.S. terrorists, carried out by men steeped in the rhetoric and conspiracy theories of the militias. In the years that followed, a truly remarkable number of criminal plots came out of the movement. But by early this century, the Patriots had largely faded, weakened by systematic prosecutions, aversion to growing violence, and a new, highly conservative president.
>
> They're back ... A key difference this time is that the federal government—the entity that almost the entire radical right views as its primary enemy—is headed by a black man. That, coupled with high levels of non-white immigration and a decline in the percentage of whites overall in America, has helped to racialize the Patriot movement, which in the past was not primarily motivated by race hate.

"Mainstream" conservatives, from Texas Governor Rick Perry and his secessionist talk, to media personalities like Rush Limbaugh and Fox News' Glenn Beck, actively encourage much of this movement with implicit messages of violence. Prone to conspiracy theories and an ingrained fear of the government (fanned for years by conservatives), a lot of militia types saw Barack Hussein Obama's election as a nightmare scenario, where the big bad government was now headed by a closeted Muslim black man and the whole white Christian nation fantasy was over.

Obama's election sparked a nationwide run on guns and ammunition, fueled by fear that he would soon be knocking on their doors to take away their guns. The FBI reported that between January and May 2009, the agency's background check system handled 6.1 million checks—an increase of 25.6 percent over the same period in 2008. And throughout 2009, gun dealers couldn't keep enough ammunition in stock to meet demand. "The ammo is being snapped up as soon as it comes in," said one Columbus, Ohio, area firearm instructor who was considering cancelling his monthly NRA pistol training class because of the shortages. "It's kind of like that run on Elmo dolls. People are in a frenzy." A blogger at a survivalist website remarked that the ammo shortage even extended to obscure caliber rounds, better suited for antique and niche weapons than mainstream guns. "When it looked like Obama was going to win I saw the writing on the wall and wanted to stock up," wrote this blogger. "I chose what are called 'oddball' calibers knowing the rush on 9mm, .223 Remington and anything 12Ga would drive prices through the roof and make getting these rounds a competition of who can get to the gun store the fastest and charge the most. Unfortunately I underestimated demand for the unique calibers because Luthi's [gun shop] is completely out of .327 Federal Magnum and .32 H&R Mag even though two or three weeks ago they had plenty that wasn't moving." An Austin-area dealer couldn't recall anything like it. "We've seen runs on various things before, but never this sustained or this lengthy. It's been a buying frenzy."

Smith & Wesson, the nation's largest handgun manufacturer, enjoyed record profits in 2009, with demand so strong they had a *quarter billion dollar backlog* in orders they were unable to ship. Even in a tanking economy, sales in handguns and tactical rifle products soared by more than 25 percent, setting records, even as the company's hunting division suffered a drop of 33 percent from the year before.

Most of that ammunition was being stashed in bunkers in preparation for that looming revolution vividly advocated by the Missouri billboard, exhorting the faithful to "Prepare for War—Live Free or Die!" This paranoia is fueled by the American Taliban's most mainstream voices in right-wing media, who seem distressed at the prospect of a more perfect union where *all* Americans have access to health care, where we have cleaner air and water, and where citizens are protected during flooding. They can't stand the idea of the government fighting to protect jobs, or bankers being forced to give back to the American taxpayers after the taxpayers bailed out Wall Street. No doubt expressing the sentiments of his entire American Taliban audience, Rush Limbaugh admitted one month after Obama took office that

> the dirty little secret is that every Republican in this country wants Obama to fail but none of them have the guts to say so. I am willing to say it. We want him to fail because we want to preserve our country as we found it. We do not want to see a successful attack on capitalism.

They certainly appear to believe capitalism is under siege. "What's in this [health care] legislation? The end of America as you know it, I believe," said Glenn Beck on his Fox News show in November 2009. "We are talking about massive, sweeping change. Americans showed up by the hundreds of thousands at various tea parties to demand the opposite of this: stop spending money. But look at these bills. Look at this. This is a fundamental transformation of America. They are moving at the speed of light and we've got to get up off of our couches and get into their offices. If we don't stop this insanity now, they will fundamentally transform America. It must end. You must make a choice."

This isn't a call for electoral organizing, nor for flooding politicians' email inboxes and voice mails, and it is most certainly not a call for any kind of peaceful and legitimate protest. It's a call to arms, first bombastically stating that the proposed health care legislation represents "the end of America as you know it," then demanding that people get off their couches and "stop this insanity now."

What the American Taliban's pompous public personalities don't get—or get, but don't acknowledge—is that such incendiary rhetoric has consequences. Violent, bloody consequences.

Richard Poplawski was a messed-up 22-year-old from Pittsburgh with a history of violence. He was booted out of the Marine Corps for throwing a food tray at a drill sergeant, and had violated a restraining order put in place by a previous girlfriend. His landlord in Florida evicted him when the German shepherd she entrusted to his care disappeared. He eventually returned to Pittsburgh and moved in with his mother and grandmother. Poplawski was active on white supremacist and neo-Nazi Stormfront internet forums. While posting run-of-the-mill racist crap in 2008 ("Negroes especially have disgusting facial features. The fat nosed flaring nostril look is putrid. Nappy hair makes me want to gag"), he appeared to have transitioned to a more confrontational anti-government posture. An Anti-Defamation League report on Poplawski tracked his transformation.

> Rather than "retreat peaceably into the hills," Poplawski urged his fellow white supremacists in November 2008 to achieve "ultimate victory for our people" by "taking back our nation." Stating that he believed they were running out of time, he noted that "a revolutionary is always regarded as a nutcase at first, their ideas dismissed as fantasy."
>
> ... Following the Super Bowl victory of the Pittsburgh Steelers in early February 2009, Poplawski used the celebrations that occurred in Pittsburgh as an opportunity to "survey police procedure in an unrestful environment," and reported the results of his reconnaissance to fellow Stormfronters. "It was just creepy seeing busses [*sic*] put into action by authorities, as if they were ready to transport busloads of Steeler fans to 645 FEMA drive if necessary."

No, the "645 FEMA drive" thing didn't refer to an old episode of the X-Files. That was a reference to one of the American Taliban's favorite post-election conspiracy theories. Yes, some people believe that 800 FEMA-run concentration camps have been built around the country in preparation for a declaration of martial law. Why? Who knows. Some think it has something to do with the establishment of a United Nations one-world government, while others argue Obama will populate these camps with heroic patriotic dissenters.

Curiously, teabaggers never found themselves shipped off to these camps, and Glenn Beck is still on the air. But Fox News was more than happy to further validate this craziness. "We are a country that is headed toward socialism, totalitarianism, beyond your wildest imagination," said Beck on his *Fox and Friends* show on March 3, 2009. "I have to tell you, I am doing a story tonight, that I wanted to debunk these FEMA camps. I'm tired of hearing about them—you know about them? I'm tired of hearing about them. I wanted to debunk them. Well we've now for several days been doing research on them—*I can't debunk them!* And we're going to carry the story tonight. . . . It is our government—if you trust our government, it's fine. If you have any kind of fear that we might be headed toward a totalitarian state, there is something going on in our country that it's—it ain't good."

Among Beck's audience was the primed-for-action Richard Poplawski, who soon posted a YouTube video of another Glenn Beck segment, discussing the FEMA nonsense with libertarian Representative Ron Paul of Texas.

> *Glenn Beck:* Good to be with you. First of all, on the FEMA prison thing, we've been in contact with your office and we would appreciate any help that you have. I want to make sure that we will be turning over every stone on everything, because there's a lot of crazy stuff that is being said about these things, and I appreciate you talking to us, and we'll be in touch with you again because I want to make sure that we have everything that you might be concerned with as well. Will you help us on that, sir?
>
> *Ron Paul:* Yeah, I don't think all the answers are in. You're concerned that they might be setting up these camps that verge on concentration camps. There's no evidence that I can find that they're actually set up. But I think there is a justified concern, not just because of the legislation that has been proposed, because that piece of legislation doesn't have a lot of co-sponsors. It's not on the verge of being passed.
>
> But the atmosphere in Washington is what we have to be concerned about. You know, since 9/11, dealing with the PATRIOT Act, and repealing the Posse Comitatus and the

Insurrection Act—these in transit are very, very bad, where personal liberties and civil liberties are not well protected and FEMA is already very, very powerful and they overrule and they go in on emergencies. So in some ways, they can accomplish what you might be thinking about, about setting up camps, and they don't necessarily have to have legislation, you know, to do the things that we dread. But it is something that deserves a lot of attention.

Clearly, things were churning in Poplawski's head, what with his predilection for anti-government and racist views, not to mention the validation he received when he watched similar views on national television and on talk radio.

It all came to a head a month after the above broadcast, on the morning of April 4, 2009.

Police received a 911 call from Poplawski's mother, describing an argument she had with her son over one of his dogs urinating on the carpet. Two officers, Paul Sciullo and Stephen Mayhle, responded. A third, Eric Kelly, on his way home after his shift, stopped by to provide backup. Poplawski's mother opened the door and asked Sciullo and Mayhle to remove her son. The two officers walked a few feet into the house when Poplawski, wearing a bullet-proof vest and armed with an AK-47, shot both of them in the head. Poplawski then turned his assault rifle on Kelly, who had just arrived, also mortally wounding him. After an hours-long gun battle, a wounded Poplawski was taken into custody.

Later, his best friend, Edward Perkovic, told the media, "We recently discovered that 30 states had declared sovereignty. One of his concerns was why were these major events in America not being reported to the public?" Ahh, here was that "sovereignty" nonsense again, bolstered by the FEMA camp craziness, with a dash of the "socialist" Obama administration turning America into a gulag. A cornucopia, if you will, of conspiracy, being promoted by the likes of Texas Governor Rick Perry and the Fox News airheads, and absorbed by people like Poplawski, pushing them over the edge. Thirty states had *not* declared sovereignty, yet Poplawski had been driven to kill three cops by right-wing media circulating this nonsense. Officer Mayhle left behind his wife and two daughters, ages 3 and 6. Officer Kelly left behind his wife and three daughters, 11, 16, and 22. Officer Sciullo was engaged to be married. Three families destroyed because of the American Taliban's obsession with creating their own alternate reality, fueling the delusions of hapless and unstable youngsters like Poplawski.

Instantly under fire, Glenn Beck aired a segment on his April 6 show debunking the FEMA camp story. Three days later, he ran to Bill O'Reilly's show to act shocked—shocked!—that anyone would assign any blame to him for such a heinous crime. For someone who had given credence to this idiocy on the chief propaganda outlet of the American Taliban, it was a case of retroactive cleansing: too little, too late.

Unbelievably, two months later, Congresswoman Michelle Bachmann of Minnesota, a high priestess of the American Taliban, continued to engage in speculation that Obama might actually set up concentration camps. "Take this into consideration," she said in a Fox News interview in June 2009. "If we look at American history, between 1942 and 1947, the data that was collected by the Census Bureau was handed over to the FBI and other organizations at the request of President Roosevelt, and that's how the Japanese were rounded up and put into the internment camps . . . I'm not saying that that's what the administration is planning to do, but I am saying that private personal information that was given to the Census Bureau in the 1940s was used against

Americans to round them up, in a violation of their constitutional rights, and put the Japanese in internment camps."

People die, and the America Taliban's trash-talk goes on.'

On June 10, 2009, James Wenneker von Brunn, 88 years old, drove to the Holocaust Memorial Museum in Washington DC and walked up to the entrance. Security guard Stephen Tyrone Johns opened the door for him, and von Brunn shot him at point-blank range with a .22 caliber rifle. Two other security guards immediately opened fire and wounded von Brunn, preventing a larger massacre. At the time, the museum was crowded with visiting school children. Von Brunn's car tested positive for explosives, and police recovered a notebook of his, which contained the following passage: "You want my weapons—this is how you'll get them. The Holocaust is a lie. Obama was created by Jews. Obama does what his Jew owners tell him to do. Jews captured America's money. Jews control the mass media. The 1st Amendment is abrogated henceforth . . ." In addition to being a fierce racist and anti-Semite, von Brunn had been arrested in 1981 for entering a Federal Reserve building to make a "citizen's arrest," while carrying a .38 caliber revolver, a knife, a fake bomb, and a sawed-off shotgun. He complained of being sentenced by a "Negro jury" and a "Jew judge."

Here was a man who clearly shared the basic beliefs of the American Taliban—that Obama would take away his rights, his freedoms, and his guns, and that the liberal (and Jewish-owned) media doesn't tell the real story about the dangers of the Obama administration. Every one of these themes is promoted relentlessly by the radical Right.

On August 4, 2009, in Collier Township just south of Pittsburgh, 48-year-old George Sodini walked into a women's aerobics class, placed his duffle bag on the ground, turned off the lights, and began firing. He reportedly fired 52 shots from four handguns, including two 9mm semiautomatics and a .45 caliber revolver. When the lights were turned back on, three women lay dead, another nine wounded, and Sodini had killed himself as well. Although Sodini apparently had been sexually frustrated and despondent over women rejecting him, it was the Obama election that appears to have been the last straw. His diary begins the day after Obama's election with a rant that would be right at home on Rush Limbaugh's or Glenn Beck's shows. "Good luck to Obama! He will be successful. The liberal media LOVES him. Amerika has chosen The Black Man. Good! In light of this I got ideas outside of Obama's plans for the economy and such."

Sodini was a full-fledged member of the American Taliban. "I got a bumper sticker that reads: 'Stop Socialism Impeach Clinton' from an ad in *National Review* magazine," he wrote in a 1994 newsgroup posting. "There are many neat buttons and stickers and things advertised in those conservative magazines." He also contributed to the activisim.militia news group at least once. "I am convinced that more drastic action is required to bring the country back to the Constitutional order that it was 200 years ago. I don't think any group of political leaders will achieve this for us," he wrote. Like most members of the American Taliban, Sodini didn't seem to have any murderous anti-government problems when George Bush was president. One can imagine that all this constant American Taliban yakking on about Obama's "socialism" and the "liberal media" and the loss of freedoms and the conspiracies about concentration camps—all of this soaks the fringe elements like Sodini and feeds their fears, steeping them in helplessness and anger, until one day they boil over in a burst of blazing weapons.

Then there's the story that unfolded a few days before the

Sodini episode, this one in New York involving 49-year-old Nancy Genovese. On July 30, 2009, officials at the Air National Guard Base at Gabreski Airport in Long Island, New York, saw her taking a lot of photographs on base property. This wasn't the first time she'd been seen taking photos, so officials called the local police. That call probably prevented a major bloodbath. When police arrested her and checked her car, they found an XM-15 assault rifle, a shotgun, and 500 rounds of ammunition.

It would seem to be just another nutcase incident, but it turns out that Genovese had been, well, yes, a Glenn Beck fan. Front and center on her MySpace page was an embedded video clip of Beck, delivering one of his rants in his usual overheated style.

> We are coming. We will be heard. We will be represented. You think that we are so busy with our lives that we will never come for you. And we were. But now you've gone and done it. We are the formally [*sic*] silent majority, all of us. Quietly work, pay our taxes, obey the laws, vote, save money, keep our noses to the grindstone—now looking up at you. You have awakened us, and a patriotic spirit so strong and so powerful. It had been sleeping too long. You have pushed us too far.

Below the embed, Genovese was effusive.

> ... we the people. I just saw Glenn Beck tell it like it is! Yes, he was firm and he is talking to congress, for all of us ... we the people. I just saw Glenn Becks show, now on the 2 am show, missed it at 5 PM today.
> United we stand, divided we fall.
> Please do re post this video.
> He is mad as hell and so are we. He is right and so are we. He says a copy of the letter he is speaking of, from a grandmother, is on his site
> GlennBeck.com, if you want to add a comment or sign it.
> God Bless all of you my friends.

In another passage, she related talking with someone from the Department of Homeland Security (DHS), where she pressed him on a Beck-esque nightmare scenario that would precipitate martial law for—surely you can guess by now—yes, FEMA camps.

> I presented a scenario of dyer straits to him, like, the dollar goes down to the predicted 15.7 cent in value, swine flu is killing people and they have a few million dead bodies to deal with, people have no homes, no food, looting is going on. Um, yes, martial law would be something the country would need.

Imagine the poor DHS guy taking this call.

> He told me FEMA owns NO camps. None. I asked, "you must see the info on the internet regarding these camps?" He told me he . . . works all day and had no time to research the videos' and docs proving FEMA owns these camps. I have the feeling his job title may be damage control.

Although FEMA concentration camps, socialism, black presidents, and sovereignty/secession efforts may provide fodder for the ranting and raving and macho-militant talk of the American Taliban, there is yet another issue that gets them frothing at the mouth: immigration, especially immigration from south of the border, the brown kind, Mexicans and other Latinos, bringing burritos, salsa music, and the Spanish language into this white Christian mac-and-cheese nation. Anti-immigrant sentiment is so pervasive within the American Taliban that xenophobic activists have systematically purged any GOP positions that would remotely offer any help, amnesty, or services to men, women, or even children who are not documented aliens.

This anti-immigrant fever was best seen during the Republican primaries in the 2008 presidential race. At one point John

McCain was forced to admit that he'd vote against *his very own* comprehensive immigration reform bill. In fact, the entire GOP field tried to one-up each other on their anti-immigrant bona fides. Former Arkansas Governor Mike Huckabee was attacked for supporting a scholarship program for gifted children that didn't discriminate based on immigration status. He was deemed out of line for *helping children*, just because their parents brought them north without proper documentation. Former Massachusetts governor Mitt Romney aggressively ran ads attacking McCain's plan for "amnesty," calling it the "wrong approach" (even though Romney and his family hired undocumented immigrants to maintain the grounds around their homes).

Although immigration fizzled as an electoral issue in both 2006 and 2008, the radical Right wasn't about to let go of it. By 2010, conservative activists within the Republican National Committee proposed a purity test of 10 issues to gauge a candidate's fealty to their rigid agenda. Among them was supporting "legal immigration and assimilation into American society by opposing amnesty for illegal immigrants." Ronald Reagan would've failed that proposed litmus test—a fact that probably helped kill it.

This relentless decades-long drumbeat about the "brown threat" gave rise to the Minutemen Project in 2005—the American Taliban's own border patrol. Fashioned after the first fighters in the American Revolutionary War who, in wingnut lore, apparently patrolled the Rio Grande trying to keep brown-skinned Redcoats out, or something. This loose coalition acts as a vigilante group, looking to catch undocumented immigrants as they come across from Mexico. In non-border states, these Minutemen seek to enact restrictive immigration laws and to physically harass immigrants—or anyone who looks like one.

The Minutemen became so radicalized, in fact, that one of its two co-founders, Jim Gilchrist, left the movement in disgust. In April 2005, the 59-year-old Gilchrist, a former accountant, had led several dozen volunteers on a month-long border-watch operation. The gambit proved a media sensation. Camera crews covered their antics, and anti-immigrant media personalities like Lou Dobbs of CNN championed their cause. California Governor Arnold Schwarzenegger lent the nascent movement his credibility. "I think they've done a terrific job," Schwarzenegger said in a radio interview a few weeks after the first Minuteman patrolled the California-Mexico border. "They've cut down the crossing of illegal immigrants a huge percentage. So it just shows that it works when you go and make an effort and when you work hard. It's a doable thing."

But things steadily spiraled out of control after those heady early days. Gilchrist went through an acrimonious split with his co-founders, and his own organization accused him of embezzlement. Charges and countercharges of power grabs were made, all of it resulting in a series of court battles and legal wrangling that shattered any hope of a strong, centralized organization running the operation.

Yet, from the ashes of the bigger groups, smaller offshoots have spawned like, well, crazy. And while Gilchrist at least made a show of keeping racist and white supremacists out of his organization, the new offshoots aren't shy about embracing neo-Nazis and flat-out "eliminationists." One example is the splinter group Border Guardians, founded by a woman appropriately named Laine Lawless, a lunatic outlaw who offered up some truly crazy proposals in an email sent to Mark Martin, "SS commander" of the Western Ohio National Socialist Movement. Title of the email? "How to GET RID OF THEM!" Here's a taste of Lawless' suggestions:

- Steal the money from any illegal walking into a bank or check cashing place.

- Make every illegal alien feel the heat of being a person without status . . . I hear the rednecks in the South are beating up illegals as the textile mills have closed. Use your imagination.

- Discourage Spanish-speaking children from going to school. Be creative.

- Create an anonymous propaganda campaign warning that any further illegal immigrants will be shot, maimed or seriously messed-up upon crossing the border. This should be fairly easy to do, considering the hysteria of the Spanish language press, and how they view the Minutemen as "racists & vigilantes."

There's more. Although Lawless and her fanatical cohorts talk mean and spew hatred, advocating "creativity" in harassing children, some of her allies have gone further.

Shawna Forde, a 41-year-old who was kicked out of the Minutemen Civil Defense Corps for "unstable" behavior (how unstable do you have to be for *that?*), created her own small splinter group called the Minutemen American Defense organization. (One is reminded of the classic "People's Front of Judea" scene in Monty Python's *Life of Brian.*) Her second-in-command was Jason Eugene Bush, a 35-year-old with ties to the Aryan Nation and at least one murder to his name—that of a sleeping Latino homeless man in Wenatchee, Washington. Also part of the team was Albert Gaxiola, a marijuana trafficker.

Forde harbored extreme prejudices against Latinos. "I had to take an oath, and part of the oath was that I couldn't eat Mexican food," said her half-brother, who left the group out of fear Forde was going off the deep end. At one point, Forde claimed she had been gang raped by a group of Latinos; police quickly determined it was a hoax. To finance their operations, Forde, Bush, and Gaxiola hatched a bizarre plot. "She sat right here on my couch and told me that she was going to start an underground militia," her half-brother recounted. "This militia was going to start robbing drug-cartel dealers—rob them and steal their money or drugs."

All that pent up racism and hatred of brown people found release in a gruesome carnage around midnight on May 30, 2009, in the small town of Arivaca, Arizona, a few miles north of the border. Forde, Bush, and Gaxiola, posing as police officers supposedly searching for a fugitive, burst into the home of Raul Flores and Gina Marie Gonzales. Forde apparently believed Flores was a drug dealer—a fact vigorously denied by family and neighbors. According to courtroom testimony that December, Flores became suspicious because the intruders' guns were wrapped in duct tape. When he asked about the duct tape, one of the attackers said, "Don't take this personally but this is for you," and opened fire, even as Flores begged them to spare his wife. They ignored the pleas, and shot her. She played dead. Then suddenly, in one of the bedrooms, 9-year-old Brisenia Flores cried out, "Why are you shooting my daddy? Why are you shooting my mommy?" One of the intruders entered her room and shot her in cold blood as she yelled, "No, no, no!" Fortunately, Brisenia's 12-year-old sister was away visiting her grandmother. Nothing indicates the assailants found drugs or money at the residence.

The larger Minutemen organizations rushed to disassociate themselves, but the reality was that Forde had been intimately involved with them. Jim Gilchrist had worked closely with Forde, and was debating adding her and her group to the Minuteman Project's list of national leaders right before her arrest. Intended or not, the Minutemen Project produced a slew of vigilante groups whose ranks are heavy with armed and dangerous white supremacists.

Gilchrist now regrets what he unleashed. "There's all kinds of organizations that have spawned from the Minuteman Project, and I have to say, some of the people who have gotten into this movement have sinister intentions," he said. But that is a bit disingenuous. He can complain about the "Saddam Hussein mentality" pervasive among the movement's new leaders, but anyone could have predicted that a movement based on an undercurrent of hatred of brown people would turn ugly fast.

You'd think that mainstream conservatives would reject these extremists, distance themselves from the violent ones, and seek to marginalize and expunge them from their ranks. At the *very* least, you'd think they would certainly support law enforcement efforts aimed at tamping down violence among right-wing extremists. Think again.

In April 2009, the Department of Homeland Security (DHS) released a report titled, "Rightwing Extremism: Current Economic and Political Climate Fueling Resurgence in Radicalization and Recruitment." The report mentioned several factors driving the resurgence.

> Rightwing extremists may be gaining new recruits by playing on their fears about several emergent issues. The economic downturn and the election of the first African American president present unique drivers for rightwing radicalization and recruitment.
>
> . . . Rightwing extremist groups' frustration over a perceived lack of government action on illegal immigration has the potential to incite individuals or small groups toward violence. If such violence were to occur, it likely would be isolated, small-scale, and directed at specific immigration-related targets.

... Heightened interest in legislation for tighter firearms restrictions ... may be invigorating rightwing extremist activity, specifically the white supremacist and militia movements.

The report also noted that returning veterans with experience in weapons and explosives could be integrated into these extremist groups, making them all the more dangerous.

But the American Taliban response to this report laid bare the fact that the extreme has merged into the mainstream of the conservative movement. The prominent *Hot Air* conservative website led the pushback, screaming that by pointing out extremist anti-government groups, "the DHS has all but declared war on federalism, which *used* to be the founding concept of our republic." Michelle Malkin headlined her response to the DHS report "Confirmed: The Obama DHS Hit Job on Conservatives Is Real." Meanwhile, former House Speaker and supposed conservative intellectual Newt Gingrich tweeted that "The person who drafted the outrageous homeland security memo smearing veterans and conservatives should be fired." Wait, what? Smearing veterans? Representative John Boehner took the same tack, calling that part of the report "offensive and unacceptable."

Apparently, Gingrich and Boehner had forgotten that domestic terrorist Timothy McVeigh was an Army veteran who murdered 168 people in his attack on the Alfred P. Murrah Federal Building in Oklahoma City in 1995. Anyone with military service (like me) can tell stories about the bad characters that inevitably abound in an organization as large and diverse as the U.S. Army. According to statistics from the U.S. Courts of Appeals for the Armed Forces, 5,737 service members in the Coast Guard, Army, Navy, Marine Corps, and Air Force were convicted in courts martial in the 2008 fiscal year. Another 2,080 were kicked out either under dishonorable or bad-conduct discharges. And those are just the ones who got caught. Our military isn't all honor and bravery. There's a fair amount of scum floating around.

None of that mattered to the American Taliban. Fox News personalities were apoplectic about the DHS report. Sean Hannity, with Focus on the Family's James Dobson on the show, acted as if Barack Obama personally wrote the report, and asked, "What do you think of that interpretation, especially coming from a guy that started his political career in the home of an unrepentant terrorist who bombed our Pentagon and Capitol and sat in Reverend Wright's church for 20 years?" Nothing wrong with *that* fair and balanced question, is there? No mention either that the report was commissioned by the Bush administration. Dobson glibly replied, "There are no Timothy McVeighs out there right now. They're making a big deal out of something that hasn't happened and may not happen." Or it *may* happen, but acting in the face of potential terror is not a strong suit for these guys. Who can forget George Bush ignoring his daily briefing report on August 6, 2001, titled, "Bin Laden Determined to Strike in U.S."? Who could blame them? Why make "a big deal out of something that hasn't happened and may not happen"?

The American Taliban's freak-out over the report was widespread. Fox contributor Andrea Tantaros screeched, "It's free speech and the Obama administration is trying to shut it down." Radio talk show host Jay Alan Sekulow, on Fox, charged that "the Obama Administration here under Department of Homeland Security has allowed a new regime to come into place that basically says this: Our focus is going to be on the right-wing groups." MSNBC's conservative morning anchor, Joe Scarborough, joined the chorus. "When you have a president and you have the Department of Homeland Security more focused on targeting veterans than on protecting our border on the South where a war is breaking out, or protecting us from, I don't know, Al Qaeda?" And former Bush spokeswoman Dana Perino, ignoring that her own former boss commissioned the report, claimed that "if Bush had done that we would be having a very different conversation ... There would have been a special prosecutor. We would have had to come out and apologize."

Actually, a report on left-wing extremists *was* issued a few months earlier. Difference is, liberals didn't criticize it as politically motivated or rush to defend the violent fringe on the outskirts of their movement. The fringe was left out on the fringe. If government authorities wanted to hunt down violent and extremist groups on the far Left, more power to them. Liberals wouldn't weep if violent ecoterrorists or whatnot were rounded up. But the American Taliban simply saw in this new report an opportunity to whack their opponents. No matter how violent the lunatics described in the report, mainstream conservatives not only couldn't bring themselves to disavow them, they moved to actively *embrace* them.

"We are all right-wing extremists now. Welcome to the club," wrote Michelle Malkin in her nationally syndicated column. Thousands around the conservative blogosphere proudly echoed the sentiment, "I am a right-wing extremist." A Google search for that exact term brings up nearly 2 million hits. Many took it a step further, bragging that they were *proud* right-wing extremists. One commenter wrote, "Cool! I am a right-wing Extremist terrorist! I will print my certified certificate out and show it off! Wish I had this when I went to the Tea Party, could have held it proudly." Conservative T-shirt shops rushed out "I am THE right-wing extremist" gear, for those who wanted to more publicly associate with violent nutjobs.

A government report that warned of violence in America—

violence that came to pass in the following months so tragically with the Minutemen murders of the father and daughter, with Poplawski's triple-murder of Pittsburgh policemen, with Sodini's rampage at the women's aerobics class, and so on—was treated as a joke by the American Taliban. Worse, it was being used as a rallying cry.

At an August 2009 town hall meeting in Redding, California, one audience member called himself "a proud, right-wing terrorist." People cheered. The response from U.S. Rep. Wally Herger of Yuba City: "Amen. God bless you. There's a great American."

In all the anti-Obama and anti-abortion and anti-immigrant and anti-government rhetoric of the American Taliban, there is always a latent militancy, references to revolution and rebellion, a flirtation with the use of force, and sometimes outright talk of "war" when things don't seem to be going their way.

The difficult political environment for Democrats in 2010 has given these extremists hope that the ballot box might validate their ideology. In fact, the belief that Republicans might have a shot at taking the majority in Congress seemed to tamp down a great deal of the political violence in late 2009. But the passage of the health care reform law sparked a new outburst of violent rhetoric, and anti-government fervor led to a new round of political violence, like the 9/11-style suicide plane attack against an IRS building in Austin, Texas, on February 18. So, given their expectations of a complete takeover of both the U.S. House and Senate, anything less (which is most likely) will surely spark even greater calls to violence. Bottom line, if Congress and the ballot box don't validate them, the American Taliban lack the respect for democracy to take such losses in stride. For the American Taliban, the bullet plays the backup to the ballot.

We saw that after Obama's inauguration in January 2009. By that summer, armed teabaggers were seen patrolling town halls and public events where Obama was speaking. A dozen armed protesters with unconcealed weapons showed up at an Obama event in Phoenix, Arizona, including one man with a holstered 9 mm pistol and AR-15 rifle slung over his shoulder. Another armed nutbag stood outside an Obama event in Portsmouth, New Hampshire, with a sign that read, "IT IS TIME TO WATER THE TREE OF LIBERTY," referencing Thomas Jefferson's famous maxim about revolution: "The tree of liberty must be refreshed from time to time with the blood of patriots and tyrants." The protesters weren't allowed near the president, of course. But they did get inside some town halls, including one held by Rep. Steve Cohen in Memphis, Tennessee, and at another event by Rep. Gabrielle Giffords in Arizona, where an attendee accidentally dropped his gun on the floor, mid-event—teabagger gun safety in action.

Edwin Vieira, president of the National Alliance for Constitutional Money (obsessed with eliminating the Federal Reserve Board and returning to the gold standard), had a solution in November 2009 to the Obama problem. In an article titled "Tea Parties Need Teeth," he advocated not just mass secession from the United States, but also the bolstering of the militia movement to make it happen:

> WE THE PEOPLE need to revitalize "the Militia of the several States" in order to regain and retain popular control over State governments, and through them to regain and retain control over the two fundamental powers of sovereignty: (i) the Power of the Purse—*i.e.*, currency and credit, and (ii) the Power of the Sword—*i.e.*, community self-defense.

Vieira has been an open advocate for taking up arms, even hinting at assassinations.

Vieira made the rounds of the teabagger circles and received considerable commendations, including one from Baptist pastor Chuck Baldwin, the 2008 presidential nominee of the Constitution Party, who gushed, "I would dare say that the first State that determines to follow Vieira's sagacious counsel (and rumblings of this have already begun in states such as Alaska, Oklahoma, Texas, Montana, New Hampshire, Indiana, Tennessee, South Carolina, etc.) would have so many liberty-loving patriots flock there that its economy would explode with prosperity—resulting in a domino effect of many other states following suit—and the revolution that this country so desperately needs would indeed take place."

If only we were so lucky. I'm partial to ceding a portion of the Texas Panhandle to these wackos, naming it Dumbfuckistan, taking it off the federal dole, building a wall around it, and arresting anyone trying to enter America illegally. I can always dream.

Believe it or not, Vieira is not a marginalized extremist. In April 2005, he spoke at a conference in Washington DC on "Confronting the Judicial War on Faith," which was attended by such American Taliban luminaries as Phyllis Schlafly, Alan Keyes, and former Alabama Chief Justice Roy Moore. The speakers mostly focused on harmless fantasies of impeaching U.S. Supreme Court Justice Anthony Kennedy, a Ronald Reagan appointee whom conservatives consider a traitor for swinging to the left. But Vieira went much further. He took the podium to harangue Kennedy for voting to strike down Texas' anti-sodomy law, claiming he "upholds Marxist, Leninist, satanic principles drawn from foreign law." Then, ominously, he quoted Joseph Stalin, saying he had a solution worth considering. "He had a slogan, and it worked very well

for him, whenever he ran into difficulty: 'No man, no problem.'"
Set aside the irony of railing against the "Marxist, Leninist" Kennedy, then turning to Stalin for his solution. Focus instead on that
solution: the full Stalin quote Vieira was referencing was, "Death
solves all problems: no man, no problem." In other words, murder.

Holding such a position, it should go without saying, is pro-
foundly un-American, no matter how much the American Taliban might disagree with court rulings on abortion, sodomy, and
integration. Progressives also often disagree with the court—don't
forget, the court *installed* Bush as president in 2000 despite the
fact that he lost both the national *and* Florida popular votes. But
progressives respect the institutions that make our democracy
work, and they deal with disagreements via the democratic process.

Consider the popularity of Psalm 109 in teabagger circles. This
psalm is known as an imprecatory prayer, and quite a disturbing one
at that, in which divine intervention is sought to destroy enemies
in horrific ways. And yes, it became popular among the American
Taliban because it was aimed at none other than the president of
the United States. The mild segment making the rounds is Psalm
109:8: "Let his days be few; and let another take his office." In polite
company, the crazies argue that this is a lighthearted reference to
their hope that Obama loses his re-election battle in 2012. Ha-ha.
But among the American Taliban, with a wink and a nod, the
faithful read on to the next few lines:

> May his children be fatherless and his wife a widow.
> May his children be wandering beggars; may they be driven from
> their ruined homes.
> May no one extend kindness to him or take pity on his fatherless
> children.
> May his descendants be cut off, their names blotted out from
> the next generation.

Ah, there's nothing like a little lighthearted, death-wishing, multigenerational cursing psalm to get you going in the morning.

Beliefnet, a religious online community, featured an Op-Ed by prominent rabbi Brad Hirschfield titled "Psalms 109:8, An Ugly Prayer for President Obama."

> The issue is not the scripture quoted or the name by which God is called by those doing the praying. The issue is invoking the God in whom any of us believe, to act as executioner of those with whom we disagree.
>
> From Yigal Amir, who murdered Israeli Prime Minister Yitzhak Rabin, to Major Hassan who murdered 13 and wounded 30 more [in a shooting at Ft. Hood], to whomever might step in on behalf of a "Christian nation" to make the words of the Psalm 109 a reality, each was inspired by prayers and scriptural readings not unlike those of the millions who made verse 8 a top Google search this morning. There is no place for such prayers in any of our faiths and until we all stand up and say so, at least a little blood will be on all of our hands.

Whatever the rest of the Bible might or might not say, Psalm 109 *is* "an ugly prayer" as the rabbi said, and its adoption by the American Taliban is not funny, not glib, and not trivial. It's serious business when people's lives hang in the balance, when the first black president faces assassination threats daily.

But don't say that to the prominent figures of the American Taliban, because they actually want Obama to be gone—from office, from life. Take, for instance, Wiley Drake, who is no small potato: besides being a vice-presidential running mate to Alan Keyes on America's Independent Party ticket in 2008, Drake served in 2006–07 as vice president of the Southern Baptist Convention, the world's largest Baptist denomination and the largest Protestant group in the United States, with 16 million members and 42,000 churches. In a June 2009 webcast, Drake celebrated the murder of Dr. George Tiller, who performed abortions, as an answer to prayer. When he later came on a radio show hosted by Alan Colmes, he was asked if he was praying for anyone else's death.

"The usurper that is in the White House is one, B. Hussein Obama," Drake answered.

Colmes was clearly unsure if he'd heard right, and circled back to clarify.

"Are you praying for his death?" Colmes asked.

"Yes," Drake replied.

"So you're praying for the death of the president of the United States?"

"Yes."

Colmes asked Drake if he was concerned that he might be placed on a Secret Service or FBI watch list, and if he believed it appropriate to talk or pray that way.

"I think it's appropriate to pray the Word of God," Drake said. "I'm not saying anything. What I am doing is repeating what God is saying, and if that put me on somebody's list, then I'll just have to be on their list."

"You would like for the president of the United States to die?" Colmes asked once more.

"If he does not turn to God and does not turn his life around, I am asking God to enforce imprecatory prayers that are through- out the Scripture that would cause him death, that's correct."

Psalm 109 isn't a joke; it's a clever code for the American Tal- iban to openly pray for Obama's death. If God calls for a fatwa against the president, as Drake clearly believes, someone will carry out God's will. It was done to Dr. Tiller in Kansas, and these reprobates clearly hope someone steps up against Obama. Their entire movement embraces this violent *modus operandi*. It's an open invitation for another unstable lunatic to go on an assassination hunt, this time for the life of the nation's president.

Erik von Brunn, the son of the Holocaust Museum shooter, issued a statement in response to his father's violent attack, clearly aware that many in the American Taliban had recklessly applauded his father's actions.

> While my father had every right to believe what he did, by imposing those beliefs on others he robbed them of their free will.
>
> ... For the extremists who believe my father is a hero: it is imperative you understand what he did was an act of cowardice. To physically force your beliefs onto others with violence is not brave, but bullying. Doing so only serves to prove how weak those beliefs are. It is simply desperation, reminiscent of a temper tantrum when a child cannot get his way. Violence is a cop out; an easy answer for an ignorant problem.

Erik *is* right. This pathological need of the American Taliban to impose their rigid and irrational ideology on the rest of us *does* rob us of freedom. Their alarming propensities to arm themselves and resort to violence *are* the actions of desperate cowards, whether it is Islamic fundamentalists chanting "Death to America!" or suicide bombers targeting religious pilgrims, or Rep. Tom Tancredo speculating about "tak[ing] out their holy sites" and "bombing Mecca." It most certainly applies to Pat Robertson, whose blood lust is endemic of his entire movement. "There will never be world peace until God's house and God's people are given their rightful place of leadership at the top of the world. How can there be peace when drunkards, drug dealers, communist, atheists, New

Age worshipers of Satan, secular humanists, oppressive dictators, greedy money changers, revolutionary assassins, adulterers, and homosexuals are on top."

For the American Taliban, democracy is incompatible with peace, and they are willing to take arms to fight for their theocratic utopia. We lose sight of this simple fact at our peril.

In April 2009, Col. Oliver North, of Iran-Contra fame, wrote a column on Fox News' website titled, "I am an extremist," referring to that DHS report on right-wing extremism.

> According to this DHS "assessment," the most dangerous threat we face here at home isn't from radical imams preaching violence in U.S. mosques and madrassas, Islamists recruiting in our prisons, Somali terrorists enticing young immigrants to become suicide bombers or Hamas, Hezbollah or Al Qaeda operatives plotting mass murder. No, according to DHS, the real threat comes from what our government labels "right-wing extremist ideology."

Of course, the DHS report didn't *rank* the threats, nor say that international terrorism wasn't a concern. Of course it is.

But here's something for Ollie to chew on: yes, our homegrown radicals are indeed the bigger threat. What those international terrorists can do is cause loss of individual human lives. If our domestic American Taliban have their way, we'd not only lose lives, we'd also lose the very freedoms that make America great.

3

SEX

While the lust for power and the flirtation with violence are defining traits of the American Taliban, what really gets their panties in a twist is sex.

Unlike power and violence, sex is something they are obsessed with *avoiding*. This creates a paradox: they are so fearful of the pleasures of the flesh that they can't stop talking about them. Or, as we'll see, often *indulging in them*. Hence they've created an entire regressive moral code, dressed it up as "family values," and set out to violate almost every one of its tenets. All this repression ultimately screws them up in the head. Take James Dobson.

Dobson is founder of Focus on the Family, one of the key pillars of the American Taliban. His organization, established in 1977 and based in Colorado Springs, boasts a $130 million annual budget and nearly 1,300 employees. His weekly column is published in more than 500 newspapers, and his radio show—a 2008 inductee in the Radio Hall of Fame—airs in 164 countries besides the United States. As *Slate* noted in November 2004, "Dobson is now America's most influential evangelical leader, with a following reportedly greater than that of either Falwell or Robertson at his peak."

Dobson's main focus is "family values," which is the usual jumble of anti-sex and anti-gay repression, rounded off with a healthy dollop of child beating. This agenda can manifest in bizarre ways, like the June 2002 "monthly letter" Dobson published on his website titled, "Can Homosexuality Be Treated and Prevented?"

The piece began with an excerpt from his book, *Bringing Up Boys*, and featured a letter he received from Mark, a 13-year-old boy who was worried he might be gay. Mark wrote that he liked wearing fingernail polish and dresses and had an older cousin who "would take us (little cousins) into his room and show us his genitals. I am afraid I have a little sodomy in me." The boy went on to write that he had masturbated "and gone too far," and added that "I tried more than once to suck my own penis." He wrote that one day in front of the mirror "I wiggled my body very rapidly, making my genitals bounce up and down. I get a little bit of that feeling mentioned above as I write this." He said he "immediately asked God for forgiveness, went in the shower but did it again there." He ended by seeking Dobson's advice, saying he did not want to be gay and "go to hell."

Dobson wrote that he felt bad for Mark, and engaged in a bunch of psychoanalytical gibberish, saying the excitement Mark felt in jumping up and down in the shower "is a classic symptom of narcissism, or a 'turning inward' to fulfill his unmet gender-identification needs." He concluded that Mark was experiencing "a condition we might call 'prehomosexuality,' and unless he and his entire family are guided by someone who knows how to assist, the possibilities are very great that he will go on to experience a homosexual lifestyle." To offer guidance, Dobson quoted an excerpt from a book written by Joseph Nicolosi, who has made a career out of "reparative therapy," which aims to change a person's sexual orientation (a notion dismissed, by the way, by the American Psychiatric Association and the American Psychological Association). Nicolosi, as quoted by Dobson, had a few gems of advice to offer fathers of boys who experience what little Mark was experiencing, beginning with this: "The truth is, Dad is more important than Mom. Mothers make boys. Fathers make men." Then he offered the following suggestions to fathers:

> He needs to mirror and affirm his son's maleness. He can play rough-and-tumble games with his son, in ways that are decidedly different from the games he would play with a little girl. He can help his son learn to throw and catch a ball. He can teach him to pound a square wooden peg into a square hole in a pegboard. He can even take his son with him into the shower, where the boy cannot help but notice that Dad has a penis, just like his, only bigger.

Got it? Worried your kid might be gay? Show him your big penis and that should cure him! *That's* the advice from one of the American Taliban's leading voices. With that kind of counsel, it's no wonder that whole crowd can't handle anything sexual— whether it's homosexuality, pornography, adultery, or teenage sex.

Yet, as bizarre as this all might be, condemnation of sexuality is part of the American Taliban's core identity. In fact, it's so ingrained in their mentality, that Bill Clinton's 1996 pollsters found they could identify Republican partisans merely by asking them a short series of questions about sexual mores. As Thomas Edsall reported in the *Atlantic* magazine,

> Respondents were asked five questions, four of which tested attitudes toward sex: Do you believe homosexuality is morally wrong? Do you ever personally look at pornography? Would you look down on someone who had an affair while married? Do you

believe sex before marriage is morally wrong? The fifth question was whether religion was very important in the voter's life.

Respondents who took the "liberal" stand on three of the five questions supported Clinton over Dole by a two-to-one ratio; those who took a liberal stand on four or five questions were, not surprisingly, even more likely to support Clinton. The same was true in reverse for those who took a "conservative" stand on three or more of the questions.

Obviously, the "conservative" answers are that homosexuality is evil, that you never look at pornography, that you look down on people having affairs, that you think sex before marriage is unacceptable, and that religion is a very important part of your life. "According to [the pollsters], these questions were better vote predictors—and better indicators of partisan inclination—than anything else except party affiliation or the race of the voter (black voters are overwhelmingly Democratic)," Edsall reported.

Besides perfectly defining the American Taliban's sexual mores, those five topics are also defining cultural issues for Islamic fundamentalists.

Both Christianity and Islam consider homosexuality immoral. Indeed, same-sex relations are illegal in most Muslim countries, generally punishable by jail time or corporal punishment, and the more extreme the regime, the more brutal the punishment. In Taliban-ruled Afghanistan, homosexuals have met with horrific fates. In 1998, in the Afghan city of Herat, 18-year-old Abdul Sami and 22-year-old Bismellah were placed against a mud wall, which was then bulldozed on top of them. "Shariah-prescribed punishment has been administered to two sodomites [in] Herat Province," the Taliban proudly announced. "The cases of the accused were investigated by the public prosecution office of Herat Province, where the accused confessed to their crimes without duress or torture."

Many in the American Taliban, who must look at this cruelty with satisfaction, have fiercely fought the inclusion of anti-gay violence in our nation's hate crimes laws. During the U.S. House debate on the Matthew Shepard Act in 2009, Rep. Virginia Foxx of North Carolina, one of its chief opponents, claimed,

> I also would like to point out that there was a bill—the hate crimes bill that's called the Matthew Shepard bill, is named after a very unfortunate incident that happened where a young man was killed, but we know that that young man was killed in the commitment of a robbery. It wasn't because he was gay. This— the bill was named for him, hate crimes bill was named for him, but it's really a hoax that continues to be used as an excuse for passing these bills.

Given that Shepard's murderers used the "gay panic defense" in court to argue that they were driven temporarily insane by sexual advances from Shepard, Foxx's whole schtick was patently absurd. The trial of both murderers showed that they plotted beforehand to rob a gay man, went to a bar, pretended to be gay to befriend Shepard, offered him a ride home, took him to a remote area, tied him to a fence post, and proceeded to torture and beat him, leaving him for dead. He suffered severe skull fractures and multiple lacerations, was found 18 hours later by a passerby, and died a few days later. But for Foxx and the rest of her conservative colleagues, none of that mattered. Only 18 out of 178 Republicans in the House, and only 5 out of 40 Republicans in the Senate, voted for the bill. The measure was signed into law by President Obama on October 28, 2009.

Although they are currently constrained by law, the American Taliban would prefer America to look like parts of the Muslim world, where sodomy is criminalized, or better yet, made a capital offense, as in Iran. Human rights groups accuse Iran of having executed 3,000 to 4,000 homosexuals since the country's 1979 Revolution. An Iranian university study found that 24 percent of Iranian women and 16 percent of men had at least one homosexual experience. Iranian President Mahmoud Ahmadinejad refuses to acknowledge this stark reality. In a 2007 speech at Columbia University, he claimed, "In Iran, we don't have homosexuals like in your country." That was a bit *too* ridiculous, even for him, so in 2008, speaking to *Democracy Now*'s Amy Goodman, Ahmadinejad conceded that "in Iran it's not an issue as big as it is of concern here in the United States. There might be a few [gay] people who are known. In general, our country would not accept it. And there's a law about it, too, which one must follow."

While Ahmadinejad wallows in denial about the existence of homosexuality in Iran, the American Taliban leaders are equally delusional in their belief that therapy can "straighten" homosexuals, as we saw with James Dobson's cuckoo endorsement of showering advice. But the radical Right has been promoting another, more dangerous narrative out there: homosexuals are predators. To understand the danger of that narrative, let's take a quick look at what these evangelical nutbags unleashed in Uganda.

In March 2009, three American evangelicals, using their longstanding connections in Uganda, conducted a three-day conference on homosexuality in Kampala to "expose the truth behind homosexuality and the homosexual agenda," arguing that homosexuals were recruiting children into their ranks. They had an audience of thousands of Ugandan officials as well as teachers and police officers. The three men, set up as "experts," portrayed gays as predators who hunted children, scaring the shit out of the public and unleashing a wave of anti-gay fervor in a socially conservative Christian country.

The three men were Scott Lively, Caleb Lee Brundidge, and Don Schmeirer, all American Taliban types who believe homosexuality can be "cured." Lively, of Defend the Family International, is co-author of a book called *The Pink Swastika*, which argues that homosexuality inside the Nazi Party contributed to its extreme militarism. That was weird, of course, because the Nazis locked up tens of thousands of homosexuals in prison and concentration camps as Hitler denounced them for their threat to the "masculine character" of the nation. Just like Islamic fundamentalists and the American Taliban! Brundidge, a self-proclaimed former gay man, runs "healing seminars" at the Maryland-based International Healing Foundation. And Schmeirer works at Exodus International, a group promoting the message of "freedom from homosexuality through the power of Jesus Christ."

The Ugandan organizer was Stephen Langa, a pastor who runs the Family Life Network. He said that homosexuals "give money to children to recruit schoolmates—once you have two children, the whole school is gone." The president of Uganda, Yoweri Museveni, said, "I hear European homosexuals are recruiting in Africa." Then, echoing Ahmadinejad, "We used to have very few homosexuals traditionally. They were not persecuted but were not encouraged either because it was clear that is not how God arranged things to be." James Nsaba Butoro, Ugandan minister of state for ethics and integrity, told the *Guardian* (UK), "We are talking about anal sex. Not even animals do that. We believe there are limits to human rights."

Within weeks of the three-day conference, David Bahati, a Ugandan member of Parliament, drafted a bill to impose a life sentence on anyone convicted of gay sex. Those who are HIV positive, or convicted of having multiple offenses, or being a "person of authority" over the other partner, would receive the death penalty.

Furthermore, anyone chancing upon homosexual activity would be required to report it within 24 hours or risk up to three years in prison. Uganda would be required to pursue extradition of any Ugandan caught engaging in homosexual activity outside its borders. Even speaking positively about something like gay marriage could lead to life imprisonment. The bill was probably the harshest piece of anti-gay legislation anywhere in the world.

President Museveni, not coincidentally, is a member of The Family, the same group mentioned in chapter 1, which was established by Abraham Vereide and is focused on "ministering" to the rich and powerful, not just in the United States, but all over the world. Bahati is also a core member of The Family, meaning that he is in the organization's inner sanctum. "They have a very unusual theology in the sense that they think that Christ had one message for an inner circle and then a kind of different message for a sort of slightly more outer circle. And then the rest of us, Christ told us little stories because, frankly, we couldn't handle the truth," explains Jeff Sharlet, author of *The Family*. "And the core members are those they think are getting the real deal." So it's clear, that for The Family, executing homosexuals is "the real deal"—a core component of its hateful theology. Now every year, Bahati organizes a "Uganda National Prayer Breakfast," patterned after the same annual event here in the United States, which is attended by U.S. congressmen. In fact, Bahati was scheduled to speak at the American edition of the prayer breakfast in February 2010—at which both President Barack Obama and Secretary of State Hillary Clinton spoke—until a public outcry caused his invitation to be rescinded.

As of early 2010, Bahati's bill was scheduled for debate in Parliament—and the three American Taliban evangelicals, as well as The Family, were trying hard to dissociate themselves from the legislation and from the anti-gay hatred they'd unleashed in Uganda. Four members of The Family were asked by Rachel Maddow, of Air America Radio and MSNBC, whether they approved of this legislation. Three of them—Senators John Ensign of Nevada, James Inhofe of Oklahoma, and Sam Brownback of Kansas— couldn't bring themselves to condemn executions for homosexuals and refused to comment. And these aren't backbenchers. Until his own sex scandal (more on that later!), Ensign was chair of the Republican Policy Committee—the fourth highest-ranking senator in the GOP. Inhofe was the highest ranking Republican on the Committee on the Environment and Public Works. Brownback was a presidential candidate in 2008, and is considered a favorite to be elected governor of Kansas in the 2010 elections.

The American Taliban's war against homosexuals has been front and center in the culture wars this past decade. They have relentlessly campaigned for legally sanctioned discrimination against homosexuals and unequal treatment under the law. In 1998, for example, Alaska and Hawaii led the way, and another 41 states have various laws that prohibit same-sex marriages. And Maine in 2009 overturned a law passed by the legislature and signed by the governor that legalized marriage equality.

All these anti-gay efforts are driven by religious and moral beliefs, and by assumptions unsupported by empirical evidence. Yet, the nasty rhetoric spews forth. "I have known few homosexuals who did not practice their tendencies," preached Pat Robertson back in 1994, setting a tone for the American Taliban that has remained unchanged. "Such people are sinning against God and will lead to the ultimate destruction of the family and our nation. I am unalterably opposed to such things, and will do everything I can to restrict the freedom of these people to spread their contagious infection to the youth of our nation." These freedom lovers sure love to restrict freedom. Just as hateful and demagogic is Lou Sheldon, a close associate of convicted felon Jack Abramoff, and president of the Traditional Values Coalition, which claims to represent 43,000 churches. In a "special report," Sheldon wrote,

> Americans should understand that their attitudes about homo-sexuality have been deliberately and deceitfully changed by a masterful propaganda/marketing campaign that rivals that of Adolph Hitler. In fact, many of the strategies used by homosexu-als to bring about cultural change in America are taken from Hitler's writings and propaganda welfare manuals.

Islamic fundamentalists couldn't agree more. As Ahmadinejad told *Democracy Now*, "Our religious decrees tell us that [homo-sexuality is] against our values, and all divine laws, actually, believe in the same. Who has given them permission to engage in homo-sexual acts? It's considered as an abhorrent act. It shakes the foun-dations of a society, the family foundation. It robs humanity. It brings about diseases."

Movement conservatives in the United States surrendered a sure-fire pickup seat in a U.S. House special election in northern New York because the Republican candidate, Dede Scozzafava, did not share the sex-related obsessions of the American Taliban; she supported gay marriage and abortion rights. A ten-point lit-mus test that Republican National Committee members tried to impose on all candidates included "Retention of the Defense of Marriage Act." Any Republican opposing discrimination and supporting equality would immediately be considered *persona non grata*.

But it's not even just about gay *marriage*. Mainstream conser-vative groups have fought to keep Taliban-style sodomy laws on the books. In an essay on the Concerned Women for America website, titled "In Defense of Sodomy Laws," the very male and very evangelical Scott Lively, who helped light the anti-gay fire in Uganda, wrote,

> Unfortunately, few people dare to defend sodomy laws these days. The push-the-envelope morality of the 1960s sexual revolution has attained a status akin to religious dogma in this country, and people who question whether we've gone too far are the new heretics.
>
> . . . Although characterized by homosexuals as a loving act, sodomy is an act of sadism and violence against the receptive partner that often results in serious damage to the body, especially over time. That one partner consents to this abuse should not sanctify it in the eyes of the law, any more than wife-beating should be sanctioned if a wife consents to it.

When the Supreme Court struck down state-level sodomy laws in 2003 in *Lawrence v. Texas*, conservatives were furious. Lively penciled in God for a good old-timey biblical smackdown. "This is an error of biblical proportions, from which we're going to suffer serious negative consequences. As a result of this decision, we're going to see an escalation of the social meltdown that began with the sexual revolution and the continuing disintegration of the family-based society." R. Albert Mohler Jr., president of Southern Baptist Theological Seminary, echoed similar sentiments. "Those who believe that sexual morality is about more than personal preference will look to this decision as a tragic turning point in our nation's culture war. Those prophetic voices warning of a judicial usurpation of politics can at least say that they warned us."

While they carry on their legislative and court battles, these homophobes are also fighting in the public square, so to speak, and spreading their hatred by scaring their flocks with doomsday scenarios about how the very existence of this nation is at stake.

The American Taliban can only dream of living in a place like Ahmadinejad's Iran, where homosexuals supposedly don't exist. Here, in the Land of the Free, *Queer Eye for the Straight Guy* represents the end of the world. In a leaked audio recording of a talk given by State Rep. Sally Kern of Oklahoma to local Republicans, she says homosexuality represents the "death knell of this country. I honestly think it's the biggest threat our nation has, even more so than terrorism or Islam, which I think is a big threat."

True, Will from *Will and Grace* was *far* scarier than Osama bin Laden, what with his well-manicured hands, stylish apartment, and fabulous wardrobe. But we as a nation *have* survived much worse. Like, for example, the threat of Sally Kern, allied with those Muslims who terrify her, but with whom she has a lot in common.

She may have a point. You let those gays have freedom, next thing you know, creepy old men start having bizarre fantasies. Like, for example, U.S. Senator Tom Coburn. "Lesbianism is so rampant in some of the schools in southeast Oklahoma that they'll only let one girl go to the bathroom. Now think about it. Think about that issue." Coburn, a full-fledged member of The Family, obviously gave underage schoolgirls fooling around in bathrooms *a lot* of thought. He wanted *everyone* to think about it! A lot! But really, he can keep that one to himself. Oklahoma school officials quickly set the record straight, asserting that no such rampant lesbianism existed in their schools. But by then we had already gotten insight into the mind of Coburn—his ilk is so scared of this stuff because they *just can't stop thinking about it*. And unable to control their own urges, they demand that government reflect those prejudices and restrict the freedoms of others, just like in Ahmadinejad's Iran.

As conservative author Dinesh D'Souza admitted in his book,

The Enemy at Home, "What angers religious Muslims is not the American Constitution but the scandalous sexual mores they see on American movies and television. What disgusts them are not free elections but the sights of hundreds of homosexuals kissing each other and taking marriage vows." The very same issues, in other words, that anger D'Souza—issues like gays serving their country honorably in the military, or loving same-sex couples earning the same rights and privileges as their straight counterparts, or gay schoolteachers ably educating our youth. A May 2009 poll for Pew found that 32 percent of Republican respondents thought school boards should have the right to fire "known homosexuals." But the United States isn't Uganda. No rational person fears that gay teachers are trying to recruit their students over to the dark side.

America marches on, gradually marginalizing the American Taliban, along with their Islamic cousins.

A Pew Research Center survey in 2003 found that 45 percent of respondents favored allowing gay and lesbian couples to enter into civil unions, with 47 percent opposed. In late 2009, the numbers were 57–37, a net shift of 18 points in just six years. Polling on gay marriage ballot initiatives consistently shows that the youngest voters, ages 18–29, support gay equality by large numbers. A CBS News poll in March 2009 found that among 18–45-year-olds, 41 percent supported legal marriage for same-sex couples, compared to only 18 percent of those over 65 years. According to exit polls in California in 2008, 61 percent of 18–29-year-olds voted against Proposition 8, which outlawed gay marriage in the state, compared to 39 percent of those over 65. As that oldest generation passes away, well, so will their well-worn biases and bigotry.

Thus the culture progresses, leaving the American Taliban desperately fighting a rearguard action to preserve bigotry in our laws. Every year, those anti-gay amendments pass by smaller and smaller numbers. The last two big anti-gay efforts—in California in 2008 and Maine in 2009—passed by razor-thin margins. It won't be long before those efforts are overturned. Equality is on the rise.

In 2006, a sex tape became a national sensation in Iran. Featuring soap star Zahra Amir Ebrahimi, the tape showed sex between her and an assistant film producer she was supposedly engaged to at the time. Although she denied it was her in the video, her mate confessed to having taped the act, claimed the two were married at the time (making the sex legal), and claimed that he forgot to erase the video off his laptop's hard drive before selling it (which would exculpate him from distribution charges). Unable to properly punish the two, Iranian authorities decided to toughen their anti-pornography laws in the wake of what the nation's clerics called a "national shame." Today, participation and production of pornographic movies is punishable by death.

Pornographers in the United States won't face the death penalty anytime soon, but the American Taliban have had a long-running battle with what they consider "indecency." After 9/11, Congress was bullied into quickly passing the PATRIOT Act, a gross attack on our civil liberties, which most members of Congress had not even read closely. George W. Bush's attorney general, John Ashcroft, acknowledged in 2004 that besides provisions aimed at apprehending terrorists, the Act also included stealth measures "that were developed to combat serious crimes across the board, general crimes, and we have used those general tools both in terrorism cases as well as in other cases, such as to catch predatory child molesters and pornographers." Sex-related crimes and pornography, normally the domain of local laws and law enforcement authorities, were Ashcroft's obsessions, so he was more than happy to misapply anti-terrorism laws to his pet causes.

After a year-long investigation of a New Orleans bordello by *10* FBI agents, the agency swept in and proudly announced their haul—12 prostitutes. This led Jonathan Turley, a law professor at George Washington University, to write a piece titled "A Comedy of Eros," in which he said,

> Only the FBI could go to the French Quarter and find only a dozen prostitutes after a year of investigation. Given the roughly one-to-one ratio between agents and prostitutes, the FBI could have produced a hundred times this number by simply having agents walk down Bourbon Street.
>
> ... While it was revealed this week that the FBI largely ignored CIA identifications of known terrorists in the United States before 9/11, it appears that it was actually able to find prostitutes in New Orleans.

Ashcroft was just the latest and highest profile anti-sex crusader in the Justice Department since Edwin Meese, author of the infamous Meese Report of 1986. The nearly 2,000-page report issued by his Commission on Pornography was intended to be a harmless sop to President Ronald Reagan's Christian Right supporters. Yet, it became a national sensation, in large part due to its graphic descriptions of fact-finding missions to some of pornography's darkest corners, from sweat sniffers to practices involving human excretions. The report featured dialogue from movies like *Deep Throat* and *Debbie Does Dallas*, as well as a helpful bibliography of 2,730 movies and 725 pornographic books for the avid porn collector. In a pre-internet era, pornographers couldn't have gotten better advertising.

From its inception, the Commission was a sham, its conclusions predetermined. All you had to do was look at the commission members. Among the commissioners was (surprise!) James Dobson, clearly indicating that this was to be a product of the American Taliban. Next was anti-pornography crusader Bruce Ritter, a Catholic priest and founder of the Covenant House charity for homeless teenagers, whose work Ronald Reagan praised in his 1984 State of the Union address. Ritter resigned in 1990 after—try not to act shocked here—being busted having sex with a male prostitute and pornographic actor, and being accused of sexual abuse from former employees of the shelter. Also on the Commission were Harold Lezar, a conservative lawyer who began his career as an assistant to William F. Buckley at *National Review*, and Judge Edward Garcia, a prosecutor in Sacramento County, California, who zealously pursued obscenity cases. There was Diane Cusack, a former city council member in Scottsdale, Arizona, who had urged citizens to photograph moviegoers at the local adult movie theater, copy down their license plate numbers, and turn this "evidence" over to the police. The commission was chaired by Henry Hudson, a U.S. Attorney in Virginia who had shut down every adult bookstore in Arlington County.

So, when the recommendations came, there were no surprises. The commission asked for laws making it an "unfair labor practice . . . to hire individuals to participate in commercial sexual performances"—not because they wanted to stamp out pornography, but because of "an abiding concern for those persons used in these sexual performances." Their concern for porn stars was touching. They also tried to kill phone sex and cable TV broadcasts of pornography, demanded that U.S. attorneys engage in a review of "the obscenity problem in their respective districts, identify offenders, initiate investigations, and commence prosecution without further delay," and instructed citizens to be on the lookout for indecency. "Many popular idols of the young commonly sing about rape, masturbation, incest, drug usage, bondage, violence, homosexuality and intercourse." The commission even sent letters to drugstore chains like 7-Eleven, threatening them with sanctions if they didn't pull *Playboy* and *Penthouse* from their shelves. *Playboy* went to court and won a judicial order requiring the commission to rescind its threat.

The final Meese Report was short on research and evidence and long on propaganda and anecdotal citations. Here's one:

> [Thirty] witnesses attributed to pornography their having been coerced into pornographic performances, bound and beaten in direct imitation of pornography, and forcibly imprisoned for the purpose of manufacturing pornography. Although this Commission can neither conclusively determine that pornography caused these physical harms nor conclusively determine that it did not, it was the opinion of the witnesses that pornography played a central role in the pattern of abuse within which they were harmed.

Thirty witnesses, cherry-picked by a pack of anti-porn crusaders? *Still* no evidence whether their testimony was causally accurate? Who cares! That's all the commission needed to determine that yes, pornography was clearly a cause of violence against women. Even material labeled "erotica"—tasteful nudity that was not violent—was singled out for a finger wag. "None of us think the material in this category, individually or as a class, is in every instance harmless."

"None of us?" Interesting, because three of the four *women* on the commission—Judith Becker, Deanne Tilton-Durfee, and Ellen Levine—wrote a lengthy rebuttal to blast the claim that pornography led to violence against women. "It is essential to state that the social science research has not been designed to evaluate the relationship between exposure to pornography and the commission of sexual crimes; therefore efforts to tease the current data into proof of a causal link between these acts simply cannot be accepted," they wrote. But what did they know? Becker was a behavioral scientist who had devoted her career to treating victims and perpetrators of sexual crimes, and Levine had been writing and editing stories about women's issues as a *CBS News* journalist and as the top editor at *Woman's Day* and *Cosmopolitan Living*.

Truth is, rather than depictions of sex, it was depictions of *violence* that seemed more likely to lead to violence against women. As Edward Donnerstein, a University of Wisconsin psychologist who had studied the issue, told *Time* magazine at the time, "If you take out the sex and leave the violence, you get the increased violent behavior in the laboratory setting . . . If you take out the violence and leave the sex, nothing happens." Yet the notion that violence could lead to violence was explicitly ignored by the commission, because most of its members were more concerned about pushing their anti-sexuality agenda than in arriving at reality-based conclusions. But that's not surprising, given the American Taliban's proclivity toward violence and aggression. Sex, on the other hand, can "destroy our nation."

Not a lot has changed since 1986, at least not in the American Taliban mindset about pornography. In 2006, a coalition of 13 conservative groups, including Tony Perkins' Family Research Council and the Concerned Women for America, took out ads in *USA Today* with the headline, "An Urgent Appeal to the Department of Justice," demanding the feds investigate pay-per-view movies in hotels to see whether they violated federal and state obscenity laws. The ad was practically a copy-and-paste from the Meese Report, claiming at the very top, "Adult hardcore pornography can tragically lead to sex crimes against children." And despite the 20 years since the Meese report, there's *still* no social science to back up that claim. (And in a hilarious footnote, the ad actually gave the URL for a website featuring "an unedited list of hardcore titles" distributed by the hotel chain suppliers of adult movies. Thanks to these jokers, patrons could now shop for hotels based on personal fetishes!)

As we will see later in the book, members of the American Taliban are allergic to science and facts, and their reaction is particularly virulent in matters of sex. Thus, we get Senator Tom Coburn fantasizing about hot lesbian underage girls going at it in high school bathrooms, and we get Coburn's top staffer claiming that, get this—*straight porn will make you gay.*

Michael Schwartz isn't just Coburn's chief of staff but is also an activist in his own right, having previously served as the very male vice president of governmental affairs for the Concerned Women for America. He was also the first executive director of the House Family Caucus in 1995, a group of American Taliban in the U.S. House of Representatives that began as an informal prayer breakfast with James Dobson. Speaking at a "Values Voter Summit" in September 2009, Schwartz told his audience,

> Pornography is a blight. It is a disaster. It is one of those silent diseases in our society that we haven't been able to overcome very well. Now, I may be getting politically incorrect here. And it's been a few years, but not that many, since I was closely associated with pre-adolescent boys, boys around 10 years of age. But it is my observation that boys of that age have less tolerance for homosexuality than just about any other class of people. They speak badly about homosexuality. And that's because they don't want to be that way. They don't want to fall into it.

Wait, how did a rant against pornography so quickly morph into talk about 10-year-old boys and homosexuality? This gets good . . .

Schwartz went on to tell the audience a touching story about a friend of his "who was in the homosexual lifestyle and then he had a religious conversion," magically turned straight, and set up an AIDS hospice for gay men. And this man, Schwartz said, told him something profound—and one can hear Schwartz slowly and dramatically relating the profundity in a video of that session: "All pornography is homosexual pornography, because all pornography turns your sexual drive inward."

Wait . . . *what*?

"Now, think about that," continued Schwartz, mimicking his boss who really wanted you to *think about* hot teen lesbians going at it in the high school bathroom. "If you tell an 11-year-old boy about that, do you think he's going to want to get a copy of *Playboy*? I'm pretty sure he'll lose interest. That's the last thing he wants!"

So, I thought about it, and I'm pretty sure this guy is batshit insane if he thinks 11-year-old boys will "lose interest" in a *Playboy* if you tell them the magazine will make them gay. And they'd mock you on their MySpace page—deservedly so—if you rationalized it by rambling on about turning their "sexual drive inward," whatever the hell that's supposed to mean. Heck, for generations parents tried telling kids they would go *blind*, and it didn't do shit to stop boys from masturbating.

A study by the University of Alberta found that 90 percent of boys aged 13 and 14, from 17 urban and rural schools, admitted in anonymous surveys to having watched pornography at least once. One-third said they had viewed such material "too many times to count." Yet strangely enough, 90 percent of Alberta men are not gay. Not even a third of them are gay. Now think about that! Then again, maybe these Canadian teens got a great look at their fathers' big cocks in the shower every day, counteracting the homosexualizing influence of looking at naked women.

And really, who could possibly characterize *Playboy* as pornography? Well, to that crowd, it's downright hardcore, given they believe the best-selling "swimsuit issue" of *Sports Illustrated* is porn. Robert Peters, president of Morality in Media, had this to say in April, 2008, about Wal-Mart selling the swimsuit issue on its racks:

> In my opinion, *SI*'s Swimsuit Edition 2008 is "soft-core pornography." With *Playboy* magazine, we have full nudity; with the Swimsuit Edition, partial nudity. Otherwise, there is no difference that I can see.
>
> Surely Wal-Mart executives must realize that males don't purchase the Swimsuit Edition to view art or to choose bathing suits for their wives or girl friends.
>
> State or local public indecency laws typically prohibit individuals from appearing in a public place, like Wal-Mart or a public beach, while in a state of "nudity," typically defined to mean: "the showing of the human genitals, pubic area, anus, anal cleft, or any part of the female breast below a horizontal line across the top of the areola with less than a fully opaque covering." Many state and local harmful-to-minors sale and display laws also define nudity in this manner. Neither type of law uses the term "pornographic."

It turned out that Wal-Mart didn't really give a damn about whether nudity included "anal cleft" or "any part of the female breast below a horizontal line across the top of the areola" or any other such nonsense given that it had an agreement to sell the magazine nationwide. What's more, that darn swimsuit issue sold like crazy. And don't be embarrassed if you don't know what an "anal cleft" is—I had to look it up as well. Sounds dirty! It's actually the butt crack. Who knew plumbers were walking around nude! And the areola is the ring around the nipple, so any cleavage *below* that, as in a bikini top, or even a low-cut dress, is naked. Who knew the Oscars were one big nudist convention?

If you consider *Sports Illustrated* "pornography," it's easy to understand Attorney General John Ashcroft's decision to drape a cloth over the exposed breast of the Spirit of Justice, the art deco statue of Lady Justice in the Justice Department's Great Hall where news conferences are often held. If he could've gotten away with wrapping Spirit of Justice in a *burka*, he likely would've done that. Curiously, her male statue companion, Majesty of Law, is almost nude except for a thin rag draped over his loins, barely covering his package. Ashcroft didn't seem to have a problem with *that*. Think about it!

Ironically, those god-fearing Red states sure love them some porno. At one time, Republicans could claim otherwise. Within days after the 2000 presidential election, Pete du Pont, former governor of Delaware, made the following assertion in the *Wall Street Journal*, regarding the percentage of sex movies in the home-video market in regions of the country: "Mr. Gore carried the areas with the highest percentages (40 percent on the West Coast and 37 percent in New England and the Middle Atlantic states); Mr. Bush carried the area with the lowest percentage (14 percent in the South), and they split the rest of the country that had middling sex movie percentages." In his eagerness to paint Democrats as porn consumers, du Pont ignored the fact that those statistics were skewed by the availability of pornography for the home-video market. The South and places like Utah severely restricted access to such material. But that was before the internet.

In a study published in the *Journal of Economic Perspectives* in the winter of 2009, Benjamin Edelman examined the zip codes associated with all credit card subscriptions of a top online adult site, over a two-year period between 2006 and 2008. Here are some of his findings:

In the 27 states where "defense of marriage" amendments have been adopted (making same-sex marriage, and/or civil unions unconstitutional), subscriptions to this adult entertainment service are . . . 11 percent more [prevalent] than in other states.
. . . Subscriptions are also more prevalent in states where surveys indicate conservative positions on religion, gender roles, and sexuality. In states where more people agree that "Even today miracles are performed by the power of God" and "I never doubt the existence of God," there are more subscriptions to this service. Subscriptions are also more prevalent in states where more people agree that "I have old-fashioned values about family and marriage" and "AIDS might be God's punishment for immoral sexual behavior."

The states with the largest number of subscribers, proportionate to their population? Utah, Alaska, and Mississippi. Mississippi is the most religious state in the country, Utah ranks among the top because of its dominant Mormon population, and Alaska is, well, Sarah Palin country. Now this doesn't mean that these states consume more pornography than the sodomites in New York and California. Access to adult bookstores is virtually nonexistent in those states, so their citizens have to use the internet in disproportionate numbers to access such content. But that's the point—they *want* that content, even as they collectively and hypocritically frown upon it. Like Father Bruce Ritter, who railed against pornography even as he boinked a porn star.

In fact, of the top-10 Internet porn-consuming states, eight were Red states carried by John McCain—the three listed above plus Oklahoma, Arkansas, North Dakota, Louisiana, and West Virginia. Just two were Blue states—Hawaii and Florida. But this is a common pattern. According to the U.S. Census Bureau, the top 10 states with the highest divorce rates are Nevada, Arkansas,

Wyoming, Oklahoma, Idaho, Kentucky, Alabama, Mississippi, West Virginia, and Delaware. John McCain carried eight of those states.

So it is a fact that the radical Right segment of Americans are both publicly opposed to sex—homosexuality, pornography, marital affairs, etc.—and privately indulge in it and *think about it*. Or, in the case of online porn, watch it a lot!

When it comes to the American Taliban and sex, one can't escape the rampant hypocrisy. A lot of their loudest and most prudish voices seem simply unable to practice what they preach. So it's no surprise that some of the most virulently anti-gay voices in the American Taliban have turned out to be gay.

Ted Haggard was a Colorado Springs–area minister, heading the 14,000-member New Life Church, who served from 2003 to 2006 as head of the National Association of Evangelicals, which represents some 45,000 churches. He served as an advisor to President George W. Bush on evangelical matters. In 2005, he was named one of *Time* magazine's "25 most important evangelicals." In the documentary film *Jesus Camp*, about the madrassa-style religious training of Christian youth, Haggard is shown telling the crowd, "We don't have to have a debate about what we think about homosexual activity. It's written in the Bible." Later, he turns to the camera and says, mockingly, "I think I know what you did last night. If you send me a thousand dollars, I won't tell your wife." The crowd loved it. In a November 2005 interview with *Christianity Today*, he said, "The greatest benefit to society and to our culture and to the children of our nation would be to instill in our Constitution that marriage is the union between a man and a woman. It would be devastating for the children of our nation and for the future of Western civilization for us to say that homosexual unions or lesbian unions or any alteration of that has the moral equivalence of a heterosexual, monogamous marriage."

Funny thing, then, that Haggard regularly snorted meth and paid for sex with a male prostitute.

Just before the November 2006 elections, the religious community was rocked by revelations from a Denver masseur and prostitute named Mike Jones, who said Haggard was his client, purchasing sex and meth from him. Jones said he decided to go public after he saw Haggard—whom he knew simply as "Art"—on television and realized who his sex-and-drug client was and what he was preaching. "I had to expose the hypocrisy," Jones said. "He is in the position of influence [over] millions of followers, and he's preaching against gay marriage. But behind everybody's back [he's] doing what he's preached against."

Haggard initially denied the allegations. "I did not have a homosexual relationship with a man in Denver," Haggard told a Denver TV station, sounding positively Clintonian. "I am steady with my wife. I'm faithful to my wife." Yet a church investigation into the allegations determined otherwise, and he was eventually canned for "sexually immoral conduct."

Haggard later underwent "therapy" and emerged "cured" of his homosexuality. Phew! "It was good for me to go through the Christian hatred of people believing that I was a gay man—and hating me so strongly because of it," he said in a TV interview, as he mounted a comeback. "And so because of it, my compassion for the homosexual community has gone up incredibly." That was crazy how everyone thought he was gay for having sex with a gay prostitute, but it was all *fabulous*, because he hadn't realized how homophobic attacks are a real downer for people who are gay! And, as is the case with a lot of these sinner-preacher types, Haggard and his wife later made the media rounds, saying he was all

better now and considered himself "a heterosexual with issues."
Yeah, issues like not wanting to sleep with women.

Indeed, there's a cottage industry of self-loathing closeted gay
conservatives who rail in public against everything they practice.
Former U.S. Representative Ed Schrock, who represented the Second Congressional District in Virginia from 2001 to 2005, was a
cosponsor of the Federal Marriage Amendment, which would have
constitutionally banned gay marriage. Schrock was also a fierce
opponent of allowing homosexuals in the U.S. military. "You're in
the showers with them, you're in the bunk room with them, you're
in staterooms with them," Schrock said, likely arousing himself at
the mental images, because in 2004, he left this phone message on a
gay dating service line: "Uh, hi, I weigh 200 pounds, I'm 6'4" (inau-
dible) blond hair . . . very muscular, very buffed up, uh, very tanned,
uh, I just like to get together [with] a guy from time to time, just
to, just to play. I'd like him to be in very good shape, flat stomach,
good chest, good arms, well hung, cut, uh, just get naked, play, and
see what happens, nothing real heavy duty, but just, fun time, go
down on him, he can go down on me, and just take it from there . . .
hope to hear from you. Bye." Bye was about right, for Schrock had
to abort his re-election effort for a third term in Congress.

Senator Larry Craig of Idaho, who spent a lifetime in politics—
10 years in the House and 18 years in the Senate—was, among
other things, known for his opposition to gay rights and his support of an amendment to the Idaho Constitution banning gay
marriage and civil unions. And when the Monica Lewinsky story
broke, Craig went on national television and said, "The American
people already know that Bill Clinton is a bad boy, a naughty boy.
I'm going to speak out for the citizens of my state, who in the
majority think that Bill Clinton is probably even a nasty, bad,
naughty boy."

As it turned out, Craig knew quite a bit about "naughty boys." Rumors had swirled about his homosexuality since his days in the House back in 1982, when he was investigated by the FBI for alleged cocaine use and sex with teenage congressional pages. Nothing came of that investigation, even if the rumors persisted. And they did so for a reason.

In June 2007, Craig was arrested at Minneapolis–St. Paul International Airport for "lewd conduct." The arresting officer, Sgt. Dave Karsnia, set up a sting looking for men engaging in "cottaging"—the act of anonymous sex between men in public bathrooms—after receiving complaints of such activity at the location. Karsnia entered a stall and soon saw Craig loitering outside, trying to catch a glimpse of Karsnia through the crack in the door. According to his report, "Craig would look down at his hands, 'fidget' with his fingers, and then look through the crack into my stall again. Craig would repeat this cycle for about two minutes." Craig took up shop in the adjoining stall, blocking the door with his roller suitcase, and tapped his right foot, moving it closer and closer to the officer's foot. "My experience has shown that individuals engaging in lewd conduct use their bags to block the view from the front of their stall," Karsnia wrote, explaining that the tapping was "a signal used by persons wishing to engage in lewd conduct." The restroom was busy with travelers, but the "presence of others did not seem to deter Craig as he moved his right foot so that it touched the side of my left foot, which was within my stall area."

Craig swiped his hand under the stall divider several times, which finally prompted Karsnia to place his police badge on the floor so Craig could see it. "With my left hand near the floor, I pointed towards the exit," the report stated. "Craig responded, 'No!' I again pointed towards the exit. Craig exited the stall with his roller bags without flushing the toilet . . . Craig said he would not go. I told Craig that he was under arrest, he had to go, and that I didn't want to make a scene. Craig then left the restroom." Craig's long career in politics was over. He decided not to seek re-election to the U.S. Senate in 2008.

Here's one you probably never heard of—Glenn Murphy, a well-known political consultant in Indiana, quite successful at using wedge issues like gay marriage to promote his candidates. His campaign to chair the Young Republicans was endorsed by the party bigwigs. "Glenn Murphy is one of the most well-respected Republican leaders in Indiana," wrote the state's Republican governor, Mitch Daniels. "I wholeheartedly endorse Glenn Murphy for Chairman of the Young Republican National Federation and his team for national leadership." Murphy's campaign was successful, and he was tasked with running the GOP's top youth operation.

On August 7, 2007, Murphy abruptly sent out a letter to local media saying he was quitting his position "citing an unexpected business opportunity that would prohibit him from holding a partisan political office," as the local paper reported.

It was a nice try on Murphy's part, given that prosecutors had started to investigate an incident from a week earlier, on the fateful night of July 29, when a man came forward to accuse Murphy of sexual assault. Apparently, Murphy and the 22-year-old man had both been at a Republican event, where they drank a lot. Too drunk to go home, they both crashed at the man's sister's house. The victim told police he woke up at 6:40 a.m., to find Murphy "was holding his dick with one hand and sucking my dick with his mouth." It certainly wasn't the first time someone had been fucked over by a Republican, and it wasn't even the first time Murphy pulled this trick. Back in 1998, he tried it while his victim was sleeping and his victim's girlfriend was in the same room.

And so it goes. It almost seems like the more someone talks

obsessively and in detail about gay sex, the more likely that they are gay themselves. Reminds me of this particular hate mail I received after one of my appearances on Keith Olbermann's program on MSNBC. "I saw your pussy ass on Pravada (er, I mean MSNBC) yukking it up with Keith Blubberman and spouting communist rhetoric. While watching it occurred to me that you look like you crawled off the pages of a gay porn magazine. Seriously, I could practically picture one million tiny, shit stained, AIDS infested cocks ejaculating as one while you were on the air. Perhaps it may be time to take a break from your current day job of proving Senator McCarthy right and get into gay porn full time." Hmmmm. This guy saw me on the TV, and his thoughts turned to a symphony of penises ejaculating in unison?

When the Ted Haggard scandal broke, one of the strangest rationalizations for that behavior came from Mark Driscoll, pastor of the Mars Hill Church of Seattle. You see, Haggard hadn't slept regularly with a gay prostitute because he was gay, but because "It's not uncommon to meet pastors' wives who really let themselves go." Straight men, sexually unsatisfied in their marriages, usually end up sleeping with other women. They don't suddenly decide to give the penis a shot. If you fantasize about gay porn, you are gay. If you obsess about gay sex, you are gay. If you have frequent gay sex, you are gay. If you pay for gay sex, you are gay. And although it may be funny to laugh at this crowd's repressed behavior, it really is tragic. I couldn't help but feel sad for Craig, whimpering "No!" as he was being dragged out of that bathroom stall by the undercover police officer. I can't help but wonder how much happier my hate emailer would be if he could openly express his sexuality. Yet, they have been convinced that being gay is evil, so they lash out at other homosexuals and at those who refuse to surrender their principles of tolerance and equality.

Straight members of the American Taliban are no less hypocritical. They just don't suffer punishment for their indiscretions. Ronald Reagan had an affair with a married woman—his first wife, Jane Wyman. Sure, *he* wasn't married, but that's a technicality; it was an adulterous affair. Yet, he is considered a saint, even though he has the distinction of being the only president in American history to have been divorced. John McCain, the 2008 Republican presidential nominee, aggressively courted his second wife while still married to his first. New York Mayor Rudy Giuliani, self-declared owner of the 9/11 franchise, has had a long string of adulterous affairs, including a very public one while he was mayor of New York. In fact, his second wife, Donna Hanover, learned from reporters on May 10, 2000, that Giuliani had announced at a press conference he was separating from her. In the divorce proceedings, Hanover charged that Giuliani had enjoyed a series of mistresses, including a fling with his communications director.

Then there's former House Speaker Newt Gingrich, a real sweetheart, who ran his first campaign for Congress in 1978 with the slogan, "Let Our Family Represent Your Family"—while cheating on his first wife. His mistress at the time told *Vanity Fair*, "We had oral sex. He prefers that *modus operandi* because he can say, 'I never slept with her.'" *Quelle horreur!* Turns out Gingrich was Clintonian even before Bill was! Gingrich finally dumped that first wife while she was recovering in the hospital from uterine cancer surgery. You'd think that was kind of awkward, if not cruel, but Newt didn't. In fact, he did it *again,* dumping his second wife soon after finding out that she suffered from a neurological condition that could lead to multiple sclerosis. He was also cheating on her *at the same time* he was leading the GOP's impeachment efforts against Bill Clinton over his affair with Monica Lewinsky. He married his third wife in 2000, and ended up writing a book titled *Rediscovering God in*

America. Still, he holds a respectable status among the American Taliban. One wonders if their Islamic cousins are as gullible.

Gingrich's resignation as Speaker in 1998—not, mind you, due to questionable morals but because he'd led his party into a disastrous election—set off "a comedy of eros." Louisiana representative Bob Livingston, who was about to take the speakership from Gingrich, abruptly resigned following revelations of his own adulterous affair. David Vitter replaced Livingston in the House, saying of Livingston's resignation, "It's obviously a tremendous loss for the state. I think Livingston's stepping down makes a very powerful argument that Clinton should resign as well and move beyond this mess." The married Vitter then went to DC, and immediately started using the prostitution services of the infamous DC Madam. In 2007, while serving in the U.S. Senate, Vitter's name cropped up in the Madam's phone records, including calls made while roll call votes were taking place in the House. Unfortunately, Vitter didn't heed his very own "powerful argument" about resigning, and when he returned to Washington post-scandal, his party's reaction broke new records of hypocrisy. Marianne Means, a Hearst Newspapers columnist, recounted the scene as Vitter was "welcomed back to a closed Republican Senate luncheon with a loud standing ovation."

> Judging by their enthusiastic greeting, his GOP chums didn't seem to mind that the hypocrisy level in the nation's capital—always high—just zoomed upwards into outer space.
>
> Isn't this the same "family values" crowd so eager to impeach President Clinton for an adulterous dalliance with a White House intern?

Pity Vitter's poor colleague, Senator Larry Craig, fresh off tap dancing with undercover cops in that Minneapolis bathroom stall. His transgression got him quickly drummed out of his party and the Senate. Dallying with prostitutes? That merited a standing ovation.

But the biggest bunch of hypocrites was probably the denizens of the C Street House—Washington DC headquarters of The Family. While these theocrats work to impose their rigid morality on the rest of us (such as the infamous Stupak-Pitts amendment to deny health insurance for abortions, from two of The Family's most senior members—Democratic Representative Bart Stupak and Republican Representative Joseph Pitts), their C Street home base resembled something out of *Animal House*, rather than its more benign nickname, "Prayer House." Indeed, in a span of a few months, three of its Republican residents were busted for having extramarital affairs.

There was Rep. Chip Pickering of Mississippi, a former Southern Baptist missionary and poster child for the Christian Right, who served six terms in the House and was essentially offered an appointment to an open Senate seat in 2008. But Pickering skipped out on the Senate appointment and abruptly retired, just when he seemed to be at the apex of his career. Turns out he was afraid word about his mistress would leak out, while his wife was back home in Mississippi with their *five* children. It eventually did, in legal proceedings after Pickering divorced his wife. His marriage didn't stand a chance, what with gays getting married in Iowa.

Next came Senator John Ensign of Nevada, head of the Republicans' Senate election committee and the fourth-ranking Senate Republican. During the Monica Lewinsky saga, poor Ensign was filled with sadness at the turmoil the scandal was generating in the country. "The honorable thing for him to do is to resign and not put the country through this." Still, being a born-again Christian and influential member of The Family didn't stop him from having a lengthy affair with the wife of his top aide, even though he himself was married. The 51-year-old Ensign had his wealthy parents send his mistress and her family $96,000 in an apparent attempt to keep things quiet. Many of Ensign's closest associates intervened repeatedly to try and force an end to the extramarital affair—even Senator Tom Coburn got involved, trying to negotiate a million-dollar agreement between Ensign and the former aide (and jilted husband)—but poor Ensign simply couldn't stop indulging in his marriage-destroying actions. Ensign had long been an opponent of gay marriage as he sought to protect the sanctity of traditional marriage. Unfortunately, once gays started marrying in Massachusetts, his wedding vows were all but worthless.

It was June 18, 2009, when South Carolina Governor Mark Sanford sort of, well, disappeared. Nobody knew where he was— he wasn't home with his wife and four kids, he wasn't at the office, his staff tried calling him 15 times on his cell phone, but there was no sign of the governor. He was supposed to be hiking on the Appalachian Trail, according to his family, but several days went by and he did not return. When he reappeared on June 24, it didn't take long for him to realize that reporters were close to breaking the story, so he came clean: he had run off to South America to spend time with his Argentinean girlfriend, whom he had met years earlier. During the Monica Lewinsky affair, Sanford considered adultery a firing offense. "Very damaging stuff. This one's pretty cut and dried," he said at the time. "I think it would be much better for the country and for him personally [to resign]." Yet in his own life, he was so busy cavorting with his mistress half a world away, that he couldn't even be bothered to phone home to talk to his kids on *Father's Day*. He also couldn't be bothered to resign, for the good of his state. I'm sure it was the fault of those gays marrying in Connecticut, threatening healthy heterosexual marriages.

Really, who needs gay marriages to destroy traditional marriages when the American Taliban are doing such a fantastic job of it themselves? Heck, homosexuals might be able to teach these hypocrites a thing or two about being in committed, loving relationships. An analysis by statistician Nate Silver of FiveThirty Eight.com found that divorce rates were higher in states that had passed Constitutional gay marriage bans. "Overall, the states which had enacted a constitutional ban on same-sex marriage as of 1/1/08 saw their divorce rates rise by 0.9 percent over the five-year interval," Silver wrote. "States which had not adopted a constitutional ban, on the other hand, experienced an 8.0 percent decline, on average, in their divorce rates." The highest increase of any state? Sarah Palin's Alaska, also the first state to enact a Constitutional ban on gay marriage.

The American Taliban damage marriage far more than any homosexual ever has, by tainting the institution with bigotry, adultery, and hypocrisy.

Of course, adultery knows no ideological or party lines and is not limited to the American Taliban. But the hypocrisy of the conservatives is so much more difficult to stomach, as they relentlessly beat the drum for "family values" and good morals, as they leap at the chance to criticize others (like Clinton) who stray, and as they use every opportunity to impose their moral code on the rest of society. Liberals don't have sex-related issues at the top of their legislative agenda, and they are capable of disapproving of adultery without hyperventilating about it, or wanting to stone the culprits to death, understanding that ultimately, it's a private matter between couples.

But here's the thing: all that talk about looking down on adulterers is horseshit. The polling firm Public Policy Polling asked South Carolina voters if they wanted Sanford impeached. Forty-five percent of respondents said "yes," but only 33 percent of the "moral and family values" crowd agreed. "Where do you think these folks stood on impeaching Bill Clinton?" wrote the pollster Tom Jensen. "It's clear there is forgiveness for politicians who cheat on their wives and abuse state resources to do so—as long as they're Republicans."

Of all the bizarre sexual hang-ups of the American Taliban, none is creepier than their obsession with premarital and teen sex. Theirs is a veritable blizzard of noes—no to vaccines that prevent sexually transmitted diseases, no to contraceptives, no to sex education, no to abortion; no, no no.

Islam has an easy solution to preventing premarital sex—marry off those kids as soon as they start having sexual urges. "It is clear in Islam that Muslims are encouraged to marry early. It is also clear, from a developmental understanding, that sexual urges begin at puberty," wrote Judith Muhammad in *Islam Online*. "In a society such as [the United States], where young people are exposed through personal contact and the media to a more sexually permissive society, it is not unexpected that sexual contact will begin soon after the urges begin . . . In Islam, where early marriage is suggested as a protection against this major sin, the problems related to sex outside of marriage are diminished."

The American Taliban have their own emphasis on early marriage—perhaps not as early as Muslim cultures—as is evidenced by data from the U.S. Census Bureau in its 2008 American Community Survey, which shows that states with the youngest median age at first marriage are firmly in the American Taliban base: Idaho at 25 years old; Oklahoma, Arkansas, Utah, and Kansas at 26 years old. States with the oldest median age at first marriage—roughly a half a decade older—are among the most liberal of America: Massachusetts, New Jersey, New York, Rhode Island, and District of Columbia. There's another benefit to marrying late—the same data shows that the older people are when they get married, the less likely they are to get divorced. But preventing divorce is not high on the sex-obsessed American Taliban list, certainly not higher than their aversion to unmarried people having sex or "living in sin."

For decades now, they have relentlessly pushed for and created programs and messages aimed at getting teenagers to suppress those sexual urges, even though those programs and messages *simply do not work*. But then, facing hard realities has not been a strong suit for this band of crusaders.

Take their favorite "abstinence-only" programs, which have eaten up a whopping $1.3 billion in taxpayer dollars this past decade and which, mercifully, were quickly shut down by the Obama administration in 2009.

One group in South Carolina called Heritage Keepers received abstinence-only funding and spent the money on student manuals, none of which discussed sexually transmitted diseases or contraceptives, but instead put out advice like this: "Males and females are aroused at different levels of intimacy. Males are more sight oriented, whereas females are more touch oriented. This is why girls need to be careful with what they wear, because males are looking! The girl might be thinking fashion, while the boy is thinking sex. For this reason, girls have a responsibility to wear modest clothing that doesn't invite lustful thoughts."

One of the major abstinence-only curricula in federally funded abstinence programs, WAIT (Why Am I Tempted?), instructs students as follows: "Sexually speaking, it has been said that men are like microwaves and women are like crock pots. What does that mean? Generally, men get stimulated more easily than women and women take longer to get stimulated. Men are visual responders and women respond when they feel connected and close to someone."

Since 2001, several millions in taxpayer dollars were wasted on such rubbish. In case such insight isn't enough to justify the federal money, there's always this: "Being able to have sex does not make you any different from a rat in a warehouse. They have sex too. Is that what you want to compare yourself to?" You know who else had sex? Hitler. Do you want to compare yourself to *Hitler*?

Mathematica Policy Research conducted a long-term study of abstinence-only programs, tracking 2,057 students in Mississippi, Miami, Milwaukee, and Virginia, from the age of 11 to high school graduation. Half the students received abstinence-only instruction for several years, the other half did not. The results? "[T]here is no evidence that the programs increased the rate of sexual abstinence," said Chris Trenholm, a senior researcher in charge of the study at Mathematica.

But as idiotic as it might be to piss away taxpayer dollars on fashion advice to teen girls (from the folks who brought us Tammy Faye Baker), this obsession gets pretty strange when you look at something like the Purity Ball, a father-daughter formal event at which dads in tuxes pledge to their daughters in white dresses that they will protect their daughters' virginity until marriage. The daughter begins the rite, telling her father, "With confidence in His power to strengthen me, I make a promise this day to God, my family, myself, my future spouse, and my future children; to remain sexually pure until the day I give myself as a wedding gift to my spouse." The father responds, "I, [daughter's name]'s father, choose before God to cover my daughter as her authority and protection in the area of purity. I will be pure in my own life as a man, husband, and father. I will be a man of integrity and accountability as I lead, guide, and pray over my daughter and my family as the high priest in my home. This covering will be used by God to influence generations to come." Then, says the website of the Generations of Light—which sponsors these balls across the country, "One of the most memorable highlights of the ball is when the fathers stand in the middle of the ballroom and form a circle around their daughters standing all aglow in their lovely ball gowns. The fathers place their hands on their daughters, and together we pray for purity of mind, body, and soul for generations to come." The father and daughter actually exchange rings.

One girl told *Time* magazine that when she was 13 years old, she received a charm for her bracelet—a heart-shaped lock. Her dad kept the key.

> On my wedding day, he'll give it to my husband. It's a symbol of my father giving up the covering of my heart, protecting me, since it means my husband is now the protector. He becomes like the shield to my heart, to love me as I'm supposed to be loved.

Does he also sign over a certificate of ownership to the groom? And what about the boys? "Every year we invite the sons to attend the Ball to watch the way their fathers treat young women," writes Purity Ball co-creator Randy Wilson on his site. Gotta let the boys learn to protect the virginity of women . . . by watching men surround young women in a circle! But there's more. Wilson also advocates a boy-centric celebration called "Brave Heart of a Warrior," which is *just* like a purity ball, except the boys get swords, and they don't have to pledge their virginity. "We believe that manhood is passed from the masculine to the masculine, and because the defining line between childhood and manhood is often indistinguishable in our world, we wanted to show our sons a clear line they can cross to enter into manhood." Did I mention there's a sword? When his 13-year-old son got his, "the immense sword was almost his height," explains Wilson.

> I explained to him that although he could not wage war right now with this imposing sword, he would grow into the weight of the sword just as he would grow into the weight of manhood. We sensed the incredible privilege and responsibility we have to stand courageously as mighty warriors of God calling our sons to "fight the good fight" (1 Tim. 1:18) for the sake of the cross.

Cute. Just like militant Muslim jihadists giving their sons their first AK-47. What's the kid supposed to do with that big-ass sword? Hack off the heads of nonbelievers?

Unsurprisingly, purity balls simply don't work. In fact, it turns out they're counterproductive. A January 2009 study by Janet Elise Rosenbaum in the journal *Pediatrics* compared 289 virginity pledgers with 645 nonpledgers. Here was the first surprise: "Five years after the pledge, 82 percent of pledgers denied having ever pledged," wrote Rosenbaum. Whereas dads were enraptured by their little flowers pledging their virginity, the girls clearly saw it all as a nice, but forgettable night out with dad, and it certainly didn't alter their behavior. "Pledgers and matched nonpledgers did not differ in premarital sex, sexually transmitted diseases, and anal and oral sex variables. Pledgers had 0.1 fewer past-year partners but did not differ in lifetime sexual partners and age of first sex. Fewer pledgers than matched nonpledgers used birth control and condoms in the past year and birth control at last sex." One could look at all this weird ritualistic stuff and find it strange but harmless. But when teens are having sex without use of birth control, lives are at stake.

Human papillomavirus (HPV) is a sexually transmitted virus that infects the epidermis and mucous membranes, leading to cancers of the cervix, vagina, and anus. According to the U.S. Centers for Disease Control and Prevention, 11,999 women contracted cervical cancer in 2005, and 3,924 died from it that year. Clearly, those numbers are tragic. Fortunately, in 2006 an HPV vaccine was approved by the Food and Drug Administration, which promised to eradicate this preventable killer. Several states moved to require the vaccination of 11- and 12-year-old girls. The American Taliban went nuts. Saving young women from disease and death was all well and good, but saving young women who are sluts was not. The American Taliban's long-standing attitude is that women who wear revealing clothes or unmarried women who have sex deserve the consequences of sexual assault, rape, sexually transmitted diseases, AIDS, etc. As Phyllis Schlafly once said, "It's very healthy for a young girl to be deterred from promiscuity by fear of contracting a painful, incurable disease, or cervical cancer, or sterility, or the likelihood of giving birth to a dead, blind, or brain-damaged baby."

Unlike Muslim extremists who want to stone or give public lashings to women who sexually misbehave, our American fundamentalists simply want to let them die. "This isn't as much about morality as it is about good medicine," claimed Hal Wallis, head of the conservative Physicians Consortium. "If you don't want to suffer these diseases, you need to abstain, and when you find a partner, stick with that partner."

Tony Perkins of the Family Research Council was livid that the vaccine had been developed, because it "sends the wrong message. Our concern is that this vaccine will be marketed to a segment of the population that should be getting a message about abstinence." Do 11-year-old girls really know what vaccinations they're receiving at the doctor's office, other than that they prevent diseases? And if perchance one read the label of the vaccine—"Quadrivalent Human Papillomavirus (Types 6, 11, 16, 18) Recombinant Vaccine GARDASIL"—would the girl feel free to do half the boys in her fifth-grade class? It's not exactly the same as handing preteen girls issues of *Playgirl* or porn videos. Yet the manufacturer of this vaccine, Merck, was compelled to lobby Reginald Finger at James Dobson's Focus on the Family headquarters when seeking regulatory approval for this drug. Finger, a "medical affairs analyst" at Focus, was appointed by the Bush administration as a sop to the Christian Right, and he helped advise federal agencies on immunization issues.

Leslee Unruh of the National Abstinence Clearinghouse gave an honest wingnut reaction. "I personally object to vaccinating children against a disease that is 100 percent preventable with proper sexual behavior." In other words, let them die if they misbehave. Where's the qualitative difference between this approach and stoning or public lashings?

As usual, all the purity-and-puritanical blather from the American Taliban leaves out the facts. Roughly *95 percent* of Americans have had premarital sex, according to a 2005 study by the Guttmacher Institute. What's more, it's been that way for decades. The study found that 9 out of 10 women born in the 1940s had premarital sex. "Purity" in America has always been an unattainable ideal, if you can even call it an "ideal." Sex is natural. People do it. Married or not. Period.

But on all things sexual, the American Taliban are blind as bats. They still persist in opposing vaccines, contraception, sex education, or any other reasonable avenue to minimize the sometimes harsh consequences of sexual activity. Their answers to premarital sex are abstinence and purity balls and virginity pledges.

End of discussion. And the repercussions aren't just potential disease. There's another obvious side effect to unsafe sex: teenage pregnancies.

According to a 2006 study by the Guttmacher Institute, the 10 states with the highest teenage birth rates were Mississippi, Texas, Arizona, Arkansas, New Mexico, Georgia, Louisiana, Nevada, Alabama, and Oklahoma. Eight of those 10 are Red states. The lowest teen birth rates were in the most liberal states—New Hampshire, Vermont, Massachusetts, Maine, Minnesota, Connecticut, New Jersey, New York, and Wisconsin. The only Red state to crack the top 10 was North Dakota.

It's not hard to see the logic in this trend: teens in Red states have less access to the information necessary to make smart choices. And it's all by design. A study by Joseph and Jillian Strayhorn in the September 2009 *Reproductive Health* found that "the magnitude of the correlation between religiosity and teen birth rate astonished us. Teen birth is more highly correlated with some of the religiosity items on the Religious Landscapes Survey than some of those items are correlated with each other." The study found that even though religious teens were less likely to have abortions, that alone didn't account for the increased pregnancy rates. The only explanation is lack of information about, and access to, contraceptives.

That is, in fact, a stated goal of the American Taliban: no condoms, no birth control. "How, in good conscience, can a supposedly responsible adult support public policies that would communicate to such girls and boys that 'safe-sex' is an appropriate option?" asks the Concerned Women for America on its website. "Even if pregnancy were not a consideration, youngsters are not physically or psychologically ready for sexual activity. Even if morality were not an issue, the earlier a child begins sexual activity, the more partners he or she will have and the more risk he or she will face for sexually-transmitted diseases." So, keep them ignorant about condoms that would prevent most pregnancies and STDs. Pretend that sex isn't happening, and magical sparkling ponies will help those kids remain as pure as god intended. Except, as the statistics show, it doesn't turn out that way, and kids get knocked up.

But passing judgment is also of utmost importance to the American Taliban. Gary L. Bauer headed the President's Working Group on the American Family under Ronald Reagan and served as his undersecretary of education. He followed that stint with an 11-year run as head of the Family Research Council, culminating in his unsuccessful Republican presidential run in 2000. "If you look at the last 30 years, as a culture we have removed any form of being judgmental about out-of-wedlock pregnancy, as well as a host of other things," Bauer said in 1993. "While at first glance that may seem to be kind, the fact is that when a society has increasing rates of illegitimacy, it is headed for the rocks of decline."

Ken Blackwell of the Family Research Council—the same Ken Blackwell who used his office as Ohio secretary of state to disenfranchise thousands of voters on behalf of George W. Bush's 2004 re-election campaign—appeared on Glenn Beck's old show on CNN in 2007, and let loose with some old-fashioned sanctimoniousness. "The fact is that we have a society that talks one way but behaves another. And until we start having an adult model for these young people, we're going to see an escalation in out-of-wedlock births." Agreeing with Blackwell was none other than Christian Right author Bill Myer, a psychologist at Focus on the Family (a sister organization of Family Research Council). "If those parents are not available to them and they're not providing them with a great model of what it means to be a person of character and integrity and have strong moral values and explain the difference between right and wrong and what it means to live in a pure and noble way, where are the kids going to turn? They're going to turn right back to MTV and those same rappers who are giving them a completely different message." Beck himself did his parent-bashing bit. "Mom and Dad are so busy doing their own thing that they just think they can buy their kids with stuff or bigger TVs."

Blaming parents is certainly easy, so the American Taliban eagerly piled it on when it was revealed that Jamie-Lynn Spears, the 16-year-old sister of pop star Britney Spears, was pregnant. "The parents here are the culprits!" thundered Rush Limbaugh. And Bill O'Reilly, in his usual understated language, said, "Now most teens are pinheads in some ways. But here the blame falls primarily on the parents of the girl, who obviously have little control over her or even over Britney Spears. Look at the way she behaves." Bill had obviously watched plenty of Britney. Think about it!

Then something happened that laid bare their double standard: one of their own Taliban comrades had a teenage daughter problem. In September 2008, the McCain-Palin campaign was forced to admit that Sarah Palin's 17-year-old daughter, Bristol, was pregnant. Principled consistency would've required the American Taliban to react in righteous indignation, blaming Sarah and Todd Palin for being bad parents, and lamenting the loss of values and purity that was driving a stake in the heart of the American family.

Instead, it turns out Bristol's baby was *the most beautiful thing in the world*, and, praise the Lord, Bristol had "chosen life."

"Fortunately, Bristol is following her mother and father's example of choosing life in the midst of a difficult situation," said

Tony Perkins. "We are committed to praying for Bristol and her husband-to-be and the entire Palin family as they walk through a very private matter in the eyes of the public."

James Dobson, who had preached that premarital sex was "dangerous and unacceptable," was suddenly quite soft and avuncular. "The media are already trying to spin this as evidence Governor Palin is a 'hypocrite,' but all it really means is that she and her family are human." Bauer, formerly so outraged at the lack of judgment over out-of-wedlock pregnancies, was suddenly lacking in that judgment and looking at the bright side of things. "Bristol Palin and her family understand that a new life has been created," he said. "The commitment to bring that life into the world is a testament to their pro-life philosophy. I commend them for the example they are setting for other women in crisis pregnancies."

Would the reaction have been the same if one of Obama's daughters (assuming she was 16 or so) had ended up a teen mother and the baby's father was a high school dropout? Imagine the vile, disgusting, even racist things they would've said about a pregnant African American teen and her parents. Imagine the whole lot of these bloviated blowhards—Beck, Limbaugh, Dobson, Perkins, O'Reilly, etc.—ranting about the topic *ad infinitum*, lamenting the poor character and loose morals of the Obamas. It would've been ugly.

Yet the hypocritical embrace of Bristol was certainly a one-off. Sarah Palin herself, during her brief—and aborted—stint as governor of Alaska, slashed 20 percent of the state funding for Covenant House, a refuge for troubled teens, including a home for teenage mothers. None of Bristol's champions rushed to the defense of these teen mothers who also "chose life." Nor did any of them advocate funding for services to these life-choosers and their innocent babies. How about providing a nurturing environment, ensuring proper nutrition, postnatal health care, and counseling services to combat the stresses of new motherhood, and educational opportunities so they could pursue a productive life?

Unfortunately, not all of America's teen mothers are named "Bristol Palin," not all of them are the daughter of a governor, not all of them are white, not all of them are from middle-class households, and not all of them have two parents. It would be commendable if the American Taliban would show half as much compassion for those young women as they did for Bristol and her celebrity mother.

And don't even get them started on the evils of contraception. It all began with Anthony Comstock, a 19th-century Puritan who pushed for and succeeded in passing federal legislation in the 1870s that effectively banned the sale and distribution of contraceptives or even information about contraception. Thirty states subsequently approved similar laws restricting or banning the use of contraception until, in 1965, the U.S. Supreme Court struck down those laws in *Griswold v. Connecticut*.

Although the laws have changed, and society long ago moved on, the American Taliban cling to their outmoded Puritanical efforts to eliminate contraceptives. Leading the charge in the war against contraception is Focus on the Family, which boldly states its views on the matter on its website.

> Sex is a powerful drive, and for most of human history it was firmly linked to marriage and childbearing. Only relatively recently has the act of sex commonly been divorced from marriage and procreation. Modern contraceptive inventions have given many an exaggerated sense of safety and prompted more people than ever before to move sexual expression outside the marriage boundary.

Of course, people had sex for pleasure long before contraception became available, but don't tell Alan Keyes. Speaking in April 2002 on his short-lived and hilariously named MSNBC show *Alan Keyes Is Making Sense,* he said, "We don't need more voices [arguing] that all kinds of sex outside of marriage and apart from God's plan of procreation are to be regarded as joyful and wonderful and somehow consistent with Catholic teachings." Shoot, I guess he *wasn't* making sense. Joseph Schiedler, the national director of the fiercely anti-abortion Pro-Life Action League, one-ups Keyes in the outrage department at the notion of sex as joyful and wonderful. "I think contraception is disgusting, people using each other for pleasure . . . for those who say I can't impose my morality on others, I say watch me."

We *are* watching, and that's the problem. Schiedler is not simply stating his views; he and his organization, working with their cohorts in the American Taliban movement, are actively working to impose those views on the rest of us. Susan Orr was President George W. Bush's chief of family planning programs at the Department of Health and Human Services—and she was opposed to family planning! Orr, who was also a senior director at the Family Research Council and adjunct professor at Pat Robertson's Regent University, fought a Washington DC ordinance proposal that required all employers to cover contraception in their insurance plans. "The mask of choice is falling off," she said. "It's not about choice. It's not about health care. It's about making everyone collaborators with the culture of death." Culture of *what*? How does that even make sense?

We're not talking here about RU-486, which is a bona fide abortifacient, but about run-of-the-mill contraceptives, from the morning-after pill, which prevents ovulation, fertilization, or implantation of the egg, to the condom. And although it sounds like an extremist fringe position to say that condoms contribute to a "culture of death," Orr was clearly not alone in her views— most of the high priests and priestesses of the American Taliban share that view. The American Life League, a coalition of 97 anti-abortion groups says in its "Declaration on Truth and Life,"

> Respect for human life is impossible without respect for con-jugal union. Contraceptive acts and reproductive technologies that manipulate or replace conjugal union are a rejection of the gift of life—and most often include the foreseen deaths of tiny children.
> Abortion will never end as long as society approves the use of contraception. The practice of contraception means children are unwanted and provides the rationalization for abortion. It is a violation of human dignity to promote or accept the use of contraception.

Calling birth control a "gateway to abortion," the American Life League has set out to eradicate this supposed scourge. At the group's website, ThePillKills.com, its hysterical authors scream about how women *might* be dying of the pill, but they can't know, because there's a conspiracy to keep that information secret! "The pill and other birth control products can and do kill," begins one shrill answer to a list of FAQs. "How is that a benefit? How many more women have to die or experience serious side effects that lead to death before YOU join us in our effort to educate others on the dangers of this chemical?"

But the site betrays its true agenda in another question that asks, "What are other alternatives to the pill?" There are plenty of non-drug contraceptive options, including the trusty condom, but those don't jibe with the movement's anti-sex agenda. "If you are married and for some serious reason you need to hold off on having a child, there are safe, natural ways to doing this," they respond. "Couples who [use] the Creighton Model, have a much higher success rate in spacing their children." Got it? This isn't even about premarital sex. Married couples are basically relegated to the rhythm method, and even then, only to "space" your children if you have "serious reason" to do so.

The formidable power of the Catholic Church opposes contraceptive use. Pope John Paul II traveled the world forbidding the use of contraceptives, despite the importance of population control in some of the world's poorest regions, where high birth rates became a major contributing factor to poverty and environmental degradation. Pope Benedict XVI is no better, stating that AIDS is "a tragedy that cannot be overcome by money alone, that cannot be overcome through the distribution of condoms, which even aggravates the problems." The only solution to the AIDS crisis, of course, is abstinence and fidelity within marriage.

In recent years, the American Catholic Church has moved strongly rightward, de-emphasizing its laudable historical support for social justice and poverty relief programs, as well as its opposition to the death penalty, in favor of emphasizing its homophobic and anti-choice tenets. Once reviled by the evangelicals that make up the core of the American Taliban, they now make common cause on these divisive social issues. (According to author Jeff Sharlet, you can thank The Family for encouraging this alliance, realizing that "Catholics and evangelicals, who historically in American life have been at each other's throats, could work together on culture war issues, that they could be co-belligerents in the culture war.")

In 2000, Congress passed the Trafficking Victims Protection Act, providing funding for services for the 14,500 to 17,500 women and children brought into the United States each year as sex slaves. In 2006, the U.S. Conference of Bishops was granted a $2 million contract for administering the program. Among the services provided are food stamps, torture treatment, and career counseling, yet the agreements between the bishops' conference and its subcontractors specifically prohibit funds from being used for "referral for abortion services or contraceptive materials," which prompted a lawsuit by the ACLU.

Ironically, not even Islam is this restrictive on the topic of contraceptives, allowing its use for married couples. But the American Taliban's top politicians are aboard this regressive agenda. Most of them, like Senator John McCain, proudly trumpet their opposition to taxpayer-funded contraception programs and work to defund and eliminate family planning programs. According to the *Daily Kos* January 2010 poll of self-identified Republicans, nearly a third of the GOP base—31 percent—believed that "contraceptive use [should] be outlawed." Another 13 percent were on the fence. Although a 56-percent majority of respondents were happy with their legal contraceptives, Republican politicians have been forced to toe the line due to the vocal opposition of that significant 31 percent minority. That minority is bolstered by the collective power of organizations like Focus on the Family and Family Research Center, along with major televangelists like Pat Robertson, pompous personalities on Fox News, conservative radio hosts, not to mention the Catholic Church and other religious institutions.

What lies beneath the superficially sentimental and silly events like purity balls, and the more serious issues like laws restricting access to contraception or forbidding equal marriage rights to same-sex couples, is a desire to bring the behavior of others in line with one monolithic, unquestioned moral code. Whether in Colorado Springs or Riyahd, this obsession with sex and sexuality is ultimately *all* about control.

4

WOMEN

As obsessed with squashing sexuality as the American Taliban
are, you'd think they'd be delighted that strip-joint business was
mighty slow during a massive convention, an event that can tempt
even the most devout to stray off the straight and narrow into
the realm of debauchery. Certainly, staying away from strippers
is good news, a sign of a moral community?

During the August 2008 Democratic National Convention,
the *Denver Post* reported that strippers were complaining because
business was sluggish (but they had high hopes for the tech convention the next weekend!). To most Americans, this would mean
Democrats kept themselves focused on the reason they were in
Denver—politics. To the macho mullah of radio, Rush Limbaugh,
it meant something else entirely.

"This is easily understood by me," he declared smugly to his
listeners. "How many real men were in Denver this past week?
That's the question you need to ask."

Well, Rush, glad you asked it. First, *half* of the Democratic
delegation was female, so it's easy to see how you could get con-

fused—after all, less than *one-third* of the delegates to the Republican National Convention in Minneapolis the next month would be women. A "convention" in the male American Taliban mind is a boisterous, lewd, frat-house blowout, replete with strip clubs and call girls. Definitely no place for a woman.

But aside from the knee-jerk assumption that only men take part in political conventions, the "real men frequent strip joints" implication was a curious tack for Limbaugh to take. Had the story read differently—that strip club business was booming—Limbaugh would've reverted to "family values" mode, claiming that Democrats did not respect their families. Either way, Rush would have taken a whack at the Democrats: heads he wins, tails they lose.

But really, how could Republicans reconcile such hypocrisy—hyping "family values" while bemoaning lack of strip-club attendance by Democratic wusses? Because when it comes to sex and gender roles, the American Taliban believe in the supremacy of the male—the very *male* male, the malest male imaginable. In fact, if the American Taliban have a grand unified theory, it is unbridled machismo, typified by Republican California governor Arnold Schwarzenegger, who's made a signature of swagger, cigars, and calling opponents, such as Democratic lawmakers in the state legislature, "girlie men." He enjoyed the ensuing uproar so much, he used the phrase again a month later at the Republican national convention in a speech that drew wild applause from true believers.

From that testosterone-laden worldview of Schwarzenegger and Limbaugh stems the American Taliban's aggressiveness, their warmongering, their chauvinism, their disrespect for the Constitution, their hypocritical obsession with female sexuality, and pretty much every other ill associated with them.

The powerhouse Southern Baptist Convention (which includes former Arkansas Governor and presidential candidate Mike Huckabee) said in its "Resolution on Women in Combat" in 1998,

> God, by creating Adam first and also by creating woman for man has set the gender-based role and responsibility of males in the most basic unit of society (the family) to be that of leader, provider and self-sacrificial protector, and likewise has set the gender-based role and responsibility of females to be that of help and nurture and life-giving under male leadership and protection.

And if a woman doesn't want to live under the "leadership and protection" of a man? Tough shit.

"I know this is painful for the ladies to hear, but if you get married, you have accepted the headship of a man, your husband," declared Pat Robertson to his *700 Club* television audience. "Christ is the head of the household and the husband is the head of the wife, and that's the way it is, period."

Sadly, it's not just men who tout this nonsense. There's a long history of conservative women pressuring others to comply with fundamentalist notions of a woman's proper place. Perhaps the best known is Phyllis Schlafly, the *grande dame* of the American Taliban and founder in 1967 of Eagle Forum, a prototype for later and more powerful conservative interest groups that melded anti-abortion, anti–gay marriage, and anti–United Nations sentiments. Its early focus, however, was to defeat the proposed Equal Rights Amendment in the 1970s. Unsurprising from the woman who explained to the world that, "Women have babies and men provide the support. If you don't like the way we're made you've got to take it up with God."

Funny thing is, this is virtually identical to the message of their loathed Islamic extremist cousins. It is no accident that "that's the way it is, period," and "you've got to take it up with God," are pretty much the same messages to women whether you're in Washington or Waziristan. The rule of man over woman is just as clear in contemporary Islamic fundamentalist advice to women. An engineering student who solicited advice from a Muslim website about the propriety of her working her way through school was met with a barrage of edicts, including one that stated that employment "should not lead to her neglecting things that are more essential for her, such as looking after her house, husband and children."

The idea that a woman's rightful place is in the home—and not in the House or the Senate or the boardroom—is not just limited to Christian and Islamic fundamentalists. Conservative screecher Ann Coulter both amused and appalled a *Politically Incorrect* audience in February 2001 by ranting about the stupidity and simplicity of women in the public sphere and the uselessness of their input. She said that women:

> should be armed but should not vote. No, they all have to give up their vote, not just, you know, the lady clapping and me. The problem with women voting—and you communists will back me up on this—is that, you know, women have no capacity to understand how money is earned. They have a lot of ideas on how to spend it. And when they take these polls, it's always more money on education, more money on child care, more money on day care.

Useless women. Wanting to invest in the future of society. How stupid. Just a month before Coulter threw her inflammatory statement out there, the Saudi interior minister, Prince Nayef, declared there was no point to discussing women's rights ("out of the question") and that "such a debate would be useless and produce a hollow exchange of ideas." They'd probably insist on spending money to care for children—you know, *communist* ideas.

It gets harder and harder to tell American Taliban inflammatainment from the real Islamic extremist version, doesn't it? Witness Pat Buchanan:

> Rail as they will about "discrimination," women are simply not endowed by nature with the same measures of single-minded ambition and the will to succeed in the fiercely competitive world of Western capitalism.

At best, such antiquated views merely hold back women from the workplace or politics, and keep them tied to the home. At worst, they encourage or excuse criminal brutality against women. In Jordan, a 19-year-old got away with killing his 22-year-old sister for the honor of the family—a capital crime reduced to a 10-year sentence—because she had "many unexplained absences from home," according to CNN. In Kabul, teenage girls have had acid thrown in their faces on their walk to school for the unforgivable sin of trying to get educated. In Basra, women were tortured, strangled, and beheaded for not wearing a headscarf.

In search of a reason to invade Iraq, conservative American warmongers were among the first to eagerly seize upon the vicious treatment of women in Islamic fundamentalist societies as a *casus belli*. Yet, for all their indignation—admittedly warranted—about women being killed for not wearing burkas, for all their condemnation of men who wreak violence on women over something as basically trivial as choice of dress, it's funny how the American Taliban spout similar views. Bill O'Reilly, war hawk and American Talibanist extraordinaire, said about Jennifer Moore, an 18-year-old rape and murder victim in New York City, "She was

5-foot-2, 105 pounds, wearing a miniskirt and a halter top with a bare midriff. Now, again, there you go. So every predator in the world is gonna pick that up at two in the morning." She was, he said, "moronic." She should have known better. That's the same argument—and the same fear—women in extremist segments of the Muslim world face daily. Wear what the fundamentalist men tell you to wear, or else.

The examples are endless, and the synchronicity on women's issues between the American Taliban and Muslim fundamentalists is incontrovertible. Women are quite simply seen as inferior creatures, subservient to dominant males. According to one collection of hadith, sayings and deeds of the Prophet Muhammad, he once said, "Your lack of common sense can be determined from the fact that the evidence of two women is equal to one man. That is a proof." More than 1,400 years later, women who assert themselves as equal members of society are still met with hostility and opposition. The ultimate goal of these ideologues, be they Muslim or American, is to keep women holed up at home while men govern society. It's a social order where brute force commands, the meek are brushed aside, and intimidation is routinely used to keep women in line.

This need to dominate sometimes takes the form of intentional hyperbole, as when Coulter said "women should not vote." Sometimes, when the conservative crank wants to be taken seriously, the anti-women rhetoric gets toned down, but it's never far from the surface. When former Republican House majority leader Dick Armey, head of the teabagger group FreedomWorks, squared off against *Salon* editor-in-chief Joan Walsh in a televised debate on *Hardball* in January 2009, the discussion centered on the economic stimulus proposed by President Obama, its effect on the economy, and the likelihood of passage in the current political landscape. Near the end of the discussion, when disagreement got heated and Walsh was explaining how the Bush policies were responsible for the recession, Armey lost it. "I am so damn glad that you could never be my wife, 'cause I surely wouldn't have to listen to that prattle from you every day."

Yep. Prattle. An epithet aimed at an accomplished journalist published in numerous major newspapers and magazines over the course of a distinguished career, and an insult aimed to demean, specifically aimed at her femininity—her worth determined by her suitability to be his wife.

This hyperawareness of gender roles is certainly one of the hallmarks of both branches of the Taliban. What does it matter whether Dick Armey would want Joan Walsh as his wife, given that they were two guests on national television discussing economic policy? Why bring up gender at all? Why would Rush Limbaugh care one way or the other whether strip clubs were thriving or empty during a Democratic convention? And why is compromise, problem-solving, empathy, rationality—anything but brute intimidation or blunt force—seen as "feminine"?

Evangelist Tony Evans, founder of the Urban Alternative ministry in Texas (and chaplain of the Dallas Cowboys—can you get more macho than that?) echoes a widely held sentiment among his circles when he says, "The demise of our community and culture is the fault of sissified men who have been overly influenced by women." Evans isn't expressing some fringe idea about the sissification of American men—his radio show is broadcast on more than 500 stations daily and he was a frequent speaker for Promise Keepers, the male bonding group that arose in the 1990s to counter the "feminization of America" by encouraging men to commit to Jesus Christ and step up to take charge of their households— and to dominate the women and children therein. Couched in terms of "protection," Promise Keepers proclaims its mission to be "to ignite and unite men to become warriors who will change their world through living out the Seven Promises"—one of those promises being to commit to "building strong marriages and families through love, protection and biblical values."

Such talk of "protection" can have an appeal, and not just to the biblical "warriors" declaring their belief in the inerrancy of scripture and their god-given right to be head of household. In a world fraught with economic uncertainty, the notion of being shielded from the harshness of the free market, with its downsizing, outsourcing, and discarding of workers, can be deeply appealing, particularly to conservative women. In the wake of 9/11, we've seen how quickly Americans are willing to surrender democratic values—such as the need for search warrants and the right to free speech—for even the appearance of security. It should not surprise us to find women willing to give up autonomy, choice, and, yes, even the right to vote, in exchange for "protection."

Take this sentiment, expressed by one Kay O'Connor of Kansas: "I'm an old-fashioned woman. Men should take care of women, and if men were taking care of women today, we wouldn't have to vote." At first glance, this crazy talk would surely seem to come from some out-of-touch nutbag, right? Wrong. Kay O'Connor served 14 years in the Kansas state legislature and was, believe it or not, the recipient of the Courageous Conservative Award in 2001, the same year she expressed the views that the world had been going to hell in a handbasket since the 19th Amendment was ratified in 1920. To add insult to injury, she chose to express her view that women's suffrage has led to most of the ills of modern life at a "Celebrate the Right to Vote" luncheon of the Johnson County League of Women Voters. This is not some lonely conservative crank screaming in cyberspace, or at a teabagger rally. This is an elected official who, despite her views that more than half the population shouldn't be eligible to vote, or perhaps *because of it*, was rewarded by her party's leadership in the Kansas state senate with the vice-chairmanship of the Committee on Elections and Local Government.

When women feed into such craziness, it gives permission for American Taliban mullahs (like Rush Limbaugh) to rail even more extremely against women and their influence in the public sphere. Responding to Obama's contention that "there are still men who have a lot of old-fashioned ideas about the role of women in society," Limbaugh fired back, "Can I tell you how dead wrong he is about that? What's happening in this country, Mr. President, is that the men of this country are becoming chickified." What does that mean, exactly? Rush pointed to a *Huffington Post* piece by best-selling author Marcus Buckingham.

> "To know a culture, look to its heroes," goes the saying, and here, too, we see change and new models of leadership. Gone are the macho monarchs—Jack "Neutron" Welch, George "The Decider" Bush, Michael "Micro-manager" Eisner, and Carly "The Fighter" Fiorina . . . In their place we now honor a new style of leader, no less visionary, but more pragmatic, more concilia-tory, building consensus as they quietly get things done—in the Oval Office, Barak Obama; at Hewlett Packard, Mark Hurd; at Disney HQ, Bob Eiger; and at the Welch mansion, the softer, friendlier hybrid, JackandSuzy.

To Rush, this was apostasy. "All of these guys that have become more and more like women are now said to be the real men of America. It is simply the chickification, the feminization of our society." And that's bad, because pragmatism, conciliation, build-ing consensus, and quietly getting things done are despicable chick traits.

Other than blowing shit up, being a "real" man apparently means to assert oneself as the dominant sex. "The aim of modern feminists is to destroy the picture of what a strong man looks like and his ability to exercise that strength in society for the greater good," wrote Kevin McCullough at the conservative site, *World-NetDaily*. "They aim to say that such strength is hideous, repulsive and manipulative. And in their attempts, they have taken men and destroyed them." I'm not feeling too destroyed, but apparently that's because my wife hasn't yet executed the Prime Feminist Directive.

Here's the late Jerry Falwell expressing his views on feminism, during the heyday of the Moral Majority:

> I listen to feminists and all these radical gals—most of them are failures. They've blown it. Some of them have been married, but they married some Caspar Milquetoast who asked permission to go to the bathroom. These women just need a man in the house. That's all they need. Most of the feminists need a man to tell them what time of day it is and to lead them home. And they blew it and they're mad at all men. Feminists hate men. They're sexist.

So feminists are sexist because they refuse to submit to men who will tell them the time of day and lead them home. Damn sexist bitches want to tell time and use a GPS!

And so it goes. "I submit to you that the feminist movement is the most dangerous, destructive force in our society today," said Eagle Forum's Phyllis Schlafly, speaking at a "How to Take Back America" conference. "My analysis is that the gays are about 5 percent of the attack on marriage in this country, and the feminists are about 95 percent . . . I'm talking about drugs, sex, illegitimacy, drop outs, poor grades, run away, suicide, you name it, every social ill comes out of the fatherless home." That's some incredible data and analysis she pulled out of her ass, especially the part about deadbeat and irresponsible dads being the fault of women! But does "every social ill" attributed to feminism also include rape? The American Taliban sure think so. "Perhaps the most damning of all is [that] the treatment of little girls went from making them a special princess in our heart, to thinking of them as one of the guys," McCullough of *WorldNetDaily* wrote. "Coarse behavior replaced manners. Using vulgarities replaced words of value. Men became demoralized and, in many ways, built up resentment and became more aggressive than ever." So if a dude rapes a girl or woman, it's because girls are no longer prissy little princesses, but foul-mouthed tomboys. Before feminism, when women were women, there was no such thing as rape. Got it.

The demonization of women and modernity—and blaming all of society's ills on advances in women's rights as they moved from being property to being fully vested human beings with rights—is not coming from a fringe element of the Republican Party. These are the beliefs of the party leadership. In a 1992 fundraising letter sent to the Christian Coalition members, Pat Robertson wrote,

> The feminist agenda is not about equal rights for women. It is about a socialist, anti-family political movement that encourages women to leave their husbands, kill their children, practice witchcraft, destroy capitalism, and become lesbians.

This is the same party element that responds with such delight to Limbaugh's bombastic assertions, such as, "Feminism was established to allow unattractive women easier access to the mainstream of society." As if he's some Brad Pitt lookalike. Yet such inanity, like Dick Armey's remarks about not wanting to be married to Joan Walsh because of her "prattle," is a bedrock tactic of the American Taliban—bringing gender, or physical attractiveness, into discussions where they have no relevance. It's certainly an effective way to deflect from feminism's core issues, like equal pay for equal work, and equal opportunity for promotion and fairness.

Even taken at face value, Limbaugh's statement about unattractive women and access to society is nonsense. Should unattractive women be locked up in cellars? Put to death? Interned in FEMA-run concentration camps? And why does he think he has a greater right to "the mainstream of society" than a woman he deems unattractive? Oh yeah, it's because he has a penis—which is, indeed, quite the advantage.

In 1989, a law student at Christian Broadcasting Network University (now Regent University), one of the madrassas of the American Taliban, wrote a thesis on the role of government and family policy. The student, Bob McDonnell, had the usual litany of complaints. According to the *Washington Post*, "He said government policy should favor married couples over 'cohabitators, homosexuals or fornicators.' He described as 'illogical' a 1972 Supreme Court decision legalizing the use of contraception by unmarried couples." He also claimed that "when the exercise of liberty takes the shape of pornography, drug abuse, or homosexuality, the government must restrain, punish and deter."

In his thesis, he wrote,

> The American landscape of the traditional family and its moral code is being marred by social permissiveness and government programs. In the 1950's, 70 percent of the typical American family consisted of a working father, a homemaking mother, and one or two children. In the changed demographics of 1980, this family pattern was representative of only 15 percent of households. Historically, the intact two-parent family has been the foundation of a healthy society, the best hedge against poverty

among children, and the time-tested institution for the trans-
mission of culture and values.

He concluded that the "dynamic new trend of working
women and feminists . . . is ultimately detrimental to the family
by entrenching a status-quo of non-parental primary nurture of
children."

That was Bob McDonnell in 1989. On Jan. 16, 2010, McDonnell took office as the governor of Virginia, after serving as attorney
general and as state representative. What Governor McDonnell
was expressing in sociological Ivory Tower–speak in 1989 was
that women should stay home, take care of kids, and forget having a job.

Nothing symbolizes the diminished role of the male in the
household more than the entrance of women *en masse* into the
workforce. Whether out of economic necessity, or in pursuit of
personal accomplishment, the working woman is neither novel
nor particularly controversial. Recent polls, like a May 2009 Pew
survey, have found little appetite, even among Republicans, for
women to "return to their traditional roles in society." But Americans continue to elect representatives like McDonnell, who has
a history of attempts to roll back hard-fought gains for equality
between the sexes. The story of McDonnell's rise through the
Taliban ranks is instructional, and typical of the aspiring-mullah
career path.

During a stint as a medical supply officer in the Army following graduation from University of Notre Dame (attended on an
ROTC scholarship), McDonnell took night classes to get a master's degree in business from Boston University, then took a job
with a hospital supply company. Soon, however, he found his way
to Pat Robertson's hyper-conservative Regent University, emerg-

ing on the other side not just with the thesis that would haunt him in his 2009 governor's race (and which he disavowed) but with a master's and a law degree. During his stint at Regent, he had one foot in the world of the Christian Coalition, and the other firmly in the world of secular conservatism, interning for archconservative congressman Jerry Lewis.

In 1992, he was elected to Virginia's House of Delegates, where he served for 14 years and fought to put many of his talibanic beliefs into legislation. In 1997, he fought against a bill that would have provided emergency contraception to rape victims. In 2001, he went further, saying emergency contraception was "as egregious" as aborting a full-term child. In 2002 and 2003, he voted for bills that would support pharmacists refusing to dispense contraception or the morning-after pill if it conflicts with their religion. In 2004, he voted for a bill that would prohibit health centers at public universities from providing the morning-after pill. He was also an ardent supporter of so-called covenant marriages, heavily promoted by Tony Perkins and the Family Research Council, in which legally dissolving a union is practically impossible. After a brief passage through the attorney general's office in Virginia—he took office in 2006 and announced his run for governor in 2007—McDonnell campaigned for governor, tapping into corporations to fund him and hiring a campaign manager with ties to evangelical leader Ralph Reed and lobbyist and convicted felon Jack Abramoff. As is typical with this crowd, the conservative corporate world provided the cash, and Christian conservative activists provided the boots.

During his campaign, when called on about the content of his master's thesis, he was quick to disavow it and claimed he was a changed man. But who could believe him? In that very same thesis he wrote, "It is also becoming clear in modern culture that the voting American mainstream is not willing to accept a true pro-family ideologue . . . Leadership, however, does not require giving voters what they want, for whimsical and capricious government would result. Republican legislators must exercise independent professional judgment as statesman, to make decisions that are objectively right, and proved effective." This is the height of cynicism—openly violating the trust of the voter by pretending to be something he is not, keeping his true intentions from an electorate that wouldn't otherwise endorse his regressive "pro-family" views.

Because if a majority of American families reject this supposed pro-family agenda, perhaps it's not so pro-family after all.

In 1979, Lilly Ledbetter began working as a salaried union worker at Goodyear Tire. Every year, workers received raises based on merit reviews. After nearly 20 years, she took early retirement in 1998, only to find a gross disparity in salary compared to 15 male co-workers who started work when she did. While she was earning $3,727 per month at retirement, the lowest salary of her 15 male peers was $4,286; the highest paid man was making $5,236— 40 percent more than her. Ledbetter saw this as discrimination and sued Goodyear. A jury agreed, and awarded her $3.5 million, but Goodyear appealed and the issue was litigated all the way to the U.S. Supreme Court. In 2007, splitting 5–4 along ideological lines, the court ruled that the suit wasn't filed within 180 days of the actual alleged discrimination and ruled for Goodyear. Justice Ruth Bader Ginsburg—the only woman on the court at the time—took the rare step of reading the dissent from the bench to underscore her fury at the majority. "In our view, the court does not comprehend, or is indifferent to, the insidious way in which women can be victims of pay discrimination," she said. Ledbetter had faced a Catch 22: file early before there was proper evidence of discrimination, or file after the evidence was clear, and be denied redress because the 180-day statute of limitations had passed. And in any case, didn't every single discriminatory paycheck reset the clock? Logic and common sense would dictate so. But the conservatives on the court hid behind a tortured technicality to avoid redressing a real wrong.

In response, the House passed a bill in 2008 reversing the decision, but the Republican minority in the Senate filibustered the bill dead. With the election of even larger Democratic majorities that fall, the bill sailed through Congress and the White House, and the Lilly Ledbetter Fair Pay Act of 2009—which eliminated the statute of limitations on bringing suit for unequal pay—became the first bill signed into law by President Barack Obama, just nine days after he was sworn into office. In the House, just three Republicans broke with their party to join the Democratic majority. In the Senate, five Republicans voted with the Democratic majority—Pennsylvania's Arlen Specter, who would soon thereafter switch to the Democratic Party, and four others: Kay Bailey Hutchinson of Texas, Susan Collins of Maine, Lisa Murkowski of Alaska, and Olympia Snow of Maine. Notice anything about those four Republicans? They are the *only* Republican women in the Senate. Although Republicans claimed their opposition was based on tort grounds—preventing unwarranted lawsuits from disgruntled (female) employees—the vote breakdown betrayed that claim. Not even *Republican* women could maintain that charade. They knew exactly what they were voting for, and they voted for equal pay protections in the workplace.

That vote is an indication of the price we pay for the lack of women in positions of power in our society. All we have to do is look at the kind of statements being made during the health care debates that went on in 2009, including this one from Senator Jon

Kyl of Arizona. "I don't need maternity care, and so requiring that to be in my insurance policy is something that I don't need and will make the policy more expensive." Sure, Jon, and women don't need to pay for your prostrate exams, or the Viagra you needed for your adulterous shenanigans. And it's not just the *content* of the American Taliban arguments that is so offensive, the debaters themselves tend to be obnoxious, shout-you-down-types. During the debate on health care reform on the House floor, for example, Republican Representative Tom Price from Georgia repeatedly and monotonously shouted, "I object! I object! I object!" every time one of the members of the Democratic Women's Caucus would try to speak in favor of the House health care bill. Both Lois Capps and Mary Jo Kilroy were screamed down, Kilroy ultimately accusing him of "trying to censor" her remarks.

Thus operating with a structural disadvantage, most woman-friendly legislative battles are a difficult slog. But sometimes, something good slips by before the Neanderthals in the American Taliban realize what's going on.

In 1972, Congress passed Title IX of the Education Amendments of 1972, which was so uncontroversial that there wasn't a single news article written about it in mainstream newspapers or magazines when it passed. Other than some narrow enumerated exceptions, Title IX states, "No person in the United States shall, on the basis of sex, be excluded from participation in, be denied the benefits of, or be subjected to discrimination under any education program or activity receiving Federal financial assistance." Although simple in construction, the legislation ushered in a dramatic renaissance in women's participation in athletics and academic programs. Known primarily for its effects on sports, the law is also credited with widespread advancement of educational opportunities for women.

"In 1972, women received fewer than 10 percent of the degrees in medicine and law and about 14 percent of the doctoral degrees. Today, women are receiving close to half of the medical, law, and doctoral degrees," said Valerie M. Bonnette, president of Good Sports, Inc., a gender equity and Title IX consulting firm. "It is doubtful that such progress would have occurred in one generation without Title IX. Title IX has opened the door to the opportunity to explore. No one should be alarmed because women have blasted that door off its hinges." It is certainly alarming to the American Taliban, who launched a rearguard action against the law once they realized its true power, and they have used men's collegiate sports as their preferred avenue of attack.

"On this 30th anniversary of the enactment of Title IX, the law prohibiting sexual discrimination in education, consider this: has even more nonsense been written about Title IX than has been committed in its name?" asked conservative syndicated columnist George Will. "Title IX, as adumbrated by ideology-besotted Education Department regulation writers, has produced this lunacy: Colleges have killed more than 400 men's athletic teams in order to produce precise proportionality between men's and women's enrollments and men's and women's rates of participation in athletics." Quoting another critic as saying "the story of this law is in many ways the story of the women's movement," Will nods along, writing that yes, it's "a depressing story."

Will's facts were suspect at best. It's true, 400 men's athletics teams were eliminated by colleges and universities, but those cuts were likely based on economic factors. Between 1981 and 1999, 100 women's gymnastics programs were also cut according to the General Accounting Office (GAO), and that's just in a single sport. Were those also cut because of Title IX in the pursuit of gender equity? Furthermore, schools shifted their athletic dollars into more contemporary and popular sports. Sure, wrestling got the ax, but men's soccer gained 100 teams and football added 39 more teams. In fact, for every 2 women teams added, men have gotten 1.5 as well.

There's no doubt that the law spurred a dramatic increase in women's sports, with collegiate women's teams increasing by a factor of *nine*, and the number of female NCAA varsity athletes increasing a staggering 456 percent in the 33-year period between 1971–72 and 2004–05 (from 29,972 female athletes to 166,728), according to a study by the National Coalition for Women and Girls in Education. (Men didn't get left out in the cold—the number of male varsity athletes *increased* 31 percent during that time period.)

Although critics maintain that women are underrepresented in sports because they are less interested in athletics than men, the fact is that 1 in 27 girls participated in high school sports prior to Title IX, or about 4 percent, whereas 40 percent participate today. Given the newfound opportunity, girls responded. "People confuse a lack of interest with a lack of opportunity," Christine Grant, athletics director emeritus at the University of Iowa, told ESPN. "They are very, very different. I don't know of an instance where women were given an opportunity and nobody came."

Don't tell that to the American Taliban, who are still opposed to that basic equality of opportunity in sports and academia. In 1988, in response to a Supreme Court ruling that would have effectively gutted Title IX, Congress approved legislation to reverse the ruling and Ronald Reagan unsuccessfully tried to veto it. The battle has been no less engaged ever since.

Even the women of the American Taliban spew sexist crap. For conservative columnist and radio talk show host Debbie Schlussel, sports is apparently all about the *opposite* sex. "I'd rather watch men play football than see a lesbian crew team—'You Gotta Regatta Lesbiatta'—steal their college scholarships." And really, Phyllis Schlafly never disappoints. "The lack of college sports teams and camaraderie makes many high school boys wonder, why bother going to college?" she wrote in 2006, apparently forgetting that colleges are institutions of higher *learning*. "Public demand is for all-male sports, not female contests. Boys do not want to go to a college that eliminates the macho sports." Apparently, all those boys wanted to go to college to see oiled-up men in tights wrestle, which is totally butch and *not* gay, but have no interest in getting educated because then they'd just get those totally gay sports of football, basketball, and soccer.

But while the American Taliban may be uninterested in listening to nearly four decades of liberals touting the benefits of Title IX and how it opened up opportunities for women, they may be more open to one of their own: Sarah Palin. Here is what she told *Alaska Business Monthly* after being elected to her short stint as governor:

> I had a great upbringing under Title IX. I can't imagine where I'd be without the opportunities provided to me in sports. Sports taught me that gender isn't an issue; in fact, when people talk about me being the first female governor, I'm a little absent from that discussion, because I've never thought of gender as an issue. In sports, you learn self-discipline, healthy competition, to be gracious in victory and defeat, and the importance of being part of a team and understanding what part you play on that team. You all work together to reach a goal, and I think all of those factors come into play in my role as governor.

Too bad sports didn't also teach her not to be a quitter, but the broader point is good: the law has had a profound effect on our society, even empowering one of today's biggest voices in the American Taliban. How's that for irony?

Funny how every time government tries to make it easier for women to properly integrate into the workplace, the American Taliban step in. In 1993, Bill Clinton signed the Family and Medical Leave Act (FMLA), which allowed workers to take job-protected, unpaid leave to recover from a serious illness, take care of an ill family member, or care for a new child. Designed to provide some workplace flexibility for family caretakers (traditionally, women), the measure was viciously opposed by doctrinaire Republicans. Conservative Senator Orrin Hatch of Utah claimed the legislation would "foster a bias against hiring women of child-bearing age." How sweet of him to try and protect the breeders. Although 25 of the 27 senators who voted against it were Republican, 16 other Republicans voted *for* it. The House vote included similar crossover support. But that was a different era, before the American Taliban had completed its takeover of the GOP.

Today, the American Taliban and the GOP are willing and eager allies in their efforts to create hurdles for women in the workplace. The American Taliban may not be the *reason* women suffer workplace discrimination (such as earning just 76.5 percent of what a male earns doing the equivalent job), but their mouthpieces certainly have a vested interest in making sure such discrimination persists, so women who abandon the home for the workplace are punished. And they are willing to go to absurd lengths to ensure such punishment is as severe as possible.

Legislation such as the FMLA and the Lilly Ledbetter Act does make it easier for women to fully integrate into the workplace. Stephanie Bornstein and Charlotte Fishman, lawyers with Equal Rights Advocates, wrote in the *San Francisco Chronicle* in 2003,

As women's participation in the workforce continues to grow, the FMLA legitimizes taking time off from work for family reasons—a need that still falls more heavily on women than men. Reducing the stigma associated with taking time off from work for family in turn enables men to assume more responsibility for family caregiving.

The law certainly seems to have been successful in reducing such stigma. A Department of Labor study found that 80 percent of employers thought the law had a neutral or positive effect on profits and productivity, and 85 percent of *employees* reported either neutral or positive effects when their co-workers took family leave under the act.

However, the FMLA only offers *unpaid* leave, which still prevents a significant number of people from caring for their families during emergencies. In 2004, California became the first state to offer up to six weeks of partial pay to take care of a new child or a seriously ill child, parent, spouse, or domestic partner. Similar legislation, titled the Federal Employees Paid Parental Leave Act, was introduced in Congress in 2009. The House passed it, with only 24 of 178 Republicans voting for it. "This shows that the government doesn't just talk about family values—it values families," said Rep. Carolyn Maloney, a Democrat from New York and the bill's sponsor. Yet, those supposed "family values" Republicans continued to oppose such sensible pro-family policies, or "fringe benefits" as New York Representative Christopher Lee called them. "Think about the retail workers who are being forced to do more with less. Think about that, when Washington turns around and offers more generous fringe benefits to public sector employees." Love that logic, Chris. Government should not lead the way in employment practices but wait for the retail industry to show the way. How about all you Congressmen having the same (pathetic) health benefit plan that Wal-Mart offers its low-wage workers?

On July 21, 2005, 20-year-old Jamie Leigh Jones began work as an administrative assistant for KBR, a subsidiary of Halliburton, where Dick Cheney once served as CEO. She had just arrived in Baghdad, when several co-workers offered her a drink laced with a date-rape drug. Once she was unconscious, she was gang raped, both vaginally and anally, without protection. Her lawsuit described the damage as follows:

> When she awoke the next morning still affected by the drug, she found her body naked and severely bruised, with lacerations to her vagina and anus, blood running down her leg, her breast implants ruptured, and her pectoral muscles torn—which would later require reconstructive surgery.

A U.S. Army physician confirmed the rape, and gave the rape kit with evidence to Halliburton security forces. The rape kit and evidence soon disappeared.

Under the order of KBR/Halliburton, Jones was imprisoned in a shipping container with only a bed, and was denied food and water. "It felt like prison," Jones told ABC News's *20/20* program. "I was upset; I was curled up in a ball on the bed; I just could not believe what had happened." Jones was told that if she tried to leave Iraq for medical treatment, she'd lose her job, "Don't plan on working back in Iraq. There won't be a position here, and there won't be a position in Houston." After a day, a friendly guard gave her a cell phone, which she used to call her father, who then contacted Rep. Ted Poe, a Texas Republican, who got the State Department involved, and eventually the U.S. embassy in Baghdad sent agents to spring her from custody.

Partly because of the murky legal status of private mercenary armies in Iraq, there was no obvious criminal law redress, so Jones filed a civil lawsuit against KBR. Given that KBR is a Dick Cheney progeny, however, it immediately invoked its secrecy privilege, trying to squash that lawsuit by pointing to a clause in Jones' employment contract that required any claims be heard in private arbitration. It was a bizarre clause designed to protect the company rather than its employees.

And, disturbingly, that clause got plenty of use. According to Jones, 40 other women contacted her with similar stories, including several who talked to the press, like Dawn Leamon, interviewed by Karen Houppert of *The Nation*.

> That dawn [in early January 2008], naked, covered in blood and feces, bleeding from her anus, she found a US soldier she did not know lying naked in the bed next to her: his gun lay on the floor beside the bed, she could not rouse him and all she could remember of the night before was screaming and screaming as the soldier anally penetrated her while a colleague who worked for defense contractor KBR held her hand—but instead of helping her, as she had hoped, he jammed his penis in her mouth.

Like Jones, Leamon had no redress.

Senator Al Franken of Minnesota decided to take action in 2009, introducing an amendment to the defense appropriations bill that would prohibit the government from contracting with companies like KBR if they "restrict their employees from taking workplace sexual assault, battery and discrimination cases to court." Speaking on the floor of the Senate, Franken said, "The Constitution gives everybody the right to due process of law . . . And today, defense contractors are using fine print in their contracts to deny women like Jamie Leigh Jones their day in court . . . The victims of rape and discrimination deserve their day in court

[and] Congress plainly has the constitutional power to make that happen."

Seems fairly noncontroversial, doesn't it? "If ever there was a time for the unanimous passing of an amendment, the Franken anti-government contractor rape liability bill would seem that," Jon Stewart said on the *Daily Show,* calling the amendment a "slam dunk." Who could possibly be against giving rape victims their day in court? The American Taliban, of course, and just when you thought they could sink no lower . . .

When the dust settled, 30 Republicans had voted *against* it. Alabama conservative Senator Jeff Sessions whined that it was "a political attack directed at Halliburton," apparently missing the fact that it was a political attack directed at companies that allow their employees to rape other employees without legal redress.

As Stewart concluded, "I understand we're a divided country, some disagreements on health care . . . How is *anyone* against this?" As the public backlash hit those Republicans voting for corporate-sponsored rape, they whined at the injustice of it all. "Privately, GOP sources acknowledge that they failed to anticipate the political consequences of a 'no' vote on the amendment," read a November 2009 report in *Politico.* "And several aides said that Republicans are engaged in an internal blame game about why they agreed to a roll-call vote on the measure, rather than a simple voice vote that would have allowed the opposing senators to duck criticism." Funny how all those tough masculine men become sissified and want to hide behind anonymous voice votes when it comes to their efforts to protect corporate-sanctioned rape.

And as *Daily Kos'* Barb Morrill wrote, how could they possibly fail to "anticipate the political consequences"?

They voted against an amendment that was prompted by the brutal gang-rape of a young woman by her co-workers while she was working for a company under contract for the United States government, after which she was locked in a shipping container without food or water, threatened if she left to seek medical treatment, and was then prevented from bringing criminal charges against her assailants. And they failed to anticipate the political consequences?

Still, Republicans pretended to miss the whole point of the vote. John Thune, a South Dakota conservative, couldn't fathom why his vote could be controversial, "I think the whole purpose of that amendment in my opinion was to create a vote which they could use to attack Republicans." It's as if these guys are impervious to the thought that Franken and his allies on this issue might've been simply interested in punishing corporate rapists. Had Republicans voted unanimously with the Democrats on the issue, there would be no controversy, no vote progressives could use to attack Republicans. Yet Thune and his buddies in the American Taliban couldn't bring themselves to cast the right vote for the right reasons. So, they got angry for having cast such a patently bad vote, and they were angry that *the vote was public*.

Yet, there was nothing "conservative" about voting for corporate-sanctioned rape. Just like we saw with the Lilly Ledbetter Act, the Republican *women* in the Senate caucus had no problem voting for the Franken amendment, with all of them joining the Democrats. But of the 36 Republican men in their Senate caucus, only six voted the genuinely moral way.

What lies beneath all these anti-women votes on the Family Leave Act or the "Keeping Employees from Getting Raped by Companies Act" is the American Taliban's regressive ideology, which demands that women get married, stay home, rear children, worship their husbands, and live a 1950s *Ozzie and Harriet* lifestyle.

Indeed, Tony Perkins' Family Research Council was seriously concerned that women who graduate from college aren't getting married and staying home to make babies, so it eagerly promoted an idea by "pro-family" conservative crusader, Allan Carlson, for a $5,000 tax credit for married college graduates who have kids. "At the end of their childbearing years, 20 percent of women with a BA or higher remain childless, compared to less than 10 percent for those without a university degree." This is bad! And the lack of babies stems from the economic stress women graduates feel from their student loan debt. And when young adults have debt? Carlson writes,

> One of the strongest correlations found in social science is the negative relationship between education and fertility. This is more relevant now that women have replaced men in the United States (and in most other Western nations, too) as the sex most likely to earn a bachelors' degree . . . This trend accelerates the retreat from marriage because as women increasingly dominate higher education, they find a shrinking pool of marriageable men. Even independent of debt, it seems, education serves as a growing barrier to marriage, as well as to children.

Hence the solution: a $5,000 per child loan forgiveness per baby born to married (and *only* married) couples. "This would mean that four children born to a couple could erase as much as $20,000 per parent," Carlson wrote. Having four (!) kids would certainly keep the woman married and home, where she belongs, even if she and her husband would now be saddled with paying to clothe, feed, and educate those four for 18 years each—a cost that would easily exceed $20,000, without even considering *their* college education.

The notion of single, childless women sure is troubling! I mean, they'll get jobs, get promoted, and make their way through the world without a man telling them what time it is or showing them how to get home! And a lack of children means less impetus for marriage, less impetus to stay home, less impetus to live under the arbitrary rules of the American Taliban. This might seem a bit confusing, because we spent the last half century hearing about punishing poor women on welfare for having babies. But those were mostly black babies (in Taliban minds, not according to the statistics), so that was bad. Good, Christian, white families, however, must be encouraged to have babies because "marital child-bearing" is a "public good."

Still, kind of sweet to see the Family Research Council concerned about the plight of parents in this world. If only they extended that concern beyond keeping women at home. Responding to efforts to pass the Healthy Family Act, which would provide up to 12 weeks of *paid* leave for family caregivers dealing with acute illnesses, that empathy seems to have shriveled up and died. "I do think accommodations need to be made in those cases," said Tom McClusky, the vice president of governmental affairs at the Family Research Council. "I would hope that there are different incentives that the government can provide rather than regulating business to death." Sounds like something the *Business* Research Council would say.

Ultimately, these moral Neanderthals, whether in the United States or in the Islamic world, are *afraid* of women. They are afraid of women in the workplace, terrified of competing with them for jobs and promotions. They are afraid of women outwitting them. They are afraid of women competing with them for sports dollars at schools and universities. They are afraid of having to share tedious child-rearing duties. Heck, they are even afraid of being sexually aroused and being forced into immoral situations.

And that fear clearly binds the American Taliban to their

Islamic cousins. The *Boston Globe* reported in 2009 that as many as 90 percent of Yemeni women and 83 percent of women in Egypt said they had been harassed. "We are facing a phenomena that is limiting women's right to move . . . and is threatening women's participation in all walks of life," Egyptian activist Nehad Abul Komsan told the paper. "The religious leaders are always blaming the women, making them live in a constant state of fear because out there, someone is following them."

The *Globe* report noted that "men are threatened by an increasingly active female labor force, with conservatives laying the blame for harassment on women's dress and behavior." As a result, women are covering themselves up or staying home. For Islamic fundamentalists, that's mission accomplished. "If you take out uncovered meat and place it outside without cover, and the cats come to eat it, whose fault is it, the cats' or the uncovered meat's?" asked the top Muslim cleric in Australia and New Zealand, Sheik Taj Aldin al Hilali, at a religious address in Sydney in 2006. "The uncovered meat is the problem. If she was in her room, in her home, in her hijab, no problem would have occurred."

That sentiment is obviously no different than O'Reilly's view of the murder victim who wore a halter-top. After all, no problem would have occurred in that case either, had she stayed home in her room or dressed more appropriately. Now Muslim clerics and O'Reilly are given an assist in the "cover yourself or stay in your room" department by a whole contingent of moralists demanding that men be protected against the sexual wiles of the female persuasion.

"Anything tight, scant, backless, see-through, low in the neckline, or revealing the midriff (in any position) is immodest and unacceptable," reads the dress code at the Christianist Liberty University. The *Baptist Press* reported on a "fashion show" at a

Louisville seminary in 2002, with clothes modeled by a preacher's wife. "We must remember what battles men face to stay pure as they are stimulated visually by women," she said. "They should never have it flaunted in their faces." The website Christians DressingModestly.com offers this sage advice:

> The fact is that Jesus can see you just fine right now, from all of the way up in Heaven, where He is seated at the right hand of God the Father. Jesus knows how you dress, and He knows whether or not you are trying to dress in a manner which ultimately glorifies Him . . . Therefore, here is a basic rule to keep in mind: Never wear anything you would not want to wear in front of Jesus. Would you want Jesus to return while you were wearing "that outfit"?

Yeah, it would suck to get caught in the rapture wearing a miniskirt.

You can imagine the kind of advice they are giving at the Focus on the Family website. "As parents we must help our daughters realize that their clothing is like a label. When they wear skin-baring fashions, it often sends a message to others about their character. When we (parents) allow our daughters to dress in a revealing manner, we play a part in sexualizing and objectifying them. Not to mention, many girls are not yet able to make a connection between what they wear and the reaction it may generate among the opposite sex."

You see, when a woman dresses sexy, it generates a reaction among members of the opposite sex. "The study found that when girls dress in such a way as to call attention to their bodies, 85 percent of guys said that they would have a temptation to picture her naked (either then or later)," continued the advice columnist at the Focus on the Family website. She discussed a survey cited by Wall Street analyst/churchgoing mom Shaunti Feldhahn (a favorite on the Fox News/Focus on the Family circuit) in her book *For Young Women Only* that "further confirmed that the majority of guys thought she was dressing that way because she wanted them to picture her that way." Oh, dear god! A man might picture a woman naked!

All this huffing and puffing about the clothes women wear is clearly to protect the men from themselves. Taking this notion to another level altogether, the Arlington, Texas, school board decided in 2006 on a "no cleavage" rule for girls. "If you can see the space between a woman's breasts, it's not allowed," said Arlington High principal James Adams. Defending the decision, school board president Sherri Wade rationalized, "It's gotten bad enough that, unfortunately, our young males are looking at more than their English book, their speech book, their science book. And it's kind of nice to have something left to the imagination." I went to high school in the late '80s, an era of baggy Benetton sweatshirts, where cleavage was but a distant dream. Didn't matter one bit. The cute girls were still far more interesting to look at than English books, speech books, or science books. That has always been the case, and it always will be the case.

So of course, short of wrapping up a girl in a burka, it's inevitable that some dude is going to picture her naked. Heck, I'm too lazy to do the research, but I'm sure somewhere on the internet there's a burka fetish site. And not only is that okay, but it's not a woman's problem anyway. It would be nice if the ideologues were more concerned about men *acting stupidly* on those impulses than trying to protect the supposed stronger sex from the supposed weaker sex.

And therein lies the dichotomy between the rampant machismo of these fundamentalist ideologues, and their obvious panic at women (and feminized men, whether straight or gay) encroaching on their god-given traditional turfs as heads of the family, chiefs of government, and captains of industry. They cling to outmoded traditions and wail as society leaves them behind, fueling a sense of victimhood that, frankly, is at odds with their self-perception as manly macho men.

The Rush Limbaughs of the American Taliban may bemoan the "chickification" of America, crying about our lost masculinity in the face of resurgent estrogen. Yet, in doing so, they are just like Iranian Ayatollahs or Afghan Mullahs doing their part to prevent women from taking their rightful place as equal partners in our respective societies.

5

CULTURE

If the American Taliban and their ideological cousins on the other side of the world can agree to agree on one thing, it's that culturally, America is going to hell. From sex, drugs, and rock and roll, to movies and TV, to a growing secularism, they both have a genuine sense of shared revulsion at the notion of a permissive, free society.

The 9/11 attacks gave the Cheney-Bush warmongers an excuse to go after their old enemy, Saddam Hussein; those very attacks also gave the American Taliban an excuse to go after their own domestic enemy, the liberals. In the sweepstakes of who could best blame American progressives, the clear winner was Dinesh D'Souza, who has solid credentials in conservative circles. As a student at Dartmouth College, where he took pride in his nickname "Distort D'Newza," D'Souza outed closeted members of the Gay Student Alliance in the *Dartmouth Review*. After college, he edited a Heritage Foundation journal, then moved briefly into the Reagan White House, before making his way through the well-worn conservative welfare circuit, cycling through various endowed "chairs" and offshoots of the American Enterprise Institute, the Heritage Foundation, the Hoover Institute, and into the subsidized pages of the *National Review*. Along the way, he was engaged to Laura Ingraham and dated Ann Coulter, managing to work into his private life two of Conservadom's most acerbic female voices.

He's also a regular on various Fox News shows, mostly promoting his intentionally provocative books, which focus on popular issues in the reactionary Right circles, especially how affirmative action undermines America, and (but of course!) how the "defiance" that served slaves in the 19th century now lingers in the African-American community to their detriment.

All of this prepared him nicely as chief attacker of liberalism. His incendiary 2007 book, *The Enemy at Home* (anointed by the *Washington Post* as "the worst nonfiction book about terrorism published by a major house since 9/11") was a dirty bomb in the national conversation. Here's a sample:

> The cultural left in this country is responsible for causing 9/11. I am saying that the cultural left and its allies in Congress, the media, Hollywood, the nonprofit sector and the universities are the primary cause of the volcano of anger toward America that is erupting from the Islamic world. The Muslims who carried out the 9/11 attacks were the product of this visceral rage—some of it based on legitimate concerns, some of it based on wrongful prejudice—but all of it fueled and encouraged by the cultural left. Thus without the cultural left, 9/11 would not have happened.

D'Souza was singing in tune with Jerry Falwell, who said, "I really believe that the pagans, and the abortionists, and the feminists, and the gays, and the lesbians who are actively trying to make that an alternative lifestyle, the ACLU, People for the American Way—all of them who have tried to secularize America—I point the finger in their face and say 'you helped this happen.'"

Of course 9/11 wouldn't have happened without the Left—our very American notions of cultural freedom are what anger our enemies, whether domestic or Islamic. *Of course* there would be little Islamic anger at America if our great nation shared its values and mores with the cultural Neanderthals of both the Islamic and America Talibans. Heck, those two cultures *could* be close allies. Fortunately, we are a nation that believes in personal freedom, which puts us on a collision course with those who would deny it in the name of religion and ideologies that belong more in the Middle Ages than the 21st century. That's why the assertion that liberals want the terrorists to win has always been nonsensical and absurd—surrendering to the terrorists would be no different than liberals surrendering to the American Taliban, and our homegrown ideologues know that well.

Even so, the most cursory glance at the geopolitics of the past 20 years makes it clear that it was policy after policy pushed by the warmongering wing of the American Taliban that led like stepping stones to the 9/11 attack. America's interference in the region, first by propping up and then taking down Saddam Hussein, then by playing factions against each other in the powder keg of the Middle East, led inexorably from the bloodlusting dogma of the radical Right. And those two decades of building bases and meddling in the Middle East fueled Osama bin Laden and the rage of Islamic fundamentalists worldwide.

But that is never, *ever* mentioned in American Taliban circles. It's *only* the fault of liberal culture, not neoconservative foreign policy or menacing military buildups.

"Let's acknowledge that America's increasing decadence is giving aid and comfort to the enemy," wrote noted Christian Right author Charles Colson, a Watergate felon and Karl Rove confidant, in *Christianity Today*. "When we tolerate trash on television, permit pornography to invade our homes via the internet, and allow babies to be killed at the point of birth, we are inflaming radical Islam." *Christianity Today's* own managing editor, Mark Galli, noted soon after 9/11 that Islamic fundamentalists were angry at the United States for bringing "hedonism and material-ism into their very homes through television, enticing Muslims to become religiously lazy and morally corrupt." Thus, it's ironic to see conservative commentators like Charles Krauthammer point out that for the jihadists, "Western freedom means the end of women's mastery by men, and the end of dictatorial clerical control over all aspects of sexuality—in dress, behavior, educa-tion, the arts," when he and his cohorts in the American Taliban relentlessly fight for dictatorial clerical control over all aspects of sexuality—in dress, behavior, education, and the arts.

"When we, through our educational culture, through the media, through the entertainment culture, give our children the impression that human beings cannot control their passions, we are telling them, in effect, that human beings cannot be trusted with freedom," argues former Republican presidential candidate Alan Keyes, laying bare the essence of the American Taliban's case against Hollywood. If you give people freedom, they may actually use it in ways these moral scolds cannot stomach. Ulti-mately, they *don't* trust freedom, lest it lead to behaviors they consider immoral. And there's big bad Hollywood, leading the charge against our nation's supposed traditional values. "The lack of morals and values in Hollywood culture has been destroying the fabric of American culture, particularly the family," claims the hilarious and ridiculous Conservapedia—an alternative-reality version of Wikipedia. Or as the Rev. Jimmy Swaggart wrote in *The Evangelist* in 1988, "The Media is ruled by Satan. But yet I wonder if many Christians fully understand that. Also, will they believe what the Media says, considering that its aim is to steal, kill, and destroy?" It's like broadcast "shock and awe," except no one is *really* killed or destroyed, and, um, nothing is stolen.

Trying to stem the Hollywood machine may seem quixotic, but the American Taliban haven't shied away from the challenge. A network of "watchdog" groups police the airwaves and use the power of government to try and restrict material they deem inappropriate; others seek a more ambitious goal: to remake Hollywood in their image. And for the American Taliban, that image is locked into a fictional, sanitized 1950s world that never existed in the first place.

Our pop culture has certainly been trending away from the American Taliban ideal, with Hollywood as a prime driver for cultural change. This isn't some new revelation. After all, the magic of Hollywood was used more than half a century ago to rally the country around World War II, even employing Ronald Reagan to help in the effort. But now, shows like *Will and Grace* and *Queer Eye for the Straight Guy* have shown America that homosexuals are not predatory pedophiles, and Americans have been receptive. According to a 2003 ABC News-*Washington Post* poll, 37 percent of respondents thought gay marriage (as opposed to civil unions) should be legal, and 55 percent disagreed. In April 2009, after eight years of Republican control of the White House and Congress, 49 percent thought gay marriage should be legal, versus 46 who did not—a 21-point swing in favor of marriage equality. Almost two decades ago, in 1992, then vice president Dan Quayle lambasted the TV show *Murphy Brown* for showing single motherhood as a positive thing, an outrage that seems as sad and outdated as boycotting children's Christmas specials like

Rudolph the Red-Nosed Reindeer and *Frosty the Snowman* because they contribute to the secularization of Christmas.

Hollywood *is* liberal, stocked to the gills with innovative, forward-looking artisans—a progressive-minded class of people. Indeed, regions with concentrations of "creative class" workers— artists, engineers, writers, scientists, researchers, educators, and so on—are overwhelmingly freethinking. In addition to creative-class centers such as San Francisco, New York, and Seattle, emerging ones like North Carolina's Research Triangle have helped turn formerly conservative regions into competitive political territory for Democrats. These punk rockers of the socio-economic world chafe at anything that hampers their creative impulses. Although programmers in San Jose might help make the San Francisco Bay Area a progressive powerhouse in electoral terms, their political views have little practical impact outside the region. Conservatives use Apple or Hewlett-Packard products without being exposed to scaaary liberalism. Hollywood's impact, on the other hand, extends far beyond its geographic borders.

According to the leaders of the American Taliban, the ascension of Hollywood and the appeal of its creative class is more than just a happy accident. "Hollywood is controlled by secular Jews who hate Christianity in general and Catholicism in particular," said Catholic League President Bill Donahue, who has made a crusade—and a high-profile career—out of condemning everything from Madonna concerts to Obama appointments. Loud-mouthed and vitriolic, Donahue is a raging Catholic shock jock minus the dirty language, who hangs out on mainstream shows on CNN and CBS, being interviewed by Rick Sanchez or Bob Schieffer, debating Christopher Hitchens, and sparring with Bill O'Reilly. He "looms," according to a recent *New York Times* article "like a cop with a search warrant, over the intersection of American culture and conservative Catholicism." It's an apt metaphor, because he wants to police what America sees, hears, and thinks about, all in the name of upholding a strict Catholicism—despite his irreligious divorce.

Interviewed by Pat Buchanan on MSNBC in 2004, Donohue said,

> Hollywood likes anal sex. They like to see the public square without nativity scenes. I like families. I like children. They like abortions. I believe in traditional values and restraint. They believe in libertinism. We have nothing in common. But you know what? The culture war has been ongoing for a long time. Their side has lost.

Um, okay. What Hollywood really likes is money. But for once, conservatives really have something to fear from these capitalists. "Movies, TV shows, music, and other entertainment products don't merely amuse us or divert us from reality; often they convey messages about political, social, and cultural issues," wrote conservative media critic James Hirsen in his 2005 book *Hollywood Nation*. "And since Tinseltown remains such a liberal bastion, as we witnessed during the last presidential election with the Dem fund-raising machine, those messages usually come with a distinct lefty twist."

Super Bowl XXXVIII in 2004 broke viewership records, and the 144.4 million people who tuned in were treated to arguably the best Super Bowl of all time. The Carolina Panthers, after dismal seasons in the past, faced off against 2001 champion New England Patriots, who'd started the season off flat and come back with a 12-game win streak. The game got off to a slow start, with the longest stretch of non-scoring in Super Bowl history (nearly 27 minutes of the first half), then sudden action as the teams scored in a couple of series of drives, back to back, right before breaking for halftime with the Patriots up 14-10 over the Panthers.

The halftime show was the usual mixture of extravaganza, patriotism, marching bands, and rock stars. Jessica Simpson opened the show, Janet Jackson sang a couple of unremarkable numbers. P. Diddy, Nelly, and Kid Rock then did medleys of their hits. Janet Jackson reappeared and sang "Rhythm Nation." No big deal, nothing to write home about. Then Justin Timberlake rolled out, and began a little dance number with Jackson, and all hell broke loose . . . or rather, her breast did, when Timberlake pulled on her clothing. And America learned firsthand the fury the American Taliban could unleash when presented with the unpardonable sin of a 9/16th-second glimpse of a female breast.

Forget searching citizens' bank records without a warrant, incarcerating American citizens with no trial, torturing the innocent at Guantanamo, tapping phones illegally, using the American military to bomb wedding parties in Afghanistan. None of that mattered half as much to the self-appointed moral authorities in the American Taliban.

But 9/16th of one second of one breast? It was jihad-time, American Taliban–style.

It wasn't even full exposure—the singer was wearing a nipple shield. Still, even though the performers claimed the incident was a result of a "wardrobe malfunction" (the move was supposed to pull off her bustier, revealing Jackson's red-laced bra), that half a second generated an explosion of outrage and hand-wringing about "indecency" in television.

Leading the charge was the Parents Television Council (PTC), then being headed by L. Brent Bozell III, who has fingers in so many radical Right pies he could open up a bakery all on his own. The web he's spun between his interconnected entities is intricate and self-reinforcing. You come into Bozell's crosshairs, and it can sound like half the conservative movement is after you, when in reality, it's one lone self-righteous rich guy with a grudge the size of Texas. Besides serving as president of the PTC, he founded the Conservative Communications Center, the Media Research Center, and Cybercast News Service (CNS). He's served on the boards of the American Conservative Union and Bill Donahue's Catholic League, and his own conservative column is distributed to major newspapers nationwide through Creators Syndicate. In other words, if Bozell takes a dislike to something, you hear about it across multiple platforms, from several different directions. And he's not shy about risking overusing these groups.

PTC's complaint about Jackson's half-second breast exposure was only one of its numerous filings with the Federal Communications Commission (FCC); in fact, since the group's founding in 2004, PTC has registered more complaints about more television shows—and YouTube—than any other individual or entity. That's our tax dollars at work, having federal regulators answering jacked-up silliness over Carl's Jr. commercials and episodes of *CSI*. Funny how the American Taliban loathe government when it wants to provide health care but demand the feds step in at the drop of a bustier.

But the PTC wasn't entirely alone in its Crusade Against the Half-Second Breast. Then New Mexico congresswoman Heather Wilson, voice shaking in anger, berated CBS executives at a congressional hearing. "You knew what you were doing. You knew what kind of entertainment you're selling, and you wanted us all to be abuzz, here in this room and on the playground in my kids' school, because it improves your ratings. It improves your market share, and it lines your pockets." One can only imagine the kids abuzz about CBS on the playground: "Down with NBC! Up with

CBS! More tit!" And how much more likely is it that Wilson was mugging for the cameras, eager to broadcast her mock outrage to her American Taliban supporters? I mean, come on. Half a second of nipple wasn't going to bring in more viewers than were already watching at halftime. And if the kids wanted more tit, they could easily turn to lots of other places.

The usual suspects piled on. "CBS-TV proved again that it is determined to offend our moral sensibilities and trash our culture," wailed Phyllis Schlafly. "The shocking primetime display of Janet Jackson's breast, decorated for maximum eye-catching attraction, was undoubtedly deliberate." Maybe it was deliberate, maybe it wasn't. But "eye-catching"? We're talking *half a second*.

And Bozell kept fueling the outrage. Taking off his PTC hat and putting on his "writer guy" hat, he used his syndicated column to amp up the message his group had created and to project his own repressions on the rest of America. "The backlash was immediate and strong. Some wanted the story to end, so as to not give MTV the thrills. But an outraged public needs to make this backlash long and commercially painful." And, yes, by "outraged public," he meant *him*.

I doubt America was particularly thrilled about seeing half a second of partially exposed Jackson boob, but America certainly wasn't outraged enough to make a big deal about it. An Associated Press poll three weeks after the Super Bowl showed that 54 percent found the incident distasteful, but only 18 percent supported spending taxpayer dollars to investigate the incident. Yet, that's what the American Taliban, and their allies in the Bush administration, did. Michael Powell, chair of the FCC, ordered an immediate investigation. "Clearly somebody had knowledge of it. Clearly it was something that was planned by someone. She probably got what she was looking for." The resulting $550,000 fine was the largest ever levied against a broadcaster, a figure still being litigated in the courts.

The following year, Super Bowl officials eliminated all possibility of controversy by playing it safe and hiring Paul McCartney. And by "safe," I mean boring. But here's the thing: four years after "Nipplegate," Prince performed at the Super Bowl. With his silhouette against a sheet, Prince handled his guitar so that it appeared like a giant phallus, stroking it to simulate masturbation. "I don't care what you do with your demonic guitar phallus, any Hassid worth his *payos* will tell you that as long as it's through a sheet it's kosher," joked Stephen Colbert on *The Colbert Report*. As usual, the penis got a pass.

Still, the FCC's indecency crusade, backed by elements of the American Taliban, certainly had a chilling effect on broadcasters. A campaign by these pro-censorship groups scared 28 percent of ABC affiliates enough to skip the Veteran's Day broadcast of the World War II masterpiece *Saving Private Ryan*. Those stations feared that the violence and language in the movie would result in fines. Even an offer by ABC owner Disney to pay any fines, and pressure from veterans groups like the American Legion and the Veterans of Foreign Wars, failed to persuade those stations to air the movie. As it turned out, there were no complaints to the stations that broadcast it.

But those broadcasters had reason to fear. Coming off the Nipplegate victory, the smut detectives at PTC weren't resting for long.

In January 2005, the FCC announced it had rejected 36 complaints of indecency brought by the PTC, whose follow-up act to Nipplegate was to ferret out corrosive indecency from the blandest network programming possible. How else to explain their complaint about a scene in *Friends*, in which a female character at a doctor's office says she's got "an invasive vaginal exam to get to"? Or another *Friends* episode in which, according to the FCC summary, "certain characters use the words 'hell,' 'crap,' 'pissed,' 'bastard,' and the phrase 'son of a bitch.' One character says he 'didn't say the F-word.' Other characters ponder where a male character may have hidden 'porn.' A male character states, 'You broke my heart. Do you know how many women I had to sleep with to get over you?'" Or how about the episode of the animated show *King of the Hill* in which "a cartoon boy is shown about to enter a communal shower at his school. An off-screen voice emanating from the shower asks, 'Is that a pimple or another nipple?' As the cartoon boy removes his towel and enters the shower, his buttocks are briefly depicted." Egads! A cartoon *anal cleft*! But nothing is more indecent than that episode of the never-watched, short-lived WB sitcom *Run of the House*, where "a female character teases her brother about dating a woman who looks like his mother and, after her brother and his girlfriend have been in the hot tub, tells him 'I know what you're doing.'" Call the government! Oh, wait. They did.

The smut watchdogs are so inept that they hear things that are not said. Checking out a PTC complaint about the reality show *The Next Joe Millionaire*, the FCC wrote, "[T]he complaint alleges that a character says 'fuck off.' Based on our review of the tape, however, this description is inaccurate in that no character appears to utter the quoted language." How many taxpayer dollars were wasted reviewing the one-hour show for phantom obscenity? And where's the compassion for the poor FCC worker forced to watch an hour of *The Next Joe Millionaire*?

But it's not just about smut. The late Jerry Falwell somehow decided, apparently on a whim, that the magic bag-wearing Teletubbie Tinky Winky was gay. "He is purple—the gay-pride color;

and his antenna is shaped like a triangle—the gay-pride symbol," wrote Falwell in the *National Liberty Journal*. "As a Christian I feel that role modeling the gay lifestyle is damaging to the moral lives of children."

As a rational person, I feel that reading sexual orientation into color and geometry is damaging to the intellectual lives of Americans. But that's just me. The BBC, which co-produced the Teletubbies, agreed. "[Tinky Winky is] not gay. He's not straight. He's just a character in a children's series." Obviously.

Yet attributing sexual proclivity to cartoon characters is apparently a favorite pastime for the American Taliban. So you can imagine that James Dobson, the head of Focus on the Family, felt he struck gold when he came upon "We Are Family," a mash-up of every character of every popular show, dancing and singing and—gasp!—*getting along with each other* to the tune of the 1979 disco hit.

"Does anybody here know SpongeBob?" Dobson asked at a party celebrating the 2004 electoral victories by conservatives. Because of the cartoon sea sponge's brief walk-on (or sponge-on) in the video, he became a prime target—an apparently homosexual one—in the American Taliban's ongoing war on tolerance. Other characters also played a part in the offensive video—Barney, Winnie the Pooh, Bob the Builder, and other popular TV cartoon stars, all of whom preached an unacceptable message of tolerance and respect. "We see the video as an insidious means by which the organization is manipulating and potentially brainwashing kids," an assistant to Dobson said. "It is a classic bait and switch." But why focus on SpongeBob? Yes, he holds hands with his best friend Patrick, the starfish. But it's not as if Winnie is exactly butch, and Bob the Builder may be the most metrosexual construction worker *ever*. And what exactly is the "switch" in that bait and switch? Well, that the message on tolerance could be interpreted to include tolerance for homosexuals. Of course!

Still, it's surprising that Dobson went after SpongeBob for being gay, but was apparently okay with Squidworth, the clarinet-playing artist who is the cartoonification of gay comedian Paul Lynde, and who—I'm not making this up—is voiced by actor Rodger Bumpass. In the world of American Taliban conspiracy mongering, that would be all the "evidence" they'd usually need. And the squirrel character Sandy Cheeks is kind of butch. I'm just sayin'. And has Dobson never watched *Sesame Street*? Bert and Ernie have been in a committed, loving, and co-habitating relationship for more than four decades, and they preach *friendship* and *community*, which as we've seen, is completely at odds with the American Taliban agenda!

Other bizarre complaints objected to the flesh-colored bodysuits depicting Greek statues at the opening ceremonies of the 2004 Olympic Games in Athens. Then there was the promotional skit during a Monday Night Football telecast featuring Nicollette Sheridan of *Desperate Housewives*, scantily clad in a towel, slowly combing her wet hair, inching closer and closer to Philadelphia wide receiver Terrell Owens in the locker room and begging him to skip the game. He finally succumbs when she drops her towel and he sweeps her into his arms. "I wonder if Walt Disney would be proud," sniffed FCC Chairman Powell, claiming his agency had received 50,000 complaints about the skit—the bulk likely from Brent Bozell's PTC complaint machine. Rush Limbaugh nearly had an aneurism from the event. "You see enough of her back and rear end to know that she was naked. There's no frontal nudity in the thing, but I mean you don't need that." Actually, there was no ass in the shot either, not even an anal cleft! Just her bare back. But that was enough to send the American Taliban into a frenzy, generating so much anger that media outlets were forced to re-review the scene time and time again. "People were so outraged they had to see it 10 times," joked CNN's Aaron Brown.

Oddly, the outrage over such scenes doesn't seem to extend to the areas most often identified as the moral backbone of the country; *Desperate Housewives* itself has been a frequent target of right-wing boycotts, but its most ardent fans are, yes, in the Bible Belt. "A hit everywhere, it is even a bigger hit in Oklahoma City than it is in Los Angeles, bigger in Kansas City than it is in New York," wrote *New York Times* columnist Frank Rich. So who exactly was filing all those supposed FCC complaints?

Oh, yeah. Brent Bozell and the PTC outrage-production shop.

Jeff Jarvis, creator of *Entertainment Weekly* and prominent blogger, filed a Freedom of Information Act request to gauge how many actual complaints the FCC received for cases on which it decided to act. Although the FCC claimed 159 complaints against a Fox show called *Married by America*, Jarvis found just 90 complaints, filed by just 23 individuals, and all but two of those complaints were identical to a form letter posted by the PTC. In other words, these were not legitimate gripes by the viewing public but an "astroturfed" fake campaign. It didn't matter—the FCC still fined Fox $1.2 million for an episode showing pixilated strippers.

Most of the American public has grown up, even if the radical Right has not. The battles they wage against pop culture prove they're laughably out of date with contemporary society. "As recently as March 2008, children who watched BET's *Rap City* and *106 & Park* and MTV's *Sucker Free* were bombarded with adult content—sexual, violent, profane or obscene—once every 38 seconds," wrote the PTC in a 2008 report. "Most of what children are seeing in these music videos are sexually charged images—45 percent of the adult content in the analyzed videos was of a sexual nature." Don't freak out about all that sex on TV—this is the same outfit that gets the vapors when someone says the word "pissed." Or when someone on TV mentions *not* mentioning the "F-word."

Recoiling at modern culture is not exactly a new trend. In a 1964 column, conservative stalwart and *National Review* founder William F. Buckley, apparently the oldest 39-year-old in history, told the neighborhood kids to get off his lawn. "They are so unbelievably horrible, so appallingly unmusical, so dogmatically insensitive to the magic of the art, that they qualify as the crowned heads of anti-music," wrote Buckley about . . . the Beatles. "The Beatles aren't merely awful. I would consider it sacrilegious to say anything less than that they are godawful." Not exactly in tune with popular culture, was he? Twenty-six years later, he still hadn't let it go. Responding to a request by Yoko Ono to play the song *Imagine* at the exact 10-year anniversary of John Lennon's murder, Buckley lost his head. "Now I do not know the melody of *Imagine,* but I have the lyrics in front of me, and what it amounts to is a kind of Bible, as written by the sorcerer's apprentice.

> *"Imagine there's no heaven—*
> *It's easy if you try.*
> *No hell below us,*
> *Above us only sky.*
> *Imagine all the people*
> *Living for today.*

"I venture to say that those who imagine in that direction ought to make every effort to restrain themselves," Buckley wrote. Whether you like the lyrics or not, how could you go through life without knowing the melody to *Imagine*? The song was named by *Rolling Stone* magazine as the third best song of all time. Nevertheless, to Buckley, that refrain wasn't the worst of it. "The chorus of 'Imagine' is—well, it is too subversive to appear in a family publication." What subversive chorus? *This* one?

> *You may say I'm a dreamer*
> *But I'm not the only one*
> *I hope someday you'll join us*
> *And the world will live as one*

My god, hide the kids from these dastardly sentimental and idealistic lyrics! These self-righteous pooh-bahs sure don't sound much different than those complaining today about rap- and rock-music lyrics. And yes, that inability to adapt to modern cultural norms has a price, an electoral price—conservatives don't appeal to many voters born after 1980. The gap between youth voters and the GOP has never been wider: only 32 percent of voters under 30 voted for John McCain in 2008. Ronald Reagan actually won a narrow majority of such voters, but today's youth have turned on Republicans with a vengeance.

Can you get any more out of touch than James Dobson working himself into a lather on his website over . . . dancing? "[T]here is no biblical prohibition against dancing in and of itself," writes a columnist on Dobson's site. That's about as lenient as *he's* going to get. "The problem is that in today's teen culture, social dancing has become very sexually provocative. Many high schools have even banned certain forms of dancing, such as 'grinding.'" Fortunately, he has a suggestion.

> One way to avoid any problems at the party and have fun at the same time would be to feature some type of musical "theme" such as a 1940s swing dance or a country square dance. The kids

could dress in the appropriate style and you could hire a professional dance instructor to teach them the dance steps.

I'm not sure how swing or country dancing would keep kids from having sex (as we saw in the last chapter, people born in the 1940s and Southerners have plenty of it), but at least this beats the heck out of Dobson's advice for fathers to shower with young sons to keep them straight. Not to be out-mullahed, Jerry Falwell's Liberty University (making a mockery of the school's name, incidentally) banned dancing altogether, and students face reprimand and fines if caught doing the jig.

Dancing really seems to infuriate these people. Most recently, the PTC turned its guns from Seth McFarlane's *Family Guy* and *American Dad* (hilarious but genuinely racy shows that I won't let my six-year-old watch—yet), *Heroes* and *Hell's Kitchen* and took aim at . . . *So You Think You Can Dance.*

Say what? How does a dance competition make the censor's hit list? "Some of the dances, particularly Hip Hop, can contain suggestive moves," reads a 2006 report by the organization's nags. Hip-hop culture is certainly a frequent target of the American Taliban (likely fueled by a dollop of racism), but the fact is, any kind of dancing that crosses into the realm of "sexy" is blasted. And frankly, some of their ideas of "sexy" are pretty darn weird, as when Bill O'Reilly decided to take on a high school cheerleader routine he deemed too racy.

To discuss this pressing outrage, O'Reilly invited self-styled "culture warrior" Margaret Hoover onto his October 9, 2009, show. Her claim to fame is being a member of Rudy Giuliani's exploratory committee for the presidency and being Herbert Hoover's great-granddaughter. "What do you call spreading your legs and shaking your booty?" Hoover demanded. I don't know, Margaret. Dancing? Ready with an answer on the show was O'Reilly's other guest, Fox News commentator Gretchen Carlson. "And don't forget bending over, which was the most offensive move to me." How could I forget *that*? But it seems a bit tamer, Gretchen, than parading up and down a runway in a bathing suit in front of the entire country as you did when you walked away with that Miss America title.

Just to make sure people understood how slutty the dancing cheerleaders were, O'Reilly ran clips of the dance routine over, and over, and over, and over again. And then, just to make sure viewers stuck around a bit longer, he ran the clips a few times more.

These people just don't understand that the things they view as horrifying—cheerleaders, Stewie and Peter on *Family Guy*, Rachel and Ross on *Friends*—are popular for a reason and well within the cultural mainstream. Gays are seen as normal, and it's okay for SpongeBob (gay or not) to hold his best friend's hand. People *love* that stuff.

Even former Pennsylvania Senator Rick Santorum gets it, as he explained to his fellow conservatives at the 2009 Paul Weyrich Awards Dinner, named after one of the most revered figures of the American Taliban. Weyrich was co-founder of the Heritage Foundation, Free Congress Foundation, and (with Falwell) Moral Majority. Santorum, who lost his Senate seat in 2006 to Bob Casey when voters decided they'd had about enough of his anti-homosexual, pro-war, anti-science stance, told the audience exactly what it wanted to hear, and what he knew in his very sanctimonious heart: the country was going to hell in a handbasket.

I will assure you that the vast majority of the American public has very little idea what is going on in the halls of Congress right now, as far as who's speaking on the floor of the Senate. But I can tell you millions are watching TV shows tonight . . . hundreds of millions, and we are absent from those screens.

This was a problem, you see, because while conservatives were focusing their resources on political power, they were neglecting pop culture.

We have always had this idea that we can shield ourselves from the popular culture, that we can protect our family from the effects of Hollywood, from the effects of the mainstream media, from the effects of the university, we just have to be careful. Well, the bottom line is media is so pervasive, it is virtually impossible to do so . . . you let them in every single day when you turn on that television, when you press that button to turn the computer on.

Ousted senators and dinosaur conservatives aren't the only ones waking up to the realization that their ideas are perceived as old, stodgy, and laughably out-of-date. Enter Andrew Breitbart, the flamboyant former acolyte of conservative news phenomenon Matt Drudge, who built his *Drudge Report* up on conservative outrage and the Lewinsky scandal. With a low-tech look and screaming headlines, the report was American Taliban Central, the place where talk radio ripped its narratives and riffed on the "news" of the day. Breitbart was Drudge's right-hand man, assisted Arianna Huffington in starting up the *Huffington Post* website and—most important for his quest to take on Hollywood culture—had a stint under his belt as a reporter at E! Entertainment Television.

Breitbart was a prime candidate to take on the "toxic" culture that Santorum and friends wanted to change, and his *Big Hollywood* website launched to much fanfare in those circles, with a demand that Tinseltown return to its "patriotic roots."

Big Hollywood's modest objective: to change the entertainment industry. To make Hollywood something we can believe in—again. In order to give millions of Americans hope. Until conservatives, libertarians and Republicans . . . recognize that (pop) culture is the big prize and that politics is secondary, there will be no victory in this important battle.

It's true. Conservatives have been masterful in selling their political ideas to the public. Fox News still has no peer, Rush Limbaugh leaves all others in the dust, conservative authors dominate political bestseller lists, and the conservative web is alive and well. The conservative machine—think tanks, advocacy groups, media outlets, politicians—is more established and far better financed than anything progressives have built.

But the good news is that mainstream America is very resistant to having its entertainment nannified by the moral police, and all the PTC complaints and the rambunctious rantings of Falwell and Schlafly and Buchanan and Limbaugh and Beck and Coulter and Bauer and Robertson and Bozell haven't slowed the march toward a less puritanical society. "Not only are harsher profanities like the f-word and s-word airing during hours when children are likely to be in the viewing audience, but they are airing with greater frequency," PTC whines, having counted 11,000 hell, damn, ass, piss, screw, bitch, bastard, suck, crap, shit, and fucks in 2007—supposedly nearly double the number counted in 1998. So if you can't beat 'em, perhaps you can join 'em, as Santorum seemed to suggest in his Weyrich speech?

"[C]onservatives are making a big tactical mistake by ignoring popular culture," argued author Paul Cantor. "They really are losing a whole generation of students or are severely impairing their ability to speak to them by not being able to speak to students in their own terms . . . To be able to relate conservative ideas meaningfully to today's students, you have to know where they're coming from and where they're coming from is popular culture."

But the American Taliban's efforts at aiming for the hearts and minds of American youth have been embarrassing at best, if not a laugh riot.

When Stephen Colbert had documentarian Bob Greenwald on his show to discuss his new movie, *The Big Buy: Tom DeLay's Stolen Congress*, DeLay's legal defense fund crowed that Greenwald had "crashed and burned" and posted the interview clip on their site, headlined, "Hollywood pulls Michael Moore antics on Tom DeLay. Colbert cracks the story on real motivations behind the movie." They were completely clueless that the show has a liberal bent, and that Colbert's "conservative" persona is a satirical act.

Meanwhile, Republican National Committee chairman Michael Steele seems to think that uttering phrases like "beyond cutting edge" and "off the hook" makes his party look hip and current.

"[B]eing a Republican is about as edgy as Donny Osmond," wrote John McCain's daughter, Meghan, in the *Daily Beast*. Meghan's efforts to help modernize her party by better aligning it with popular culture are constantly sabotaged by stuff like the (unintentionally) hilarious "Young Con Anthem" rap video by The Young Cons, promoted online by conservatives. Picture, if you will, a couple of tall, clean-cut, geeky Dartmouth Christian guys in bad lighting, with bad sound, in a classroom setting, rapping earnestly about the heinous burden of government regulation, the evil of deficits, the sin of handouts, and the glory of Jesus Christ. Keep in mind, they are not really singing, but rapping with righteous indignation.

I don't speak lies but I spit the facts
28 percent the new capital gains tax
Porkulus bill lacks a few stats
The more money we spend, the more mine is worth Jack
The Bible says we're a people under God,
Usin' radar for radical Jihad . . .
Three things taught me conservative love:
Jesus, Ronald Reagan, plus Atlas Shrugged
Saving our nation from inflation devastation
On my hands and my knees praying for salvation

"The video's lameness is staggering," wrote writer George Hawley at the *American Conservative* magazine. Calling it "tripe," Hawley wrote that the number of people it would appeal to "is assuredly in the low single digits."

The conservative movement knows that it has a problem with young voters. Specifically, they have no young voters. The Young Cons, or any similar group, will not help. Hip-hop will never be a good medium for promoting supply-side economics—or any other Republican buzzword these tools will ever want to advance. BET and the GOP are not natural allies. A disingenuous rap song explaining that Martin Luther King was "really a conservative" (which is simply not true, by the way) will not change that essential fact.

As Hawley argues, conservatives are incapable of creating good art. "I am not sure what can be done to change the fact that most musicians and screen writers tend to lean toward the statist left," he wrote. "If that's the best it can do, the mainstream Right will be better off giving up on popular culture entirely. Such a move will not save the conservative movement, but it will at least keep it from humiliating itself further as it continues to decline."

The conservative movement is truly an artistic wasteland.

Its most successful TV show is probably *Touched by an Angel,* a Christian drama series that aired from 1994–2003. Although Christian rock is certainly popular, its young listeners are actually trending *left.* While only 16 percent of white evangelicals under 30 voted for John Kerry in 2004, 32 percent voted for Obama in 2008. At a Christian rock concert in New York, ABC News found that the young concertgoers were most concerned about internet pornography, media glamorization of sex and drugs, and children orphaned by AIDS. Health care and the environment were also important. Far less important were gays or abortion.

It doesn't help conservatives that they can't do funny. Are there any comedians among their ranks besides Dennis Miller? Then again, he is a *former* comedian—he stopped being funny ever since 9/11 turned him into a crazed wingnut and a regular pundit on Fox News. In an effort to counteract the impact of Comedy Central's *The Daily Show with Jon Stewart,* Fox News created its own news parody show in 2007, *The 1/2 Hour News Hour.* Get it? Explicitly making the comparison to Stewart, the show's creator Joel Surnow (of *24* fame) said, "You can turn on any show and see Bush being bashed. There really is nothing out there for those who want satire that tilts right." Guess what? There *still* isn't anything out there.

The show was a pathetic attempt at right-wing comedy. "Illinois Senator Barack Obama admits that as a teenager he sometimes used cocaine. This news sent Obama's approval rating among Democrats *plummeting* to an all-time low of 99.9 percent," began a segment from the pilot episode. "But, in a related story, Senator Obama has just been endorsed for president by former Washington DC Mayor Marion Barry." Canned laughter punctuated every line, underscoring just how unfunny they were. Another piece had President Rush Limbaugh alongside Vice President Ann Coulter.

Limbaugh says that his Democratic opponent, Howard Dean, is "finally getting the medical attention he has so desperately needed for so long," which was a bit bizarre given Limbaugh's addiction to pain killers. The punchline had Coulter reciting her post-9/11 line about "invade their countries, kill their leaders, and convert them to Christianity"—the same dumb line that had gotten her fired from the conservative *National Review*. It wasn't any funnier on Fox.

"A look at the first episode suggests that, just as A.M. is the unassailable province of the right, TV might better be left to the left," read a typical brutal review, this one from the *Hollywood Reporter*. "One fake public service announcement hammers the ACLU for backing First Amendment rights for Nazis to march in Skokie, Ill., an issue that may have lost some of its heat since it transpired 30 years ago. What next? A swipe at Eleanor Roosevelt?" The show was cancelled after 17 episodes, leaving late-night comedy as the domain of the left. Indeed, the *Daily Show* and *Colbert Report* have achieved iconic stature, and few doubt David Letterman's liberal leanings. The American Taliban's recent electoral successes can't be duplicated in the current pop-culture world.

But that doesn't mean they don't try to co-opt pop culture and twist it to their ends.

Regardless of Hollywood's liberal leanings, most of the entertainment it produces is just that, entertainment, neither liberal nor conservative, but *apolitical*. A lot of it is pretty plain vanilla, recycling proven plot lines about love, betrayal, courage, and sacrifice. Yet, for the American Taliban, nothing is benign, *everything* is ideological. This leaves them with two choices: attack Hollywood because of its ideological transgressions or attempt to co-opt it as the embodiment of conservative principles. It doesn't matter if a show is sometimes just a show; they will go to great lengths to brand it as conservative, or attack it as heresy.

Take, for instance, the sci-fi blockbuster series *Battlestar Galactica* (BSG). Based loosely on a short-lived 1978 series trading off the cinematic success of *Star Wars*, the re-imagined series features a distant civilization nearly wiped out by a robotic enemy called the Cylons. With their homeworlds decimated in a massive nuclear strike, the only humans left are those who were traveling in space at the time. This small flotilla gathers together, and the Battlestar Galactica warship is its only means of protection. Together they set out in search of the rumored cradle of human civilization—Earth.

Jonah Goldberg, of the *National Review*, would liveblog BGS episodes, examining them through his ideological lens.

> So I watched the latest Battlestar Galactica last night. [A] new plot line was introduced ... They are radical peaceniks who want to call a truce with the misunderstood and victimized Cylons (for those who don't watch, the Cylons are dedicated to the eradication of the human race and have nuked numerous human planets killing untold billions). The peace-terrorists are clearly a collection of whack jobs, fifth columnists and idiots ... if we're going to keep score, I'd say last night's episode goes down in the Right column as a win.

Yaaay for conservatives! For a crowd that couldn't enjoy science fiction without saddling it with ideological meaning, the show had everything: a black-and-white picture of the human "good guys" and the theocratic murderous robotic Cylon "bad guys," who morphed into Islamic terrorists in their minds. Even though some conservatives scoured the show for evidence of "liberal bias," they didn't find it. The show flirted with disdain for the human civilian government and celebrated strong military leadership. It even seemed to mock democracy, which got Goldberg excited. "I like that the good guys wanted to steal the election and, it turns out, they were right to want to." Just like Florida 2000.

But alas, the fantasy didn't last long. By the end of the second season, the humans had settled a barren planet, New Caprica, only to be quickly conquered by the Cylons. Rather than slaughter the defenseless humans, the Cylons opted for an occupation, and the season ended in great suspense. As the third season approached, conservatives got worried—a series of five-minute webisodes began sketching out the opening theme of the season. It wasn't very conservative, drawing "complimentary parallels between the jihadi 'insurgents' and the human resistance forces on New Caprica," as one *National Review* reader put it. Their worst fears came to pass. Humans—the supposed heroes!—were called "insurgents," and they used improvised explosive devices and even suicide bombers to disrupt the occupying Cylons. Humans working for the Cylons were assassinated as collaborators. In one episode, one of the Cylons joked about the lack of welcome when they first invaded. Clearly, the parallels with the American invasion and occupation of Iraq could not have been more blatant.

"This is a disgrace," wrote one conservative blogger. "Brave American soldiers are dying for the moral infants who are portraying them this evening as the evil oppressors and their murderers as admirable rebels." Some conservatives were so invested in the notion of *Battlestar Galactica* as a "conservative" show that they claimed the humans were modeled after the *French* resistance, leading an exasperated Jonah Goldberg to fire back, "The whole suicide bombing thing . . . made the comparisons to Iraq incredibly ham-fisted."

National Review's John Podhoretz piled on:

Whenever people on the Right love a work of popular culture that is unabashedly Leftist, they try to come up with some theory that makes it not so. Message to BSG fans on the Right: You can love the show, as it is undeniably high-quality goods. What you cannot do is come up with some cockamamie explanation whereby it's not about how we Americans are the Cylons and the humans are "insurgents" fighting an "imperialist" power.

The notion of BSG as a conservative show was clearly *very important* to these guys. And at a time when support for the Iraq War was cratering—2006—this was particularly painful.

Same with *Lord of the Rings*. "As the hobbits are going up Mount Doom, the Eye of Mordor is being drawn somewhere else," former Pennsylvania Senator Rick Santorum told the *Bucks County Courier Times* editorial board. "It's being drawn to Iraq and it's not being drawn to the U.S. You know what? I want to keep it on Iraq. I don't want the Eye to come back here to the United States." Such analogies didn't save him in his re-election bid, which he lost by double digits to Democrat Bob Casey. And why would they save him? Those analogies were ridiculous. Sauron was a technologically superior invading force, more analogous to the United States—if you really must cram a story published in 1954–55 into our contemporary geopolitical landscape. The author of the books, J.R.R. Tolkien, didn't even like people trying to turn his masterpiece into allegories about either World Wars I or II; he certainly wouldn't have taken kindly to conservatives cramming it into their "war on terror."

How about *Star Wars*? The *Weekly Standard*'s online editor, Jonathan V. Last, wrote a piece in 2002 arguing that writer-director George Lucas screwed up by making the "anarchic royals" rebellion the good guys. "The Empire doesn't want slaves or destruction or 'evil.' It wants order," he wrote. "The important thing to recognize is that the Empire is not committing random acts of terror. It is engaged in a fight for the survival of its regime against a violent group of rebels who are committed to its destruction." Heck, even the murder of Luke Skywalker's Aunt Beru and Uncle Owen is excused because "they aid[ed] the rebellion by hiding Luke and harboring two fugitive droids."

Small wonder that this gang screwed up the wars in Iraq and Afghanistan. As a bonus, Last's piece also informs us that, "like the United Nations, the Republic has no armed forces of its own, but instead relies on a group of warriors, the Jedi knights, to 'keep the peace.'" The United Nations has Jedi Knights? Cool!

But really, you've lost the pop-culture war when you feel compelled to make the case that the good guys are really bad guys because they were anarchic hippies opposed to a "law and order" galactic administration, even if they *did* worship the Dark Side. Like Dick Cheney.

Yes, it's easy to mock conservatives for these silly obsessions over television shows and movies. I personally loved *Battlestar Galactica* when it was supposedly conservative, and still loved the show when it was supposedly liberal. I watched *Law and Order* for years despite its repeated and approving resort to the death penalty, and I watch shows like *24* and *The Unit* despite depictions of actions (like torture) that I personally oppose. If the writing is good, if the action is good, if there's nothing better on at the time—well, what's the harm? It's called "fiction" for a reason. Then again, as shown by growing support for gay rights, popular culture *does* have an impact on attitudes about contentious social and political issues. The conservative frustrations with a hostile Hollywood culture are thus understandable on one level. But clinging to shows they believe validate their ideology is more than a bit pathetic. It's the same as clinging to actors they believe share their politics. For all the venom they direct at Hollywood, they sure swoon when Kelsey Grammer or Jon Voight or Chuck Norris (a real gaggle of hipsters) enters the room.

This is certainly a fundamental problem for the American Taliban, or, as James Poulos, political editor of the short-lived conservative culture website *Culture11*, put it, "Conservatives are particularly good at doing a kind of cultural criticism that results in inaccurate or radically incomplete observations about things going on in this crazy culture of ours." This brings to mind a rant by Oklahoma's then Representative Tom Coburn against the network broadcast of *Schindler's List*, blasting NBC for airing "full-frontal nudity, violence, and profanity" in a 1997 press release. "I cringe when I realize that there were children all across this nation watching this program . . . It simply should not have been allowed on public television." *I* cringe when I realize Coburn missed the *entire* point of *the* seminal Holocaust film.

Less outrageous, but equally clueless, was a 2006 debate among the editors at the *National Review* over "the greatest 50 conservative rock songs," discussed for days by the energized hipsters at *National Review*'s online hangout, *The Corner*. "What makes a great conservative rock song?" asked staff writer John J. Miller, who curated the list. His own answer: "The lyrics must convey a conservative idea or sentiment, such as skepticism of government or support for traditional values." Skepticism of government? That means the Sex Pistol's "God Save the Queen" or "Anarchy in the UK" made the list, right? Look, skepticism of government isn't always a conservative trait. And if skepticism of government were required for inclusion, as Miller required, how did Lynyrd Skynyrd's "Sweet Home Alabama" make the list? It's lyrics say that "In Birmingham they love the governor," not exactly an anti-government sentiment. Then again, that governor happened to be segregationist George Wallace. So skepticism of government is good, yes, unless that government stands in the schoolhouse door to keep black children out. Supporting *that* kind of government is good, because it's conservative.

The blogger *Rude Pundit* was hilariously brutal in his assessment.

> The entire list—fuck, the entire effort—is sad and embarrassing, like watching Grandpa do the Macarena now, thinking that he's still hip, that he's been hip for the last 30 years. Because to come up with fifty songs, the readers and editors of the *National Review* had to neglect, almost entirely, the politics and lifestyles of nearly every single one of the music acts on the list, like, say U2, the Clash, and the Sex Pistols, just for kicks, or noted cross-dressing androgyne David Bowie. They had to twist the meaning of lyrics so that vague references to "freedom" all of a sudden became calls to a modified libertarianism (you know, no taxes, but also no fucking). And, of course, the mention of every fucking song they could find that seems to oppose abortion or alludes to the fall of Communism or doesn't like taxes.

It's like the time Ronald Reagan's staff used the Bruce Springsteen song, "Born in the USA" at campaign rallies. Apparently, none of them had ever listened beyond the blockbuster song's title—the lyrics are a depressing take on the hardships of returning Vietnam veterans and their challenge of reintegrating in American life. Not exactly the patriotic anthem most clueless conservatives make it out to be. At least *National Review* didn't include the Boss on its list.

In late 2009, like flies drawn to a flame, conservatives couldn't help but freak out over James Cameron's blockbuster movie, *Avatar*. The pro-environment and anti-war themes weren't exactly subtle. "I wasn't infuriated by *Avatar*. I was infuriated by the way it framed the culture-war debate," wrote Goldberg, editor-at-large of the *National Review*. Conservative movie critic John Nolte, writing in *Big Hollywood*, was equally disgusted. "*Avatar* is a thinly disguised, heavy-handed and simplistic sci-fi fantasy/allegory critical of America from our founding straight through to the Iraq War. It looks like a big-budget animated film with a garish color palette right off a hippie's tie dye shirt." John Podhoretz, reviewing the film for *The Weekly Standard*, resorted to an old right-wing trope. "The conclusion does ask the audience to root for the defeat of American soldiers at the hands of an insurgency. So it is a deep expression of anti-Americanism . . . "

Yet, as conservatives railed, the crowds flocked to theaters. By mid-February 2010, the movie had exceeded $2.2 billion in worldwide revenues, easily becoming the largest grossing movie of all time. Although just four movies had ever reached a total of $1 billion in adjusted-for-inflation box office receipts (*Lord of the Rings: Return of the King*, *Pirates of the Caribbean: Dead Man's Chest*, *Titanic*, and *The Dark Knight*), *Avatar* broke through that mark in just 17 days.

Nolte, stung by the movie's success, shot back in another post at *Big Hollywood*. "After years of watching helplessly as liberal films flopped at a heartwarming 100 percent rate while conservative-themed films such as *Rambo, Gran Torino, Taken, Knowing*, and *Dark Knight* made money, it only makes sense that to lost-in-the-desert Lefties, Cameron's garishly colored 3D cartoon makes hamburger look like a steak dinner." The premise that those movies are "conservative" is laughable at best. *Rambo*, for example, is about an unemployed Vietnam Vet suffering from post-traumatic stress syndrome after witnessing the ravages of war, and the *Dark Knight* features Batman realizing that torture yields inaccurate intelligence and that his big spying machine is a travesty that must be destroyed.

But aside from that, is Nolte now arguing that Hollywood is *conservative*? Who can keep track of the spin? Did you hear that Judd Apatow's raunchy humor is "conservative"? No, really. Anyone seeing any of his movies, such as *Superbad* (featuring teens trying to score beer and get laid) or *Pineapple Express* (featuring a stoner and his drug dealer chased by a murderous gang), would laugh at the notion that they are in any way "conservative."

But never underestimate the desperation of conservatives to glom on and try to co-opt the latest trends. Ross Douthat, the conservative columnist at the *New York Times*, gives his analysis of Apatow.

No contemporary figure has done more than Apatow, the 41-year-old auteur of gross-out comedies, to rebrand social conservatism for a younger generation that associates it primarily with priggishness and Puritanism.

No recent movie has made the case for abortion look as self-evidently awful as *Knocked Up*, Apatow's 2007 keep-the-baby farce. No movie has made saving—and saving, and saving—your virginity seem as enviable as *The 40-Year-Old Virgin*, whose closing segue into connubial bliss played like an infomercial for True Love Waits . . . By marrying raunch and moralism, Apatow's movies have done the near impossible: They've made an effectively conservative message about relationships and reproduction seem relatable, funny, down-to-earth and even sexy.

I'm not sure how a movie relentlessly mocking a sad-sack, friendless 40-year-old virgin makes virginity seem "enviable." In fact, Steve Carell's character in the movie is pretty much a punching bag from beginning to end. As for *Knocked Up*, the protagonist—a career woman no less—engaged in premarital sex, which is sort of the opposite of *The 40-Year-Old Virgin*. Mixed messages? No, because Apatow wasn't making *freakin' political message movies.* He was writing fiction. In one, he thought the notion of a 40-year-old virgin was hilarious, so he wrote a movie. In the other, he thought a movie about a responsible career woman getting knocked up by a loser stoner would be hilarious, so he made sure his pretend fake character didn't have an abortion. If she had, *there'd be no movie.* It had nothing to do with Operation Rescue, and it certainly had nothing to do with propping up the American Taliban's anachronistic morality.

In fact, Douthat's "conservative" hero, Apatow, maxed out in contributions to Obama in 2008 ($4,600), contributed $7,500 to the Democratic Congressional Campaign Committee, $2,500 to the Democratic National Committee, $500 to MoveOn.org, and boasts a history of donating to such Democrats as John Kerry, Wesley Clark, and Howard Dean.

You'd be hard-pressed, in fact, to find a more generous "conservative" donor to liberal candidates and causes.

Not even dead celebrities can escape the clutches of these bozos. When writer, director, and producer John Hughes died, Ben Stein rushed to the Fox Business News cable network to claim that the creator of *Pretty in Pink*, the *Breakfast Club*, and *Ferris Bueller's Day Off* (among others) was "an avid Republican." Campaign finance forms *do* show contributions to George W. Bush in 2004, as well as Colorado Republican Tom Tancredo and Arizona Republican Representative J. D. Hayworth in 2006. But in 2007, he maxed out with $2,300 to Democrat Joe Biden, followed by $2,300 to both Obama and Democratic congressional candidate Dan Seals in 2008 via the Democratic online donation clearinghouse *ActBlue*. If he was an "avid Republican," he sure had an odd way of showing it. But beyond that, who gives a flying fuck what party Hughes was a member of, really? Most people marked the sad occasion by remembering the man fondly for his art, his contribution to filmmaking. But doing that would be a missed opportunity in Stein's world. After all, what better way to take advantage of the warm and nostalgic feelings toward Hughes than by claiming him as one of your own? I've no doubt that Ben Stein's claims sent a warm tingly feeling up the legs of countless conservatives watching the broadcast.

The American Taliban's pathological need to view all art through an ideological prism is both ironic and self-defeating on several different levels. For irony, ask yourself: what were the hallmarks of both Soviet and Chinese Communist totalitarianism? One of the most prominent was certainly the insistence that all creative works be designed in service of the state, promoting nationalism and glorifying the very narrow definitions that nitpicking bureaucrats deem "acceptable" and "moral." Hello, Parents Television Council? A call from Joseph Stalin on line one.

Beyond that is the stark, sad, scary fact that in our society at this time, the American Taliban simply cannot get a hold on the next generation, at least not through art, entertainment, or culture, which have *always* shaped the worldview of the up-and-coming generation, from the *Lost Generation* to the Beat Poets to the Beatles to *Star Wars*. The Millennial Generation is, by all accounts, lost to them. The statistics are alarming: in the 18- to 29-year-old cohort in the 2008 election, voters broke two for one for Democrats. Of the 2.2 million new voters, *2 million* voted Democratic. This is not just the hope/change Obama campaign phenomenon; even in the lower-energy midterms, in 2006, 18- to 29-year-old voters supported Democratic candidates at a 58 percent level, six points higher than the population at large.

These people are the political future. They are the voters. They will be the candidates. They will write the nation's laws. And the American Taliban have lost them, completely, on the culture front. The only battlefield left to them is the information front.

It's in the media landscape that they are trying to make their final stand.

6

TRUTH

If you can't get a handle on current culture, and modernity is messing with the meticulously ordered world inside your head, what do you do? You create a parallel world, complete with an alternative history, make-believe science, and an animatronics fantasy that allows you to pretend that your fables about the beginning of the universe, and how it currently works, are true.

Then you cloak your alternate world with the trappings of "science," and you build a 70,000-square-foot museum to complete the illusion.

Welcome to the Creation Museum, a $27 million compound in northeastern Kentucky that opened in 2007, a place where you can preserve your faith in the inerrancy of the book of Genesis by "walking through Biblical history," which crams the supposed 6,000-year history of the world into a three-hour tour. Remember those dioramas from grade school? Imagine them scaled to life size and tricked out by engineers from Universal Studios. Hang out in the Garden of Eden with Adam and Eve, play with kids by Eden's rivers, and be tempted by the evil serpent. Stroll through Noah's

Ark, where dinosaurs (!) share space with zebras (but don't eat them). Watch a theatrical presentation in which "Men in White" explain the "thrills of the Bible and science." Walk into the Star Gazer Planetarium where "cutting-edge digital technology" proves the universe has only been around 60 centuries. Hell, bring your family and make a whole day of it; there are food courts, a medieval gift shop, dragon and dinosaur shows, massive murals, playgrounds, Six Days of Creation Theater, all brought together under the massive command of "Prepare to Believe!"

It's a garish, lavish, bizarre monument to anti-science, which uses scientific-sounding pseudo-babble and 21st-century technology to reinforce a Bible-driven worldview that has been completely undermined by modern physics, geology, and cosmology. It's been labeled the "Creationist Disneyland" and "one of the weirdest museums in the world" (which says a lot), and its entire existence, insisted upon repeatedly in every display, exhibit, theater presentation, diorama, and brochure, is dedicated to blaring that the world is only 6,000 years old and the Bible, every word of it, is to be taken literally.

The museum falls in the well-traveled category of freakish Americana, such as the Shuffleboard Hall of Fame in St. Petersburg, Florida, or the Nut Museum in Old Lyme, Connecticut—except this one has lots of pulsating lights and bells and whistles, making it a sort of roadside attraction on crack. Situated in Petersburg, Kentucky, the museum is a project of Answers in Genesis, founded by Australian Young Earth creationist/evangelist Ken Ham, who's had his fingers in creationist pies on different continents for a few decades. In Australia, he co-founded the Creation Science Foundation with John Mackay, who eventually was excommunicated for accusing a fellow congregation member of necrophilia and witchcraft. Ham found America more eager to embrace his creationist philosophy; predictably, Jerry Falwell's Liberty University bestowed him with an honorary degree, and the Creation Museum itself was praised and patronized by Republican Geoff Davis, congressional representative of Kentucky's Fourth District.

It's no surprise that this multimillion-dollar monument to American Talibanism requires employees to sign statements saying they believe in the tenets of the Answers in Genesis ministry, and that along with references, resumes, and work histories, an essay on religious belief is a prerequisite for employment. Such behavior follows a long tradition of denying science and disdaining scholarship by religious authorities. For example, in 1633, Galileo Galilei was convicted by the Catholic Church of being "vehemently suspect of heresy." The ruling conclusively stated, "The doctrine that the earth is neither the center of the universe nor immovable, but moves even with a daily rotation, is absurd, and both philosophically and theologically false, and at the least an error of faith." His writings were banned and he was placed under house arrest for the remainder of his life.

The fundamentalists eventually conceded that the Earth rotates around the sun, but to this day they remain hostile to most other elements of scientific discovery. Whether it's global warming or stem cell research, the American Taliban revel in rejecting scientific evidence and cling to ideology. They approach every scientific discovery the same way the Catholic Church did in 1633: any such findings are absurd, and, most inexcusably, they constitute an error of faith. Nothing is more central to the American Taliban's denial of reality than its dogmatic opposition to evolution.

Certainly, the advancement of science has long presented a challenge to religious authority by providing explanations for many of the phenomena religion once sought to answer. Why

take your sick child to a shaman for prayer when science has provided the medicines to make her well? Indeed, between 1850 and
1950 medical research led to treatments and cures that doubled
our nation's average life expectancy. From radio to television, from
the microwave to satellites, from microchips to the internet, from
wireless technologies to GPS, science has delivered the tools and
gadgets that shape the way we live and immeasurably improve
our way of life. Science demystifies the world, and well, religion
becomes a little less central to people's lives. But science still can't
answer questions about death and spirituality, and many still look
to their church or mosque or holy book for guidance in these areas.
Yet for the American Taliban, this diminished relevance is unacceptable and the pursuit of knowledge is considered antithetical
to spiritual goals.

Hilarious creation museums and a few Astroturf organizations
like the Parents Television Council aren't the only ones throwing
hissy fits over glimpses of a female breast. If the anti-knowledge,
anti-science, anti-sex crowd were limited to the fringes, there
would be little cause for alarm (a lot of room for laughter, granted).
But the tentacles of the American Taliban stretch from mega-
churches to radio shows, from the pages of newspapers to the halls
of power. These modern-day spiritual luddites are *everywhere*!

Former Pennsylvania Senator Rick Santorum has never shied
away from using his pulpit to subjugate science in the name of religion. During his 2005 book tour for *It Takes a Family*, a book that
claims that the power of the family has been crippled by the power
of the federal government, Santorum aligned himself squarely
with the dinosaur-with-zebras crowd of the Kentucky museum.
"[I]f we are the result of chance, if we're simply a mistake of nature,
then that puts a different moral demand on us," he told NPR.

Ann Coulter was typically dismissive:

Liberals' creation myth is Charles Darwin's theory of evolution, which is about one notch above Scientology in scientific rigor. It's a make-believe story, based on a theory that is a tautology, with no proof in the scientist's laboratory or the fossil record—and that's after 150 years of very determined looking. We wouldn't still be talking about it but for the fact that liberals think evolution disproves God.

The existence of god is irrelevant to the scientific pursuit, but Coulter's claim is an article of faith with this crowd: liberals seek to eliminate the existence of god. As then Chief Judge Braswell Deen of the Georgia Court of Appeals, put it in a March 1981 *Time* magazine article, "[T]his monkey mythology of Darwin is the cause of permissiveness, promiscuity, prophylactics, perversions, pregnancies, abortions, pornotherapy, pollution, poisoning, and proliferation of crimes of all types."

Of course, many people of faith have little trouble reconciling their religion with science. Genesis was but a parable, and the concepts of God and the Big Bang Theory are certainly not mutually exclusive. Conservative columnist Charles Krauthammer, himself a psychiatrist and pretty well-versed in the benefits of science, penned an entire column on the topic in 2005 expressing his frustration at the constant re-litigation of the Scopes trial.

> How ridiculous to make evolution the enemy of God. What could be more elegant, more simple, more brilliant, more economical, more creative, indeed more divine than a planet with millions of life forms, distinct and yet interactive, all ultimately derived from accumulated variations in a single double-stranded molecule, pliable and fecund enough to give us mollusks and mice, Newton and Einstein?

Yet Krauthammer is in the minority within his conservative movement. A June 2007 Gallup survey found that 68 percent of

Republican respondents did not believe in the theory of evolution. That confirmed a 2005 Pew Forum on Religion and Public Life study, which found that roughly 6 in 10 Republican respondents believed living things have always existed in their present form.

For nearly two thousand years, much of the Western world believed in Young Earth Creationism, which claims the world was created in six 24-hour days roughly 6,000 years ago, as delineated in the book of Genesis. "The only way we can determine the true age of the earth is for God to tell us what it is," explained Henry Morris, founder of the Institute for Creation Research, betraying the extent of his actual "research" into the issue. "And since He has told us, very plainly, in the Holy Scriptures that it is several thousand years in age, and no more, that ought to settle all basic questions of terrestrial chronology." That was quick. Research is hard work! All it took was the reading of the first 11 chapters of Genesis. Done with science for a lifetime! Phew!

Real science is a little more rigorous than that. As scientific knowledge was gained and (real) research methods became more understood and accepted, creationism theories began to be questioned, even in some religious circles. In 1950, the Catholic Church expressed neutrality on the question of evolutionary biology, and by the 1990s had openly accepted it. "In his encyclical *Humani Generis* (1950), my predecessor Pius XII has already affirmed that there is no conflict between evolution and the doctrine of the faith regarding man and his vocation, provided that we do not lose sight of certain fixed points," said Pope John Paul II in October 1996, at an address to the Pontifical Academy of Sciences. "Today, more than a half-century after the appearance of that encyclical, some new findings lead us toward the recognition of evolution as more than a hypothesis."

So long as you aren't talking about the evolution of the *soul*, the Vatican is cool with natural selection. Most major Christian denominations followed suit, distancing themselves from Young Earthism or abandoning it completely. Reason being, it is at odds with virtually every branch of natural science, from astronomy to zoology and every *ology* in between. Radiometric dating, observation and measurement of distant, ancient stars, data from genetics and molecular biology, and a wealth of other empirical observations directly render the "young earth" view little more than wishful thinking or willful ignorance.

Yet, creationists continue to push their agenda, undaunted by the march of scientific progress, the broader acceptance of evolution among the mainstream churches, and the 1987 Supreme Court declaration that teaching creationism alongside evolution in the public school was an unconstitutional establishment of religion. For example, in the alternate world of Conservapedia, the authors work avidly to promote their special brand of crazy. Check out the entry on "dinosaurs," and you'll learn that they "were reptiles *which are now generally believed* to be extinct." Keep an eye out for T-Rex next time you go out for milk. And how do they know that dinosaurs co-existed with humans? Conservapedia argues that "descriptions of dragons are widespread and match descriptions of dinosaurs, suggesting that dragons were real creatures and were actually dinosaurs." And if that wasn't enough evidence for you, there's this: "Dragons appear in the flag of Wales, in traditional Chinese New Years' Day celebrations, and in the Chinese calendar. Every other creature on the calendar is a real creature." Case closed! With logic like that, the half-eagle, half-lion griffin was real, as was Pegasus the flying horse, as was just about every fantastical creature to grace the legends of many a culture.

Conservapedia's defense of creationism runs deep. Look up kangaroos, and you'll learn that, "after the Flood, these kangaroos, bred from the Ark passengers, migrated to Australia. There is debate whether this migration happened over land with lower sea levels during the post-flood ice age, or before the super-continent of Pangea broke apart." Debate among *whom*? I'm afraid to find out. Click on "Pangea," and you learn that their version of Pangea didn't break up 250 million years ago, but during the flood of Noah's time. Look up T-Rex, and you'll find this:

> If T-Rex lived in the Garden of Eden, he must have been a vegetarian rather than a scavenger since there was no death in the garden, right? If so, it looks like God created T-Rex knowing that man would fall and the world would need some predators. I wonder what Adam thought when he saw those huge teeth and massive claws. I wonder if he had some thought in the back of his head that something was off.

T-Rex was then hunted to extinction by man or, of course, "a combination of reasons."

Thus progress marches on, except where it doesn't.

Perusing the offerings of the Creation Museum, one can't help noticing that virtually all the features—cartoons, dioramas, videos, animatronics dinosaurs, games—are aimed at children. This is by design, not accident. As religious traditions have long known, grabbing kids early and getting the indoctrination going young are crucial. Who gets to teach, and what is taught, is one of the American Taliban's most viciously fought battles.

"We are engaged in a social, political, and cultural war," said Gary Bauer, failed presidential candidate and former president of the Family Research Council. "There's a lot of talk in America about pluralism. But the bottom line is somebody's values will prevail. And the winner gets the right to teach our children what to believe." Bauer should know: he was Reagan's undersecretary of education, and a general in the culture war of public education. Autocrat James Dobson of Focus on the Family, which sponsors a radio show aimed at children, called *Adventures in Odyssey*, agreed. "Those who control the access to the minds of children will set the agenda for the future of the nation and the future of the Western world."

Ralph Reed, the first executive director of Pat Robertson's Christian Coalition, once said, "I would rather have a thousand school-board members than one president and no school-board members."

Robert Simonds, of the National Association of Christian Educators and a member of Ronald Reagan's "Nation at Risk" panel, was far more aggressive about his goals.

> There are 15,700 local school boards in this country. It is our intent to take them over, one by one. All we need is a majority . . . and then we will determine what is taught, we will determine who is hired and who is fired . . . We will be the "stealth candidates," and you must carry out our mission in such a way that the public won't know what we're about until we've won control. I am a fundamentalist Christian, and as far as I'm concerned, that's the only kind of Christian there is.

Among the people carrying out Simonds' mission is school board member and activist Cynthia Dunbar, currently orchestrating radical historical revisionism in the Texas State Board of Education. She is clear about her goals. "The philosophy of the classroom in one generation will be the philosophy of the government in the next." The Texas board is considered the most influential in the country, as the *New York Times* reported in February, 2010. "The state's $22 billion education fund is among the largest educational endowments in the country. Texas uses some of that money to buy or distribute a staggering 48 million textbooks annually—which rather strongly inclines educational publishers to tailor their products to fit the standards dictated by the Lone Star State." As Texas A&M education professor James Kracht noted, when it comes to textbooks, "Texas was and still is the most important and most influential state in the country. Texas governs 46 or 47 states."

Dunbar and her allies are well aware of their undue influence on the nation's educational system and have been busy injecting dogma disguised as curriculum. For example, in February 2010, they passed new requirements that students "describe the causes and key organizations and individuals of the conservative resurgence of the 1980s and 1990s, including Phyllis Schlafly, the Contract with America, the Heritage Foundation, the Moral Majority and the National Rifle Association."

While pluralism—or diversity of thought and opinion—might be an American value, for unreconstructed theocrats like Bauer, Dunbar, Reed, and Dobson, it's an unacceptable one. The American Taliban can't win the battle of ideas in an education setting that fosters inquisitiveness, curiosity, tolerance, and critical thinking. Those usually prove deadly to fundamentalist ideologies.

Indeed, part of the dynamic of democracy is rigorous debate and discussion of ideas, visions, philosophies, and public policy; a thriving intellectual climate is necessary and schools and colleges are the incubators where this takes place. This is precisely why the Afghan Taliban have long targeted educational institutions. Entire swaths of the Uruzgan province in south-central Afghanistan, a hotbed of the Taliban insurgency and rumored home region to Mullah Omar, don't even have schools. According to the Pajhwok Afghan News in August 2006, the Taliban distributed night letters demanding parents send their children to mosque schools instead. "Impart religious education to your children instead of the modern teachings; otherwise all of you will be killed," read one such letter. And by the way, that's just for the boys. "Female education is against Islamic teachings and spreads vulgarity in society," proclaimed Shah Dauran, a Taliban leader in Pakistan. In Nigeria, one group of Islamic militants seeking to impose Shariah law in all 36 provinces of the country is named Boko Haram, which literally translates to "Education Is Prohibited."

In the place of secular schools are religious educational institutions, the maddrassas of the Islamic fundamentalists, where science and mathematics, as well as critical thinking and creativity, are eschewed for theocratic indoctrination. The American Taliban are no different, as they seek to turn our public schools into dogmatic madrassas. Take D. James Kennedy, for example, founder of Coral Ridge Presbyterian Church, which was the fastest growing Presbyterian church in America in the 1960s. So worked up was he about education that he founded a nonprofit known as the Center for Reclaiming America, and co-authored the 1993 book, *Education: Public Problems and Private Solutions*. In its pages, he proclaimed, "The Christian community has a golden opportunity to train an army of dedicated teachers who can invade the public school classrooms and use them to influence the nation for Christ."

"Invade" was indeed an apt descriptor for the hostile takeover attempts of the American Taliban. And although Kennedy's ideas may have been extremist, they were well received within the conservative mainstream. Upon Kennedy's death, President George W. Bush and his wife, Laura, issued a statement declaring him to be "a man of great vision, faith, and integrity," who carried a "message of love and hope and inspired millions through the institutions he founded."

This kind of hatred toward learning institutions was and still is widespread and embraced by the conservative movement's leading lights. The late senator from North Carolina, Jesse Helms, bizarrely declared, "Your tax dollars are being used to pay for grade-school classes that teach our children that cannibalism, wife-swapping and murder of infants and the elderly are acceptable behavior." That'd be one heck of an interesting curriculum if it had ever existed anywhere outside of Helms' fevered mind.

Still, when they've convinced themselves that a public education system is basically the devil's workshop, it's easy to see why they're out to destroy it. "I hope I live to see the day when, as in the early days of our country, we won't have any public schools," dreamed Falwell. "The churches will have taken them over again and Christians will be running them. What a happy day that will be!"

And Simonds, the "Christian educator," was so up in arms about public education that he had a solution. Well, it's not *his* solution, exactly. He got the idea directly from God, but he declared in 1998 that every Christian student in America should be withdrawn from public school by 2010. "We'll take away their power and their money. Money comes from students. We'll break their backs by taking 24 million kids out of the public schools," he declared. Everyone seems to have ignored god, and there's no sign of an exodus yet.

I'll go out on a limb and predict that public schools won't be broken in 2010, or anytime soon thereafter. Funding cuts are a bigger threat to them than our homegrown theocrats. Having died without realizing his happy day, perhaps Falwell would've had better luck sending night letters threatening to kill those who attended secular, instead of religious, schools.

The 1990s were tough going for the creationism movement. Science was on a forward march and the American people were loving it, their imagination all fired up. Kiddies were crazed over dinosaurs, and no one was really buying the crap about them having been on Noah's Ark. Space exploration was resurgent, and unmanned spacecraft and the Hubble telescope were bringing us exciting new discoveries. Scientists mapped the human genome, giving us unprecedented insight into our bodies and opening new doors to fight disease and slow the aging process. Other research detailed how, as a species, we were damaging our planet, and warned of the dangers of inaction.

So, rather than fight science, the Creation Museum attempts to adopt scientific language and props to bolster its credibility. The use of the lingo and trappings of science—fossils, skeleton casings, aquariums, planetariums, molecules, bacteria—confounds, confuses, and leaves an opening for fast-talking faith peddlers to step in.

But the museum was just that, a museum. It wasn't a school. And when, in 1987, the Supreme Court slammed the schoolhouse doors shut in the face of the creationists, ruling that they could not teach creationism in the public schools, a new approach was needed.

Say hello to Intelligent Design.

Intelligent Design, or ID as it is often called, claims that some features in living organisms are too complex to have arisen in the traditional Darwinian step-by-step fashion, each incremental modification offering an adaptive advantage. Therefore, the only other logical (to them) explanation is that those complex features were designed by some "intelligent" entity. As to the identity of

the Intelligent Designer, mum's the word. If you push them privately, they'll admit that, yeah, their god just happens to fit the
bill. Publicly, they try to maintain the fiction.

Intelligent Design seeks to undermine science, casting doubt on
scientific theories and methods and findings, and hoping to then
fill the vacuum with its own cockamamie theology. Chief among
its proponents is the Discovery Institute, and its Center for Science
and Culture, which was founded in 1996 on the basis of a manifesto, the Wedge Document. This document proposed to "reverse
the stifling dominance of the materialist worldview and replace it
with a science consonant with Christian and theistic convictions."
The center works with churches to promote its mythology to the
general public, publishes Op-Eds, pushes legislation in school
boards, state houses, and Congress, and litigates when necessary.
It's a real crusade, with the "wedge" as its primary weapon.

> The social consequences of materialism have been devastating.
> As symptoms, those consequences are certainly worth treating.
> However, we are convinced that in order to defeat materialism,
> we must cut it off at its source. That source is scientific material-
> ism. This is precisely our strategy. If we view the predominant
> materialistic science as a giant tree, our strategy is intended to
> function as a "wedge" that, while relatively small, can split the
> trunk when applied at its weakest points.

When speaking to secular audiences or when filing legal documents, advocates of Intelligent Design tend to downplay their
extremism, stressing what they claim are scientific flaws in evolution, arguing that Intelligent Design is a legitimate and more
complete scientific explanation for the origin of the universe.
Parallels are drawn to the search for extraterrestrial life, where
large radio telescopes and complex computer programs attempt
to discern signs of alien chatter amid the vast background noise of

interstellar static, sunspots, chirping satellites, and other cosmic sources of radio waves.

The Wedge Document was authored by former University of California, Berkeley, law professor Phillip E. Johnson, also credited with inventing the notion of Intelligent Design. Johnson drafted an amendment to the No Child Left Behind Act that required Intelligent Design be taught in school. The amendment, introduced by Senator Rick Santorum, mercifully failed.

Although Johnson is careful to use science-laced language in public, he drops that façade when addressing the "red meat" crowd—fellow right-wing fundamentalists. Speaking in Florida in 1999 at the Reclaiming America for Christ Conference presented by D. James Kennedy (the same Kennedy who advocated the invasion of classrooms by armies of Christian teachers), Johnson said, "The first thing you understand is that the Darwinian theory isn't true. It's falsified by all of the evidence and the logic is terrible. When you realize that, the next question that occurs to you is, well, where might you get the truth? . . . I start with John 1:1. In the beginning was the Word. In the beginning was intelligence, purpose, and wisdom. The Bible had that right." Doesn't sound so sciency, does it?

But science is popular, and theocracy less so. So what's a good Christian to do? Deceive. Johnson, when addressing the American Taliban at the Florida conference, was explicit about the need to hide the origins of his "theory" from the broader public.

> What I am not doing is bringing the Bible into the university and saying, "We should believe this." Bringing the Bible into question works very well when you are talking to a Bible-believing audience. But it is a disastrous thing to do when you are talking, as I am constantly, to a world of people for whom the fact that something is in the Bible is a reason for not believing it . . . You see, if they thought they had good evidence for something, and then they saw it in the Bible, they would begin to doubt.

A stealth jihadist, to be sure. Sowing doubt is what it's all about, at least as a first step. And the beachhead of the effort was the Kansas Board of Education.

In 1999, conservatives took control of Kansas' top education authority, and immediately sought to ban the teaching of Darwinism, but the plan was short-circuited when moderates ran them out the following year. A second attempt, in 2005, took a different tack. Instead of outlawing the teaching of evolution, the board would mandate that students be offered an alternative: Intelligent Design. It was a much more sophisticated approach, and a 6–4 majority, led by religious conservatives, quickly invited (at taxpayer expense) members of the Discovery Institute and other proponents of Intelligent Design to recommend changes to the science curricula. The results were a forgone conclusion, with one board member stating flatly at the outset of the hearings that, "evolution has been proven false. ID is science-based and strong in facts." Another member sent a flier to constituents stating that evolution was an "age-old fairy tale" that was defended by those with "anti-God contempt and arrogance." The board voted for a curriculum that included greater criticism of evolutionary biology and the introduction of Intelligent Design as an alternate theory. However, voters again undid the damage, rejecting four of the original six religious conservatives in the 2006 elections. The new standards were quickly dropped.

But it was in tiny Dover, Pennsylvania, in 2005, where Intelligent Design hit the metaphorical brick wall.

As in Kansas, a group of right-wing fundamentalists gained control of the Dover Area School Board and decreed a watered-down version of Intelligent Design be taught to students. It would be presented as an alternative to evolution and an "explanation of the origin of life." In addition, a statement would be read to students noting that evolution was "only a theory" and that a book on Intelligent Design called *Of Pandas and People* (heavily promoted by James Dobson when first published in 1989) would be made available in the library for anyone interested in learning more. Unsurprisingly, given Dobson's endorsement, the book was published by the Foundation for Thought and Ethics, a nonprofit formed by a Texas minister. Also, unsurprisingly, biologists called it "worthless and dishonest," and "a wholesale distortion of modern biology."

The ACLU filed a lawsuit on behalf of 11 parents, the first lawsuit in the nation to directly litigate against the concept of "Intelligent Design" in the public schools. The school board was represented pro bono by the Thomas More Law Center, a Christian conservative law firm active on culture war issues. The case landed in federal court in the Middle District of Pennsylvania, presided over by Bush appointee Judge John Edward Jones III, a fact that caused much cheering among supporters of Intelligent Design. One writer at a major conservative website gushed that Jones was a "good old boy brought up through the conservative ranks" and extolled his character and past accomplishments. As the chairman of the Liquor Control Board, Jones had banned Bad Frog Beer label because he felt it broke the boundaries of bad taste; the label featured a frog (vaguely, very vaguely) flipping the bird. Jones was a favorite of Senator Rick Santorum. For the American Taliban, this guy had serious potential!

The praise would not last long.

Witnesses at the trial, which began on September 26, 2005, included scientists, lawyers, teachers, and parents. Right from the start, the defendants ran into the same problem Phillip Johnson and others had grappled with in the 1990s: school board members had been blatant about their religious motivations. One had told constituents, "Nearly 2000 years ago someone died on a cross, shouldn't we have the courage to stand up for him?" Research done by the expert witnesses revealed that the text, *Of Pandas and People*, had been hastily scrubbed from an earlier version to erase or remove openly Christian terms and replace them with more neutral terms. In addition, 60 copies of the book had been donated to the school anonymously . . . by a school board member's church.

With the Intelligent Design proponents suddenly on the defensive, the only question was the magnitude of their defeat. As he completed his closing arguments on November 4th, defense attorney Patrick Gillen asked the judge, "By my reckoning, this is the 40th day since the trial began, and tonight will be the 40th night, and I would like to know if you did that on purpose." Judge Jones fired back, good-naturedly, "Mr. Gillen, that is an interesting coincidence, but it was not by design." Intentional or not, the joke foreshadowed the judge's decision, and when it was issued roughly six weeks later, it was *brutal*.

Judge Jones issued a 139-page trashing of the Intelligent Design effort, ultimately concluding that "ID is an interesting theological argument, but . . . is not science." The judge then took aim at the American Taliban members of the school board.

> The citizens of the Dover area were poorly served by the members of the Board who voted for the ID Policy. It is ironic that several of these individuals, who so staunchly and proudly touted their religious convictions in public, would time and again lie to cover their tracks and disguise the real purpose behind the ID Policy.

The school board wasn't just wrong; it was populated with liars guilty of "breathtaking inanity," Jones wrote.

Overnight, Judge Jones went from being a conservative hero to a rogue, activist traitor. Bill O'Reilly on Fox News called Jones "an activist, anti-religion judge." Richard Land, president of the Southern Baptist Convention's Ethics and Religious Liberty Convention, was equally bombastic, saying, "We're being terrorized by secularist judges who have megalomaniacal ideas of their own importance," and damned the ruling as "a poster child for a half-century secularist reign of terror." Phyllis Schlafly called Jones' decision "biased and religiously bigoted." And Pat Robertson, speaking on the *700 Club* show, didn't turn the other cheek. "I'd like to say to the good citizens of Dover, if there is a disaster in your area, don't turn to God. You just rejected him from your city . . . If they have future problems in Dover, I recommend they call on Charles Darwin. Maybe he can help them." (So far, Dover has been spared divine punishment.)

Never one to miss an opportunity to sound nutty, Ann Coulter wrote,

> After Dover, no school district will dare breathe a word about "Intelligent Design," unless they want to risk being bankrupted by ACLU lawsuits. The Darwinists have saved the secular sanctity of their temples: the public schools. They didn't win on science, persuasion, or the evidence. They won the way liberals always win: by finding a court to hand them everything they want on a silver platter.

Bombast aside, Coulter was right about one thing: the Dover decision cooled efforts by the Discovery Institute and its allies to force their mythology into the classrooms. Jones' decision was too clearheaded, and came from too unimpeachable a source, to give any other jurisdiction hope of prevailing on the merits. It didn't help that the fight cost the school board $1 million (and could've been higher had the plaintiff's law firm not waived another $1 million in costs). It was much harder for fundamentalists to stand on principle against the Constitution when it would cost them so dearly. So now, the opponents of evolution have resorted to "teaching the controversy": trying to get school boards to mandate the teaching that evolution is flawed. Certainly the hundreds of millions of dollars spent to muddy the waters on evolution have had some effect.

In a 2004 Gallup poll of American adults, 45 percent agreed with the statement, "God created man pretty much in his present form at one time within the last 10,000 years." Only 38 percent chose the alternate statement, "Man has developed over millions of years from less advanced forms of life, but God guided this process, including man's creation," and just 9 percent agreed with the atheistic statement, "Man has developed over millions of years from less advanced forms of life. God had no part in this process." In 2006, positive views on evolution in the United States were compared to those in 33 other countries, and America ranked second to last. Only Turkey, where an Islamic version of creationism (surprise!) was steadily gaining popularity among Muslim fundamentalists, ranked lower.

The battle for the minds of our children doesn't end in high school but continues into the institutions of higher learning. Long a target of the radical Right, universities have earned the ire of the American Taliban for their emphasis on critical thinking, questioning, challenging conventional wisdom, conducting research, exploring new cultures and lines of thought, and their embrace of the scientific method. All these qualities make the American college campus the antithesis of everything glorified by the radical, rigid Right.

Chief among the right-wing critics of academia is David Horowitz, who has made a career out of living on the fringe. In his younger years in the 1960s, he belonged to the New Left, was editor of the left-wing magazine *Ramparts*, and a fundraiser for the Black Panther Party. After alleging the Black Panthers murdered a bookkeeper at *Ramparts*, he "reassessed" his leftist views and swung himself all the way to the Far Right fringe. He now runs the David Horowitz Freedom Center, which publishes *Front-Page Magazine*, *Jihad Watch*, and Discover the Networks—his own personal enemies list in the media, academia, and politics.

In his 2006 book, *The Professors: The 101 Most Dangerous Academics in America*, Horowitz claimed the targeted professors believed that "an institution of higher learning is an extension of the political arena, and that scholarly standards can be sacrificed for political ends; others are frank apologists for terrorist agendas, and still others are classroom bigots." A triumph of McCarthyist demonization of obscure academics, the book was lauded by the American Taliban. *The National Review* claimed the book proved that "our universities have been hijacked by a band of rabid, anti-intellectual liberals more concerned with advancing ideological agendas—usually of the 'social justice' variety—than with educating students." Actually, given that there are over 1 million post-secondary teachers nationwide, Horowitz's list of 101 cherry-picked professors didn't prove much. *Publisher's Weekly* was brutal in its review: "[T]he most egregious crimes perpetrated by the majority of these academics is that their politics don't mesh with Horowitz's." Ouch.

Yet for the American Taliban, the book did what it was designed to do: confirm and reinforce their prejudices, regardless of their distance from reality. In March 2006, Pat Robertson interviewed Horowitz on his *700 Club* program, stating that there weren't just 101 dangerous left-wing profs, but at least 30,000 to 40,000 of them. He referred to these faculty as "termites that have worked into the woodwork of our academic society." Robertson was just getting started.

They are racist, murderers, sexual deviants, and supporters of Al Qaeda—and they could be teaching your kids! These guys are out-and-out communists; they are propagandists of the first order. You don't want your child to be brainwashed by these radicals, you just don't want it to happen. Not only be brainwashed but beat up, they beat these people up, cower them into submission.

Who knew universities were such brutal, violent places? Not one to be out-outraged by anyone, Horowitz amped up the fear. "I estimate there are 50,000 to 60,000 radical professors who want the terrorists to win and us to lose the war on terror." This was even worse than Robertson thought! Heavens! "It is an intellectual corruption, and it is really a political corruption that is bigger than the Enron scandal and much worse. Enron was about money. This is about young people's minds and the future of the country."

Over at DiscoverTheNetworks.org, Horowitz describes his little enemies list as "a guide to the political Left," where he keeps track of all their misdeeds and highlights supposed outrages from the Left and the Muslim world—like the Egyptian parent who allegedly reduced his three-year-old to tears by forcing her to recite the Quran on TV, when it turns out she cried because he denied her a lollipop. But more important is the entire section devoted to these "tenured radicals," who have "made the contemporary university an institutional outpost of leftist thinking and organizing by reshaping disciplines, particularly in the humanities and social sciences, and by using control of the hiring process to constitute faculties whose views are uniformly Left, leading to the use of the classroom for purposes of indoctrination, not education." Despite the claim that there are 60,000 radical professors, his website only links to several hundred of them. Included in the list are the late historian Howard Zinn, journalist Barbara Ehrenreich, film director Spike Lee, and oh, yeah, a guy named Barack Hussein Obama (even though the latter three aren't tenured professors).

Ironically, conservatives rail at "politically correct" speech codes and behavior that, they claim, stifle free speech. Horowitz has a whole section on DiscoverTheNetwork dedicated to just this topic. Yet, their efforts to stifle the speech of targeted academics smack of exactly the kind of suppression they claim to oppose. In their twisted reasoning, speech codes designed to prevent the use of racial epithets like the "N" word were corrosive infringements on the First Amendment, but stating that the United States was responsible for the anger that led to 9/11 was unacceptable and worthy of a sustained effort to destroy an academic's career. But of course, the George W. Bush era was a study in political correctness, American Taliban style—criticizing Bush was providing "aid and comfort" to the enemy, opposing his agenda was "showing division when we needed to be united," and agitating against a destructive and illegal war was "surrendering to the terrorists." The attacks on 9/11 gave the American Taliban a brief taste of success at censorship, and to this day they continue to work tirelessly to recapture that environment of fear and repression, in academia and beyond.

As the Taliban themselves are fond of noting, universities fiercely resist repression. "State Universities are breeding grounds, quite literally, for sexually transmitted diseases (including HIV), homosexual behavior, unwanted pregnancies, abortions, alcoholism, and drug abuse," argued Dobson. Without the overbearing influence of clerics and moral scolds, college-aged kids might actually have sex! They might have a drink! They might smoke a joint!

They might actually *be normal kids leading normal lives*! But worst of all, they might *learn*.

In 2002, then House Majority Leader Dick Armey wandered off topic when speaking to an audience about the Middle East and managed to insult not just liberals but Jewish Americans as well. "I always see two Jewish communities in America: one of deep intellect and one of shallow, superficial intellect." Guess what the difference is between the two? "Conservatives have a deeper intellect and tend to have occupations of the brain in fields like engineering, science, and economics. Liberals, on the other hand, tend to flock to occupations of the heart." Challenged on his statements, he dug his heels in, "Liberals are in my estimation just not bright people . . . as opposed to the hard scientists." As usual, he was wrong.

A Pew Research study in July 2009 asked more than 2,500 members of the American Association for the Advancement of Science about their politics. Results found that 55 percent of scientists identified themselves as Democrats whereas just 6 percent were Republican. Ideologically, 52 percent considered themselves "liberal" (compared to just 20 percent of the public at large), 35 percent were "moderate," and just 9 percent were "conservative" (compared to 37 percent of the public). In short, less than 1 in 10 scientists was conservative.

Why would scientists be conservative, when the American Taliban have declared war on them? "Evolution is a bankrupt speculative philosophy, not a scientific fact," once railed the Reverend Jimmy Swaggart. "Only a spiritually bankrupt society could ever believe it . . . Only atheists could accept this Satanic theory." In his book, *Finding Inner Peace and Strength*, Jerry Falwell proclaimed, "The Bible is the inerrant . . . word of the living God. It is absolutely infallible, without error in all matters pertaining to faith and practice, as well as in areas such as geography, science, history, etc."

The American Taliban had an ally in the Bush-Cheney administration in their efforts to dethrone reason and crown faith as the ultimate arbiter of reality in all areas.

Scorn for caution and proof was most clearly evident in the march to war in Iraq, when military advice was disregarded and intelligence that contradicted Bush's and Cheney's assumptions stifled. But it was in the Environmental Protection Agency (EPA) and other federal agencies that rely on facts and proof—on science—that the blatant rejection of evidence and need for federal protections was most felt.

The Union of Concerned Scientists (UCS), founded at the Massachusetts Institute of Technology (MIT), has been vigilant of political interference in government-funded research, periodically surveying government researchers to find out about improper meddling. Between 2005 and 2007, the UCS found that at agencies like the EPA, the Food and Drug Administration (FDA), the Department of Defense, and NASA, *60 percent* of scientists responding to their survey reported at least one incident of political interference in their work over the previous five years. Seven percent, or 88 scientists, said that agency directors had directed them to "provide incomplete, inaccurate, or misleading information" to the public.

That political interference has real-world repercussions for the public. Thirty-three percent of EPA scientists didn't believe that the EPA was acting effectively to "clean up and/or mitigate existing pollution or environmental problems"; 39 percent of FDA scientists didn't believe the FDA was "acting effectively to protect public health"; 69 percent of scientists at the Fish and Wildlife Service didn't believe their agency was effectively protecting endangered or threatened species. And at the National Marine Fisheries Service, 70 percent of scientists didn't trust their political bosses to "protect marine resources and ecosystems." This pessimism was warranted, given the Bush administration's well-documented meddling in government research. As one EPA scientist told the UCS, "There are still good scientists producing good science at EPA. The main problem I see is an administration that considers science only if it supports its agenda."

For example, the EPA released a set of smog standards in March 2008 that were significantly less stringent than levels proposed *unanimously* by its scientific advisory council. "The EPA's own risk estimates show that [at the new levels], there will be hundreds more deaths and thousands more visits to emergency rooms, and hundreds of thousands of more lost school days," said John M. Balbus, the chief health scientist at the Environmental Defense Fund, to the *New York Times*.

After that decision, scientists at the EPA—an agency loathed by conservatives despite the fact that President Richard Nixon created it in pre–American Taliban days—were so fed up with government interference in their work that the agency's unions pulled out of a decades-long partnership with management because of frustrations dealing, in large part, with scientific integrity. The unions' letter to the administration, among other things, said,

> Under your Administration, EPA *ignores* . . . its own Principles of Scientific Integrity whenever political direction from other federal entities or private sector interests so direct. Examples include fluoride drinking water standards, organophosphate pesticide registration, control of mercury emissions from power plants, and requests for waivers to allow States to more stringently control greenhouse gases.

Such a conflict was inevitable. Science understandably refuses to play ball with rigid ideologies. And fundamentalists seek to veto, control, or suppress science just as their ideological ancestors did during Galileo's day. They make assertions that fly in the face of the evidence at hand. They can claim climate change is a hoax and that the entire senior climatology faculty at NASA is in on it; cigarette smoking is harmless; certain races and ethnic groups are inferior to others; homosexuality is a choice not affected by genetic propensities; and evolution has been debunked by Intelligent Design.

Some find it much easier to follow along blindly than deal with messy exploration and inquiry.

Being a member of the American Taliban is not easy. It must seem like the whole world is constantly against them, challenging their cherished assumptions with facts and science and reality. So conservatives must create an entire alternate reality, one that is often absurdly at odds with the real one, then sell that pile of bullshit to their foot soldiers and the broader public. Theirs is a bubble mentality that could certainly be appreciated—and envied—by Islamic fundamentalists half a world away.

Author Vali Nasr, writing in his 2009 book *Forces of Fortune*, notes that Iranian President Mahmoud Ahmadinejad feeds the desire among his supporters to scoff at knowledge and belittle those who are well informed.

> His frequent speeches before large crowds all across the country are full of obtuse circular arguments about good and evil, and in interviews and small gatherings, like ones he has held for academics and journalists when he visits the United Nations in New York, he answers questions with questions, ending with a joyous smile that reads as a distinct putdown. His logic is seldom convincing, but then he cares little about what elites and

experts think of him. He knows that the poor masses like his folksy style. Though he may seem comical, to many in Iran he comes across as daring and confident. They like his audacity, and especially the way he stands up to the elites, belittling their education, their wealth and their blue blood.

Such propagandist efforts are difficult to pull off when dealing with an aggressive and independent press. So, seeking to counter the efforts of nongovernment media organizations, the Iranian government launched a new global news network, Press TV, in 2007. Unlike Al Jazeera, which, despite popular belief, is actually an independent network (and often the target of censorship efforts by many of the Islamic world's repressive regimes), Press TV is an outright shameless propaganda machine. "Knowing the truth is the right of all human beings but the media today is the number one means used by the authorities to keep control," said Ahmadinejad, celebrating the network's launch. "We scarcely know a media that does its duty correctly. Our media should be a standard bearer of peace and stability." Reviewing Press TV's first day, the cheeky Labour newspaper the *Guardian* in London joked that the propaganda wouldn't be the new network's biggest barrier to success, but rather its overly long and boring news reports. "As Fox News discovered, you do not need to worry too much about the truth, just as long as you keep your reports to 60 seconds, and use a lot of loud music."

It's a winning formula for a dogmatic fundamentalist movement that depends on the ignorance of their followers to maintain its hold on power. Ignorance, and its cousin, fear, are the elements that make Islamic totalitarianism successful. They are also what the American Taliban count on to advance their own anti-democratic agenda. "Fundamentalist politics—whether Christianist or Islamist—often assumes the same basic structure," wrote Andrew Sullivan in November 2009 on his *Atlantic Monthly* blog. "What must be resisted is logic, argument or follow-up questions." With the American Taliban, the entire process of educating our children and young adults is suspect *because* of its dependence on teaching such things as logic and inquisitiveness. The conservative mythology must be protected at all costs, to the exclusion of reality.

Reality, however, doesn't always cooperate with these ideologues. As Stephen Colbert put it, "Reality has a well-known liberal bias." Or as comedian Lily Tomlin phrased it, "Reality is the leading cause of stress among those who are in touch with it," which is why conservatives avoid it like the plague. Swaddled in the comfort of a world where no unpleasant contradictions are allowed to intrude, the American Taliban lull themselves into a comfortable coma, making the rounds between the Creation Museum, Fox News, and Rush Limbaugh. They put on blinders and plug their ears, refusing to process the world around them honestly. They invent epic villains and strawmen. They build entire media organs designed to validate their views. They lash out against reality-based education of children and impede the acceptance of science. They live under a siege mentality, surrounded by the evils of liberalism.

We're not just talking the old "liberal media" fiction. According to Bill O'Reilly, the *internet* is liberal. "The newspaper industry is certainly left. So is the internet. NBC News is almost completely liberal. So is PBS, so is NPR," he claimed. NPR, in fact, isn't just liberal, it's a "left-wing jihadist deal," all because it once ran a cartoon making fun of teabaggers and their propensity to scream "Nazi!" and "Communist!" when making their political points.

Heck, it's not just the media or the internet that's liberal, but even the Bible itself! Luckily, the folks at the Conservative Bible

Project are on the job, busily rewriting the holy book to strip it of anything that might be construed as "corruption by liberal bias." Apparently, the *Bible* is replete with such corruption, like when Jesus said, "Father, forgive them; for they know not what they do." That must be rewritten because, "the simple fact is that some of the persecutors of Jesus did know what they were doing." Also, "This quotation is a favorite of liberals but should not appear in a conservative Bible." Well, if liberals like it, it's gotta go, who cares if Jesus said it? And if he *did* say it, his words were probably taken out of context by the liberal media, which was clearly already misinforming people in the final decades of the first century. Everyone knows that the real Jesus would've called for the "Shock and Awe" bombing of Rome, *not* forgiveness. *God* the Bible is *so* liberal!

Wait, did I say "liberal"? I meant "socialist." "Socialistic terminology permeates English translations of the Bible, without justification. This improperly encourages the 'social justice' movement among Christians," the Conservapedia organizers claim. "For example, the conservative word 'volunteer' is mentioned only once in the ESV [English Standard Version of the Bible], yet the socialistic word 'comrade' is used three times, 'laborer(s)' is used 13 times, 'labored' 15 times, and 'fellow' (as in 'fellow worker') is used 55 times." Without justification? Maybe the justification, if you believe in Christ, was that Christ believed in social justice? But, nah, that's a liberal plot. The conservative Jesus didn't want to see lazy hippies get affordable health care, and he obviously wanted the poor to go screw themselves. He was also really into tax cuts.

Of course, if you think the *Bible* is biased against you, there's no end to your paranoia. Indeed, 84 percent of conservatives believe the media is biased against them, according to a July 2009 Pew Research study. This has been a long-running theme: a key component of the conservative resurgence in the final two decades of the 20th century was the methodical creation of an alternate news machine to promote the conservative message.

In 1988, Rush Limbaugh's show was picked up for national syndication, leading the way for conservative radio's takeover of the AM dial, radio territory once considered a broadcast ghetto. Limbaugh gets over 13 million weekly listeners, reaching a significant (if not majority) portion of the American Taliban base. Just a few years earlier, in 1985, Australian media mogul Rupert Murdoch had bought six broadcast stations and launched the Fox Network. In 1989, he launched Sky News in the United Kingdom. With lessons learned from both those (growing) operations, he launched Fox News in 1996, arguing that "the appetite for news— particularly news that explains to people how it affects them—is expanding enormously." Although the market for news seemed satiated, with CNN dominating the scene, Murdoch did guess correctly that conservatives would embrace a news operation that validated their prejudices and biases. Thus, everyone's favorite "fair and balanced" network began its rise to the top of the cable news ratings.

Fox News certainly does its job well. The American Taliban's chief 24/7 propaganda arm has plenty to teach the propagandists at Iran's Press TV. Hosting bomb-throwing windbags Glenn Beck, Bill O'Reilly, Sean Hannity, and a gaggle of blonde automatons spewing the latest right-wing spin, Fox has become the centerpiece of the Right's media machine, reaching 102 million households in the United States alone and consistently leading the ratings race against its competing cable news networks. In 2009, Fox averaged 4.4 million viewers every day, and Bill O'Reilly's show ran 10 years straight as the top cable news program, with 3.3 million average nightly viewers. In 2009, Glenn Beck saw his audience double to 2.3 million. Fox News topped its competitors in 2009 for the eighth straight year, winning out in every single segment of the day—morning, day, and primetime—all experiencing double-digit growth from 2008. In fact, all its primetime programs enjoyed double-digit growth.

On the progressive side, MSNBC's top two shows, *Countdown with Keith Olbermann* and the *Rachel Maddow Show*, were no slouches. Olbermann's show averaged 1.2 million viewers in its 8 p.m. airing in 2009, and Maddow averaged about 1 million at 9 p.m. Both shows average about half that in rebroadcasts at 10 and 11 p.m. Olbermann, in fact, had the most popular show on the cable news networks outside of Fox. But Fox is a powerhouse—for conservatives, an oasis of fantasy in the desert of reality. It allows O'Reilly to boast an audience that, combined with his rebroadcast, reaches about 10 percent of John McCain's 60 million voters in 2008. That is nothing to sneeze at.

While MSNBC has turned to the left with its prime-time lineup featuring Ed Schultz, Keith Olbermann, and Rachel Maddow, the cable network still has a three-hour morning block hosted by conservative Joe Scarborough and features straight news reporting throughout the day. There is no left-wing equivalent to Fox, which is a significant weapon in the American Taliban's arsenal, able to harass opponents, muddy debates, misinform viewers, rally activists, and provide a friendly soapbox for conservative personalities.

Former Vice President Dick Cheney, for one, certainly made sure to stay within his carefully constructed reality-free bubble. A document leaked to *The Smoking Gun* titled "Vice Presidential Downtime Requirements" had 12 requirements for Cheney's hotel suite stays. In addition to requiring a "private bathroom" (because that's rare in hotels these days), it required "All Televisions tuned to FOX News." Cheney would mainline Fox if he could; as is, he has to settle for having multiple TVs in his suite tuned to the network. And given his track record over the eight years he served as vice president, it's obvious he was ill served by his media choices.

No less ill-served is the American public, which, it turns out, gets dumber the more it watches Fox.

As the prime breeding ground for anti-intellectualism, it's no wonder that an April 2007 Pew Research study of various media outlets found that Fox News Channel viewers were among the stupidest respondents to a series of current events questions, such as whether Supreme Court Chief Justice John Roberts is conservative, whether Democrats hold a House majority, and the rough number of U.S. troops killed in Iraq. Only 35 percent got 15 or more of the 23 questions right, same as local TV news viewers. Only viewers of network morning shows were less informed, at 34 percent. On the other hand, the most informed were viewers of two liberal comedy shows, *Daily Show* and *Colbert Report* (54 percent), who were even more informed than NPR listeners (51 percent) and newspaper readers (43 percent). It's bad enough that two comedy programs are doing a better job of informing their viewers than anyone else. It's woeful that Fox sits at the bottom of the barrel. And given that 63 percent of Republicans or conservative-leaning independents regularly watch the network, according to an October 2009 Pew Research study, it follows that a dominant portion of the Republican base is being rendered stupid by its media consumption habits.

Aided by the deep-pocketed propaganda organ of Fox News, abetted by multiple satellites on talk radio and in pulpits, it's no wonder that an alarmingly high percentage of Americans share more core beliefs—ignorant, dangerous ones—with Islamic fundamentalists than with their fellow citizens. Now, if we were only talking about someone's odd views on the age of the planet, or their misguided and private notions about the proper amount of skin a woman is allowed to show in public, few would care. But both sects of the Taliban, Muslim and Christian, embrace the absolute commitment to forcing adherence to these views on the rest of us—whether by the force of law or just by force.

It can be masked in the lingua franca of science, as at the Discovery Institute, but make no mistake about what the final agenda is: a restriction of knowledge, as the school board cases show. As the case of Janet Jackson's breast shows, it is for the government to be used as an adjunct arm of the moral police. As David Horowitz's crusade against academics and pluralism shows, it is about delegitimizing critical thought and multiple viewpoints. It is, in the end, about undermining the very values upon which this country was founded: freedom of thought and expression.

The agenda of the American Taliban is radically, deeply undemocratic. It is, to put it bluntly, anti-American.

To understand the *fundamental* threat of the American Taliban, we can look at the Amish in America. The Amish feel called to a life of simplicity and faith. In the midst of the modern world, they have carved out a small piece of Pennsylvania for themselves where they can live their faith and stay true to their spiritual beliefs. They show no desire to impose their distrust of technology and modernism on their fellow Pennsylvanians. They don't show up at school board meetings, demanding that their views be incorporated into textbooks as scientific truth. They don't organize fake outrage campaigns demanding that the U.S. government enforce their dress codes. They don't agitate to invade countries or confiscate telephones because they don't use them. They live and they let live.

But the American Taliban are not like them. And we understate the danger posed by their demands for uniformity of thought—*their* thought—at our own peril. By polluting our knowledge with misinformation and doubt, they create a climate of distrust around reason itself. By intimidating free and independent thinkers, they smother not just dissent but habits of thought that lead to creativity, innovation, and problem-solving. They long for a citizenry that is equal parts frightened, ignorant, militant, and dogmatic, a citizenry eager to hand over the reins of power in exchange for the illusion of certainty and security.

Whether they succeed or not, whether the American experiment succeeds or not, may largely depend on men and women who are willing to relentlessly call out ignorance, who are willing to stand up to protect democratic ideals and processes, and who fight, day in and day out, to resist the imposition of a bloodthirsty, repressive, dogmatic worldview.

Recognizing the kinship between Islamic extremists and their American Taliban cousins may be only a first step in rolling them back, but it's the foundational one.

Notes

Notes, including source material, for this book can be accessed at www.dailykos.com/AmericanTaliban/endnotes.

Index

Acknowledgments

I'd like to thank my wife, Elisa, for her unfailing support during the writing of this book, but she was born in Kenya, and no one wants to talk about her missing birth certificate. And she speaks *Spanish*. I've invited Orly Taitz to file suit on my behalf, to expose this shocking truth.

My kids inspire me just by existing, even though their very existence is a threat to democracy. Turns out women who vote insist on funding for their health and education! Crazy, huh? So, thanks to my little comrades, six-year-old Ari and three-year-old Eli, for being the vanguard of a new American communist order.

Never doubt the motivational power of a proud mother. I may sometimes pretend it's not that important to me, but, yes, it is. Even if she wants the terrorists to win.

Don't tell anyone, but the *Daily Kos* staff is *really* an undercover corps of elite ACORN operatives. And even though their plate was already full—subverting democracy is hard work!—their help was critical to making this book happen.

Susan Gardner was the first person I consulted on this book idea, and she worked closely with me all through to the end. In gratitude, ACORN will steal the 2012 presidential election in her name. She deserves it.

Barb Morrill was my research assistant extraordinaire, even though it was sometimes tough to get her to help, her being a woman and all. I may not like it, but Christ is the head of the household and the husband is the head of the wife, and that's the way it is, period.

Stephen Darksyde took a break from falsifying global climate change data to lend a hand with the science stuff. Perpetrating that hoax is hard work!

Joan McCarter would've helped, but she was too busy registering voters, especially Mickey Mouse, Mighty Mouse, Chuck E. Cheese, Pinky and The Brain, Stuart Little, Speedy Gonzales, Jerry from Tom and Jerry, the rats from Ratatouille, and the Three Blind Mice. The cartoon rodent demographic is critical to Obama's 2012 re-election battle.

Will Rockafellow took care of the numbers and contracts, as well as negotiated directly with George Soros, because I was too busy to deal with the millions of democracy-destroying Soros bucks funneled my way.

The rest of the team at ACORN *Daily Kos* helped pick up the slack during my book-writing absence and only complained a little bit, at least to my face. Thanks to the whole crew for their support—Jennifer Bruenjes, Laura Clawson, DavidNYC, Greg Dworkin, Tim Lange, Michael Lazzaro, Jed Lewison, Jake McIntyre, Steve Singiser, Mark Sumner, Page van der Linden, and David Waldman. You can now all get back to giving pimps and hos career and tax advice.

Thanks to my invaluable editor, Safir Ahmed, even though his name is, well, "Safir Ahmed." That's little different than "Barack Hussein Obama," and you know how *that*'s turned out!

The *Daily Kos* community is the best fake, astroturfed, and artificially inflated community online, even if they *do* use four-letter words that make poor Karl Rove's ears bleed. But, please, stop laughing at idiot conservatives, because if you do, Republicans will stop being mean to liberals and will be eager to work in a bipartisan fashion to do what's best for America. And stop disagreeing with each other! That's disagreeable. Also.

You know who else is a threat to America? Ed Schultz and Keith Olbermann, for breaking the rules of cable news punditry by sticking to the "facts" and "reality." Suckers! They'll never be the most trusted name in news if they keep that up! But thanks for having me on anyways. Rachel Maddow is just evil in so many fantastic ways.

Thanks to Micaela Gardner for the jihadist cookies, Gillermina Ruiz, Glenn Greenwald, Jeff Sharlet, John Aravosis, for their socialist help, suggestions, and information.

Finally, thanks to this American Taliban member, who so perfectly encapsulated his whole movement with this email he sent me:

> dear socialist fuckstick,
>
> i am well awear of the fact that liberals are immune to logic and reason, but allow me to try to prove to you that you are communist scum thrugh something called the scientific method:
>
> 1 a) FACT: you suck obamas cock every chance youget. you defend everythign he does and says and you are nothing more than an apologist. this makes you complicit in obamas actions.
>
> 1 b) FACT: obama is a well known socialist. this is evident his policies and his love of SELFDESCRIBED COMMUNISTS LIKE BILL AYERS!!!! so dont thinkthat he can hide his

true nature for much longer. he will eventully be exposed and impeached. SOCIALISM CANNOT WORK OR RUSSIA WOULD STILL EXIST AND THEY WOULD NEVER HAVE LOST THE COLD WAR TO REAGAN!!! retard.

1 c) you are thusly a pro forma socialist; whether you like it or not. logic dictates this.

(2) FACT: you, sir, are a illegal immigrant. i dont give two shits whether you are an american citizen or not: you came here on taxpayer expense and you continue to drain our limited resources. you should be ashamed and go back to guatemala or whatever fucking middleeastern asshole you came from and try to sell yor leftwing bullshit there.

(3) FACT: you are also OBJECTIVELY ANTIAMERI-CAN!!!!!!!! dont even try to deny this for there is ample prof: in 2004 you openly supported the murder of four brave american soldiers in falluja. you tryed to weasel out of your responsiblity, but you cant hide the fact that you hate america and american soldiers and you love al queda and other muslim terrorists who have killed THOUSANDS OF AMERI-CANS!!!! and will never stop unless they are killed. and whose going to kill them? you? LOL you dont even own a gun because you leftofascists want to repel the second amendment.

(4) FACT: it is clear that you are a socialist illegal immigrant america hater. there is prima facies proof as above. and if logic and science says you are scum then you are scum (remember global warming? no proof, just science and that makes it true for you liberals) no matter what you think. however, i dont think you are a homo, just a homo enabler.

this doesnt mean that we cant have common ground. if you stop publishing antiamerican communist screeds, then i will stop hating you. fair?

sincerely yours

glenn

Markos Moulitsas is founder and publisher of *Daily Kos,* two-time book author, former *Newsweek* columnist, regular guest on news shows, and weekly columnist at *The Hill* newspaper.

Other Books from PoliPointPress

The Blue Pages: A Directory of Companies Rated by Their Politics and Practices, 2nd edition

Helps consumers match their buying decisions with their political values by listing the political contributions and business practices of over 1,000 companies. $12.95, PAPERBACK.

Sasha Abramsky, *Breadline USA:*
The Hidden Scandal of American Hunger and How to Fix It

Treats the increasing food insecurity crisis in America not only as a matter of failed policies, but also as an issue of real human suffering. $23.95, CLOTH.

Rose Aguilar, *Red Highways: A Liberal's Journey into the Heartland*

Challenges red state stereotypes to reveal new strategies for progressives. $15.95, PAPERBACK.

John Amato and David Neiwert, *Over the Cliff:*
How Obama's Election Drove the American Right Insane

A witty look at—and an explanation of—the far-right craziness that overtook the conservative movement after Obama became president. $16.95, PAPERBACK.

Dean Baker, *False Profits: Recovering from the Bubble Economy*

Recounts the causes of the economic meltdown and offers a progressive program for rebuilding the economy and reforming the financial system and stimulus programs. $15.95, PAPERBACK.

Dean Baker, *Plunder and Blunder:*
The Rise and Fall of the Bubble Economy

Chronicles the growth and collapse of the stock and housing bubbles and explains how policy blunders and greed led to the catastrophic—but completely predictable—market meltdowns. $15.95, PAPERBACK.

Jeff Cohen, *Cable News Confidential:*
My Misadventures in Corporate Media

Offers a fast-paced romp through the three major cable news channels—Fox CNN, and MSNBC—and delivers a serious message about their failure to cover the most urgent issues of the day. $14.95, PAPERBACK.

Marjorie Cohn, *Cowboy Republic:*
Six Ways the Bush Gang Has Defied the Law

Shows how the executive branch under President Bush systematically defied the law instead of enforcing it. $14.95, PAPERBACK.

Marjorie Cohn and Kathleen Gilberd, *Rules of Disengagement:*
The Politics and Honor of Military Dissent
Examines what U.S. military men and women have done—and what their
families and others can do—to resist illegal wars, as well as military racism,
sexual harassment, and denial of proper medical care. $14.95, PAPERBACK.

Joe Conason, *The Raw Deal: How the Bush Republicans Plan to Destroy*
Social Security and the Legacy of the New Deal
Reveals the well-financed and determined effort to undo the Social Security
Act and other New Deal programs. $11.00, PAPERBACK.

Kevin Danaher, Shannon Biggs, and Jason Mark, *Building the Green*
Economy: Success Stories from the Grassroots
Shows how community groups, families, and individual citizens have protected
their food and water, cleaned up their neighborhoods, and strengthened their
local economies. $16.00, PAPERBACK.

Kevin Danaher and Alisa Gravitz, *The Green Festival Reader:*
Fresh Ideas from Agents of Change
Collects the best ideas and commentary from some of the most forward green
thinkers of our time. $15.95, PAPERBACK.

Reese Erlich, *Dateline Havana:*
The Real Story of U.S. Policy and the Future of Cuba
Explores Cuba's strained relationship with the United States, the island nation's
evolving culture and politics, and prospects for U.S.–Cuba policy with the
departure of Fidel Castro. $22.95, HARDCOVER.

Reese Erlich, *The Iran Agenda:*
The Real Story of U.S. Policy and the Middle East Crisis
Explores the turbulent recent history between the two countries and how it has
led to a showdown over nuclear technology. $14.95, PAPERBACK.

Todd Farley, *Making the Grades:*
My Misadventures in the Standardized Testing Industry
Exposes the folly of many large-scale educational assessments through an alter-
nately edifying and hilarious first-hand account of life in the testing business.
$16.95, PAPERBACK.

Steven Hill, *10 Steps to Repair American Democracy*
Identifies the key problems with American democracy, especially election practices, and proposes ten specific reforms to reinvigorate it. $11.00, PAPERBACK.

Jim Hunt, *They Said What?*
Astonishing Quotes on American Power, Democracy, and Dissent
Covering everything from squashing domestic dissent to stymieing equal rep-
resentation, these quotes remind progressives exactly what they're up against.
$12.95, PAPERBACK.

Michael Huttner and Jason Salzman, *50 Ways You Can Help Obama Change America*
Describes actions citizens can take to clean up the mess from the last administration, enact Obama's core campaign promises, and move the country forward. $12.95, PAPERBACK.

Helene Jorgensen, *Sick and Tired: How America's Health Care System Fails Its Patients*
Recounts the author's struggle to receive proper treatment for Lyme disease and examines the inefficiencies and irrationalities that she discovered in America's health care system during that five-year odyssey. $16.95, PAPERBACK.

Markos Kounalakis and Peter Laufer, *Hope Is a Tattered Flag: Voices of Reason and Change for the Post-Bush Era*
Gathers together the most listened-to politicos and pundits, activists and thinkers, to answer the question: what happens after Bush leaves office? $29.95, HARDCOVER; $16.95 PAPERBACK.

Yvonne Latty, *In Conflict: Iraq War Veterans Speak Out on Duty, Loss, and the Fight to Stay Alive*
Features the unheard voices, extraordinary experiences, and personal photographs of a broad mix of Iraq War veterans, including Congressman Patrick Murphy, Tammy Duckworth, Kelly Daugherty, and Camilo Mejia. $24.00, HARDCOVER.

Phillip Longman, *Best Care Anywhere: Why VA Health Care Is Better Than Yours, 2nd edition*
Shows how the turnaround at the long-maligned VA hospitals provides a blueprint for salvaging America's expensive but troubled health care system. $15.95, PAPERBACK.

Phillip Longman and Ray Boshara, *The Next Progressive Era*
Provides a blueprint for a re-empowered progressive movement and describes its implications for families, work, health, food, and savings. $22.95, HARDCOVER.

Marcia and Thomas Mitchell, *The Spy Who Tried to Stop a War: Katharine Gun and the Secret Plot to Sanction the Iraq Invasion*
Describes a covert operation to secure UN authorization for the Iraq war and the furor that erupted when a young British spy leaked it. $23.95, HARDCOVER.

Susan Mulcahy, ed., *Why I'm a Democrat*
Explores the values and passions that make a diverse group of Americans proud to be Democrats. $14.95, PAPERBACK.

David Neiwert, *The Eliminationists:*
How Hate Talk Radicalized the American Right
Argues that the conservative movement's alliances with far-right extremists have not only pushed the movement's agenda to the right, but also have become a malignant influence increasingly reflected in political discourse. $16.95, PAPERBACK.

Christine Pelosi, *Campaign Boot Camp:*
Basic Training for Future Leaders
Offers a seven-step guide for successful campaigns and causes at all levels of government. $15.95, PAPERBACK.

William Rivers Pitt, *House of Ill Repute:*
Reflections on War, Lies, and America's Ravaged Reputation
Skewers the Bush Administration for its reckless invasions, warrantless wiretaps, lethally incompetent response to Hurricane Katrina, and other scandals and blunders. $16.00, PAPERBACK.

Sarah Posner, *God's Profits:*
Faith, Fraud, and the Republican Crusade for Values Voters
Examines corrupt televangelists' ties to the Republican Party and unprecedented access to the Bush White House. $19.95, HARDCOVER.

Nomi Prins, *Jacked: How "Conservatives" Are Picking Your Pocket—*
Whether You Voted for Them or Not
Describes how the "conservative" agenda has affected your wallet, skewed national priorities, and diminished America—but not the American spirit. $12.00, PAPERBACK.

Cliff Schecter, *The Real McCain: Why Conservatives Don't Trust Him—*
And Why Independents Shouldn't
Explores the gap between the public persona of John McCain and the reality of this would-be president. $14.95, HARDCOVER.

Norman Solomon, *Made Love, Got War:*
Close Encounters with America's Warfare State
Traces five decades of American militarism and the media's all-too-frequent failure to challenge it. $24.95, HARDCOVER.

John Sperling et al., *The Great Divide: Retro vs. Metro America*
Explains how and why our nation is so bitterly divided into what the authors call Retro and Metro America. $19.95, PAPERBACK.

Mark Sumner, *The Evolution of Everything:*
How Selection Shapes Culture, Commerce, and Nature
Shows how Darwin's theory of evolution has been misapplied—and why a more nuanced reading of that work helps us understand a wide range of social and economic activity as well as the natural world. $15.95, PAPERBACK.

Daniel Weintraub, *Party of One:*
Arnold Schwarzenegger and the Rise of the Independent Voter

Explains how Schwarzenegger found favor with independent voters, whose support has been critical to his success, and suggests that his bipartisan approach represents the future of American politics. $19.95, HARDCOVER.

Curtis White, *The Barbaric Heart:*
Faith, Money, and the Crisis of Nature

Argues that the solution to the present environmental crisis may come from an unexpected quarter: the arts, religion, and the realm of the moral imagination. $16.95, PAPERBACK.

Curtis White, *The Spirit of Disobedience: Resisting the Charms of Fake*
Politics, Mindless Consumption, and the Culture of Total Work

Debunks the notion that liberalism has no need for spirituality and describes a "middle way" through our red state/blue state political impasse. Includes three powerful interviews with John DeGraaf, James Howard Kunstler, and Michael Ableman. $24.00, HARDCOVER.

For more information, please visit www.p3books.com.

About This Book

This book is printed on Cascade Enviro100 Print paper. It contains 100 percent post-consumer fiber and is certified EcoLogo, Processed Chlorine Free, and FSC Recycled. For each ton used instead of virgin paper, we:

- Save the equivalent of 17 trees
- Reduce air emissions by 2,098 pounds
- Reduce solid waste by 1,081 pounds
- Reduce the water used by 10,196 gallons
- Reduce suspended particles in the water by 6.9 pounds.

This paper is manufactured using biogas energy, reducing natural gas consumption by 2,748 cubic feet per ton of paper produced.

The book's printer, Malloy Incorporated, works with paper mills that are environmentally responsible, that do not source fiber from endangered forests, and that are third-party certified. Malloy prints with soy and vegetable based inks, and over 98 percent of the solid material they discard is recycled. Their water emissions are entirely safe for disposal into their municipal sanitary sewer system, and they work with the Michigan Department of Environmental Quality to ensure that their air emissions meet all environmental standards.

The Michigan Department of Environmental Quality has recognized Malloy as a Great Printer for their compliance with environmental regulations, written environmental policy, pollution prevention efforts, and pledge to share best practices with other printers. Their county Department of Planning and Environment has designated them a Waste Knot Partner for their waste prevention and recycling programs.